The German Army on the Eastern Front

The German Army on the Eastern Front

An Inner View of the *Ostheer*'s Experiences of War

Jeff Rutherford and Adrian E. Wettstein

Pen & Sword
MILITARY

First published in Great Britain in 2018 by
Pen & Sword Military
an imprint of
Pen & Sword Books Ltd
47 Church Street
Barnsley
South Yorkshire
S70 2AS

Typeset in 10/12 & Sabon LT Std
Typeset by Aura Technology and Software Services, India

Printed and bound in Great Britain by TJ International Ltd, Padstow, Cornwall

Pen & Sword Books Ltd incorporates the imprints of Pen & Sword Archaeology,
Atlas, Aviation, Battleground, Discovery, Family History, History, Maritime,
Military, Naval, Politics, Railways, Select, Social History, Transport, True Crime,
and Claymore Press, Frontline Books, Leo Cooper, Praetorian Press, Remember
When, Seaforth Publishing and Wharncliffe.

For a complete list of Pen & Sword titles please contact
PEN & SWORD BOOKS LIMITED
47 Church Street, Barnsley, South Yorkshire, S70 2AS, England
E-mail: enquiries@pen-and-sword.co.uk
Website: www.pen-and-sword.co.uk

Contents

Introduction

For the English-speaking world, the German army of the Second World War is generally viewed through the prism of war against the Western Allies. The brilliance and audacity of German panzer commanders and their troops led to the shocking defeat of French and British forces in 1940, while the Africa Corps proved extremely vexing to British forces in North Africa. Even after defeats at El Alamein, Tunis, Salerno, and on the Normandy beaches, the German army mounted a tenacious defence – symbolized by the battle of the hedgerows in Normandy, the defence of the Gothic Line, Arnhem and the Hürtgen Forest – that precipitously slowed the Allied advance and, as the Battle of the Bulge illustrated, it still possessed the striking power to mount an offensive that threatened Allied positions. By the end of the war, however, the German army was a mere shell of the force that had conquered continental Europe. Certainly Allied actions – both on the battlefield and in the air and at sea – contributed to this state of affairs. Much more important in the grinding away of the German army's combat power and efficiency, however, was the war against the Soviet Union's Red Army.

From the beginning of the invasion on 22 June 1941 until the end of the war on 8 May 1945, the German army deployed the majority of its troops in the eastern theatre of war. As a result, this became not only the most decisive conflict of the Second World War, but also the largest in terms of size, scale, and totality. While the Sino-Japanese war approached the German-Soviet clash in terms of violence and breadth, the totality of the latter struggle was far and away the greatest of the Second World War. Modern industrialized war on the scale of the war in the East – millions of men deployed at the front, well-equipped with cutting-edge weaponry, on a front that stretched from the Arctic Circle to the Caucasus mountains – could only be undertaken by two countries who possessed the robust state structures needed to fuel such a war. This war was also given a much more ferocious edge than the one fought between the Germans and the Western Allies. In the east, Nazi ideological beliefs structured the manner in which Germany prosecuted the war and the racism that animated the Nazi state gave the war against the Soviet Union a brutal sheen that stretched from the highest levels of command down to the ordinary soldiers, and it was one that was reciprocated by Soviet state and society.

The German-Soviet war was essential in defeating Germany, the strongest of the Axis powers. While one cannot uncouple this theatre from the Allied war against Germany as a whole, it was here where the German army lost its backbone as continuous massive losses depleted the German manpower pool, decreasing the quality of officers and men alike. The Luftwaffe also suffered greatly in the East, and the use of trainer crews and flight teachers during the winter crises of 1941/42 and 1942/43 to fly supplies to encircled forces proved catastrophic to the German pilot training program. Of course, Anglo-American supply of the Soviet Union with weapons and goods of all kinds was essential for the Soviet war effort. Tanks and aircraft filled Soviet production gaps, especially in 1941/42, while other goods such as shoes helped in the mobilization effort of 1943/44. Furthermore, Western Allied aid allowed the Soviets to concentrate their production on fewer goods. It is doubtful that Soviet industry could have produced more than 100,000 tanks in the war, if it had to divert resources to – for example – locomotives and trucks, goods delivered en masse by the Western Allies. The Western Allies' war effort additionally forced the Germans to devote considerable resources to the U-boat war, coastal and air defence in the west and in the skies over the Reich. Air defence of Germany alone included no fewer than 1,400 batteries of anti-aircraft guns and searchlights at the end of 1942, with many more stationed in France, Norway or in the Mediterranean. The men and material devoted to these tasks could therefore not be utilized in the East. These caveats aside, the bulk of the German army's fighting took place in the east and it was in this theatre that the army was ultimately destroyed.

Adolf Hitler and the German military leadership planned Operation Barbarossa – the invasion of the Soviet Union – as a short campaign, consciously designed to build upon the previous rapid, mobile operations in Poland, France and the Balkans. While many issues, including, most problematically, the primary strategic goal of the campaign, were not fully decided, the belief that the German offensive would achieve its goals in eight to twelve weeks notably led to a neglect of planning for logistics and replacements. Intelligence on the Soviet Union was criminally negligent and the military leadership completely underestimated the vastness of the theatre of operations and its terrain. In expectation of civilian authorities swiftly taking control of the conquered Soviet territories following the brief campaign, a military occupation policy was also not fully developed. When this short campaign failed to defeat the Soviet Union and losses in men and material increased to an unprecedented level, the army was forced to adapt in real time. In spite of these attempts to modify its practices, the German army never fully recovered from the losses of 1941, due largely to the scarcity of reserves in both men and material. While the crisis in the replacement system was overcome in 1942, a growing manpower shortage plagued the Germans for the remainder of the war. The issue of low-level leadership also became a nagging and eventually debilitating problem. In combination, these elements led to a steady decrease in German combat power, only partly compensated for by superior weapons that became available in larger numbers from 1942 onwards and a volatile Soviet battlefield performance. The defeat of the German offensive against Moscow in autumn 1941 also shaped the German war experience – the majority of units and men would, after that point, primarily fight a defensive positional war.

In contrast to the positional warfare that settled in on the northern and central sectors of the front, the Germans launched a scaled-down blitz offensive on the southern section of the front, Operation Blue, which culminated in the catastrophic destruction of the Sixth Army and forced the Germans into a hasty and improvised retreat in the face of a resurgent Red Army. During the offensive and subsequent retreat, the army found itself suffering from the same issues that it had in 1941: high casualties, especially among experienced officers and NCOs, difficulties in bringing forward the requisite supplies needed for operations, and the increasing interference of both the political and military leadership in the operational and tactical spheres that had been traditionally considered the prerogative of the commander on the ground.

The last gasp of German offensive power on the Eastern front – the ill-fated Operation Citadel – demonstrated the manner in which the army had been transformed in the cauldron of the war in the East. While the operation was built around the use of armour, it was fought in the style of a First World War battle of attrition using Second World War technology: armoured spearheads frontally assaulted a Soviet defence echeloned in depth before being hit head-on by much larger Soviet tank formations. The stalling of the offensive, followed almost immediately by a large counter-attack north of the Kursk bulge, led to the third stage of the war when the German army was definitively on the defensive and only a few minor offensive operations could be considered complete successes. From this point on, the German army faced nearly constant pressure and there were only a few calm sectors to refresh troops. Combined with the decrease in quantity and quality that stretched back to 1941, and which only increased following the beginning of the Soviet offensives, an infantry crisis developed throughout the army in autumn 1943, which threatened to break its backbone. Operation Bagration in June 1944 was the final blow that expelled the majority of the German army from Soviet territory, while at the same time destroying most of Army Group Centre. Combined with the landings in Normandy, the summer of 1944 marked the beginning of the end of the Third Reich.

The military events of the war in the east – centred on the signpost battles of Moscow, Stalingrad, Kursk, and Bagration – were clearly unprecedented in European history in terms of size and scale, and they differentiate the Nazi-Soviet war from other conflicts during the Second World War. The essence of the war waged by the Nazi state in the east, however, was also far different from the war it waged in the west. The ultimate goal of the campaign was the complete destruction of the Soviet state and society, so that the area could be integrated into a racial empire that encompassed Central and Eastern Europe under the allegedly superior Aryan – or German – race. Plans to plunder, exploit, enslave, and eventually to commit the mass murder of various population groups in the Soviet Union underpinned the Nazi state's approach to the conflict – what has been termed the *Vernichtungskrieg*, or war of annihilation – and it seeped into both army planning and practice.

While German intentions towards the Soviet Union were laid bare in the planning process – most notably through the complex of orders referred to as the 'criminal orders' – it was during the course of the campaign that German policy underwent a marked radicalization. Autumn 1941 brought a new phase in what soon developed into a ruthless occupation policy – one that the army significantly contributed to – up until the end of the winter crisis period. Following its conclusion, army policy fluctuated between periods of reconciliation and coercion, depending not only on the German perception of the situation, but also on the attitudes of commanders on the spot. At the base of most German military policies lay the concept of military necessity; the attempt to secure the combat efficiency of the army in order to achieve victory on the battlefield, no matter the ethical or moral cost. This concept at times led the army to wage a war that corresponded to the ideological struggle demanded by the state, while at other points in time it drove army policies that contradicted state goals. Military necessity is therefore essential in connecting the war of annihilation with the war against the Red Army.

The research of the last twenty years has shed new light on the German war in the east as it centred on German criminal orders and the practices initiated, supported or at least tolerated by the military, including the rather conservative army. This research has not only focused on the criminally negligent and even genocidal German treatment of Soviet POWs and the beginnings of the Holocaust through the murders of Soviet Jews and other groups specially persecuted by the National Socialist regime, but it has also examined occupation policies that included the Starvation Plan, which intended that some 30 million Soviet citizens die of hunger and the diseases it caused, the carrying out of criminal orders such as the Commissar Order, the exploitation of Soviet economic resources, particularly agriculture, the forced deportation of workers to Germany, and finally the excessive and brutal anti-partisan warfare waged by the Germans and their Axis allies. While few still doubt that the German military leadership and army itself was actively involved in the war of annihilation in 1941, many other issues are still open to debate. Only a limited number of studies on the German army examine the war in the east beyond the winter crisis of 1941/42, and the few that have indicate that local approaches provided a multitude of occupation policies rather than one unified line of action. The involvement of the individual soldier is also debated, as is the question of which arms or branches were more involved – at this point, for example, we lack a study that examines the Luftwaffe's involvement in the war of annihilation. A further difficult debate concerns the relationship between the German military and the National Socialist system and its ideology. While there were clearly numerous overlapping ideas between the military and National Socialism, it is difficult to see the cause and effect between the two value systems: where did Nazi ideology fundamentally transform German military thinking, and where did it merely radicalize pre-existing German military thought? An even more difficult discussion considers the influence of Soviet warfare on the conduct of war. While most historians agree that it accelerated the spiral of violence through its own atrocities, we simply lack sufficient research on the Red Army's contribution to this state of affairs – and unfortunately will for many years to come.

The recent focus on the war of annihilation, however, has led to a neglect of archive-based operational studies, so that many newer works still rely on the notoriously unreliable memoirs of generals or on studies more than forty years old. The relatively few new operational studies have demonstrated the necessity of further research into this area of military history. One of the persistent problems in the analysis of the Nazi-Soviet war is that there are few connections made between these two main lines of research – operational studies often enough pay no attention to these 'irrelevant matters' of occupation policy (or are written by people defending the 'clean' *Wehrmacht*), while many historians of the war of annihilation lack a fundamental understanding of military matters (which at times even weakens their approach to the topic). Finally, numerous areas important for both lines of research and which sometimes connect them, such as logistics, command, training or troop care, have received only limited research attention.

This book addresses some of these issues by presenting sources that generally originate from the mid-command level, that is, the corps to regimental level, and concentrates on the period between June 1941 and summer 1944. Several sources are presented in full or are quoted extensively to give readers a first-hand perspective on German military thinking about the war and how the army perceived and understood the conflict. It also allows the reader to get an idea about the nature of such sources, as well as of the nuances, subtleties, and even contradictions that emerge in German military documents. These are issues that are often lost when simply quoting small sections of documents.

The documents are grouped by topic into seven thematic chapters, covering the issues of combat, command, tactics and organization, supply, occupation, training, and motivation. A cursory glance at the various documents will highlight the interconnection of many of the various orders, directives, and reports. For example, it is difficult to separate combat from supply, training from command, and occupation from motivation; rather the various facets of the German army's experience of war reinforced one another in creating the particular way in which the Germans fought and understood the war in the east. They also provide evidence of a rather fragmented approach to the war against the Soviets. While this should not come as a surprise in consideration of the number of men involved and the constant evolution of the army's policies and practices, it does indicate that the narrative of a monolithic German army that operated in lock-step with central directives requires revision.

The book's approach sketched above has some limits. This study is not a chronological history of events on the Eastern front. It is also not a comprehensive look at the Eastern front, as the analysis of the Soviet Union and the Red Army, as well as that of the Third Reich outside the Eastern front, i.e. the German armaments industry, receives only cursory discussion. Its focus remains squarely on how the war was fought, experienced, and understood by the German army from the army level to that of the individual soldier.

In the translation and editing of the sources there were many obstacles to overcome. Translation and editing is always an exercise in interpretation, and we had many discussions about possible ways to translate words or sentences. In some cases, we decided to leave a term in the original German. In a few cases, the German term has become common in English (like *Führer*). In most cases, however, we decided that if the German word had a meaning – in our case often influenced by National Socialist ideology or coined by long German military tradition – that was difficult to translate accurately into English, we would leave it in the original German and enter it into an accompanying glossary. Ranks are also not translated. Another difficulty was to remain as close as possible to the German sources, but at the same time achieve a readable English, especially for those new to the field of German military history. We made many necessary compromises on these issues, which someone else may have approached differently.

Even though we have written out most of the less well-known abbreviations, the numbering of military units has been included. German units are normally numbered as follows: companies, regiments, divisions and armies in arabic numerals, battalions and corps in Roman numerals. So, for example, 3./203 refers to the 3rd Company of the 203rd Regiment while, III./203 would be the 3rd Battalion of the same regiment. To avoid unnecessary complication, we decided to translate all battalion-size units with the term battalion (German artillery, artillery related, and mobile units used *Abteilung* instead of *Bataillon*).

Manpower strength numbers are typically given as, for example, 1/7, which means one officer and seven men. In a few cases, this ratio is different, but it is explained in the text.

One of the great pleasures for professors is to teach engaged, intellectually curious students. Both of us have had this opportunity in our respective institutions and it was our discussions with them about the German army and its war in the east that convinced us to undertake such a project. We hope that this book will provide a good introduction to the Germany army on the Eastern front, not only in terms of basic knowledge, but also in developing an understanding of the sources, which helps to overcome textual difficulties and also connects them across time and space. We therefore dedicate this book to our students. In Wheeling, the history majors at Wheeling Jesuit University have generally been an outstanding group, but three stand out and this book is dedicated to them: KM, JZ, and ET. In Zurich, most of the candidates at the Federal Military Academy at the ETH Zurich shared a deep interest in military history and keenly discussed issues that were essential for their professional formation. This book is especially dedicated to RG, NJ, PS and SB. The authors would also like to publicly thank Ben Shepherd, Marco Sigg and David Stahel for providing documents and photographs for this volume.

Chapter 1

Combat on the Eastern Front

During the Second World War, the decisive theatre of war for the German army was the Eastern front. Perhaps the most effective way to measure the importance of this front for the German war effort is by looking at the army's casualties in the east. According to the historian Stephen Fritz, the Germans suffered over 3.5 million dead fighting the Red Army, with another 363,000 dying in Soviet POW camps. This total meant that 'almost four of every five German military deaths thus came at the hands of the Red Army.'[1] The Germans inflicted much heavier casualties on their Soviet adversaries, with 11.5 million the generally accepted number of military deaths, though other estimates reach upwards of some 25 million.[2] These numbers – which far and away dwarf those from the Western Allied-German conflict – not only suggest that the German-Soviet war was the largest and deadliest theatre of war, but they also highlight the German army's primary goal during the conflict: defeating the Red Army on the battlefield. This seemingly obvious point, however, has been somewhat lost in the recent historiography which has focused – rightly – on the accompanying war of extermination waged by the Nazi state. While the Third Reich's ideological war will be examined in chapters 5 and 7, this chapter will examine the army's struggle on the field of combat and the success, as well as the trials and tribulations it suffered during the little more than three years of war within the borders of the Soviet Union.[3]

German planning for the invasion of the Soviet Union was based upon two fundamental ideas. First, success in the campaign would depend on the panzer divisions, concentrated in panzer groups, driving quickly into the interior of the Soviet Union and destroying the bulk of the Red Army before it could retreat behind the Dvina and Dnieper rivers. Following this initial operational phase, the army would then carry out a mopping-up of the shattered Soviet forces, eventually pushing what remained behind the Ural mountains.[4] Second, the army possessed a not entirely mistaken belief in its superiority vis-á-vis Soviet forces. Germany's blitz victories over a whole series of opponents in between 1939 and 1941, but especially its shocking defeat of British and French forces in 1940, generated a true self-confidence throughout the army's ranks. This was contrasted by the Red Army's poor performances during its 1939 occupation of Eastern Poland and, more importantly, during the 1939–40 Winter War with Finland. The confidence, even hubris, with which the army approached the eastern campaign thus led to a criminal underestimation of Red Army capabilities, as well as a negligent attitude towards issues of intelligence and supply (see chapter 4 for a thorough analysis of the latter point). From the German perspective, the army's superiority at the operational and tactical level would ensure a quick and decisive victory, making other considerations secondary at best.[5]

On 22 June 1941, some three million German and allied soldiers invaded the Soviet Union, the largest invasion in history up until that point. On the macro-level, German forces achieved success along the entire breadth of the front, from the Baltic States to Ukraine. With the exception of Army Group South, whose initial advance was more pedestrian, German forces, particularly the Panzer Groups attached to Army Group Centre, plunged deep into Soviet territory and not only reached their initial geographic goals, but destroyed numerous Soviet armies in the process.[6] The following battle report compiled by Panzer Group 3 highlights both the unit's role in the Minsk battle and the conflict that emerged at the upper levels of the German army concerning the employment of armour: should manageable encirclement battles be waged in succession, or should the panzers drive as deeply into the Soviet rear as possible in an attempt to completely dislocate the Soviet defence?[7]

> The border heights were quickly taken. [...] On all places along the front, only minimal enemy resistance was reported. Only a very few prisoners, all of whom were completely in the dark about the beginning of the war and the situation.
>
> The question arose at the Panzer Group if the German attack really was a complete surprise for the Red Army or if the enemy had pulled back some of his forces from between the border and the Niemen [River] to the east under a wide-ranging radio deception.
>
> Gradually, the evidence increased during the course of 22.6. That still stronger enemy forces existed west of the Niemen than at first presumed. If the reported divisions existed in full strength or only partially [as they were] still in the process of formation, because they were too poorly armed, remained unclear. It was determined that these elements were without live ammunition, allegedly released for an exercise.
>
> Where the enemy chooses, he fights tenaciously und courageously until death. Deserters and surrender has been reported by no command. The struggle became therefore harder than in the Polish and the Western campaigns.
>
> As in Poland, the enemy was driven into the forests by our air attacks, from which he conducts a successful guerrilla war against rear elements and [supply] columns. This may also be a reason for the initially surprisingly small appearance of enemy forces. How much of them are hidden in the forests and how much equipment that they were forced to leave in them cannot be overlooked yet. [...]

From Vilna to Minsk

During all discussions for the Barbarossa deployment, there existed differing conceptions about the continuation of the operation after the crossing of the Niemen for Army Group B and Panzer Group 3. Panzer Group 3 had the intention to push on to the Dvina [River] on the nearest road without turning to secondary issues too quickly. The intention of the OKH[8] to create the prerequisite for the destruction of the enemy between Bialystok and Minsk with Panzer Group 2 and 3 would have been better achieved, in the view of Panzer Group 3, through a thrust to the Dvina to prevent withdrawal and new resistance there, than [through a thrust] with the narrowly pinned goal on Minsk. The army group left the decision open before the beginning of the attack and ordered an intermediate objective Molodeczno-Narach Lake to proceed either to Minsk or to Vitebsk-Polotsk.

After reaching Vilna on 26.6., Army Group Centre ordered a thrust on the high ground near Minsk to encircle the retreating troops in front of Fourth and Ninth Armies and to make a connection with Panzer Group 2.

Panzer Group 3, still believing that elements of the enemy pulled back to the east and that it was necessary to pursue them over the Dvina, once again tried to plead its point of view to the OKH through the OKH liaison officer. OKH, however, maintained its conviction for the objective for Panzer Group 3 from the deployment directive: to reach the heights of Minsk.

Once the connection was made with Panzer Group 2, Panzer Group 3 decided to start the advance on the Dvina with the bulk of the group. In contact with Ninth Army and Panzer Group 2, two divisions should have continued to block against the encircled enemy by Minsk. In contrast to Army Group Centre, Panzer Group 3 believed this was acting properly because it no longer attached any combat value to the encircled enemy and therefore the larger goal lay on the Dvina. Waiting until the last Russian had surrendered was not permissible, especially since the encircled enemy seemed to escape to the southeast through the gaps of Panzer Group 2 from 30.6. on.

The intention of Panzer Group 3 was to drive on to the upper Dvina from 2.7. without further delay. It was expected that the enemy would defend the Berezina and Dvina River sectors with resistance groups of reserves and elements of soldiers broken out of the encirclements, without depth and a coherent front, but they has already been shattered through the drive of Panzer Group 2 at Bobruisk and Panzer Group 4 by Dvinsk.

As the report notes, the war experienced by German units at the sharp end was costly during the opening days of the invasion. Despite the surprise achieved along the breadth of the front, and the tremendous numbers of prisoners taken, Soviet forces resisted tenaciously in various places and the casualties of German units involved in the initial battles were among the highest in the war.[9] More importantly, the document highlights the central issue between the various Army Group, Army, and Panzer Group commanders concerning the use of armour. For the generals commanding infantry armies, the encircled enemy forces to their front needed to be eliminated and this could only be accomplished by the Panzer Groups not merely closing the trap, but also turning the vice and driving Red Army troops into the cauldron created by the eastward marching infantry. For the panzer generals, however, what mattered was utilizing the speed and mobility of the Panzer Groups to the utmost; instead of wasting them in relatively static engagements against an already encircled foe, they wanted to leave a minimum of force to maintain the encirclement and put the remainder of their units on the road to the east to forestall the formation of any form of coherent Soviet defence. Such visions of deep Panzer thrusts to the east, however, failed to correspond to the realities of the Germans' already creaking logistic system, as well as the much slower speed of the infantry armies that were essential to both occupying Soviet territory and destroying the cauldrons created by the Panzer Groups. In the example given here, Army Group Centre sided with the infantry generals and ordered Panzer Group 3 to close the encirclement of Soviet troops at Minsk with Panzer Group 2. This led to one of the most noteworthy successes of the campaign: the twin encirclement battles of Bialystok-Minsk in which some 324,000 Soviet soldiers were taken prisoner and more than 5,100 tanks and artillery pieces were wiped out of the Red Army's order of battle.[10] The employment of German armour thus led to spectacular battlefield victories, but the Soviet Union's very geography presented the Germans with stiff challenges to their preferred method of war.

The German army soon found that the Soviet theatre did not lend itself to the type of armoured warfare that had worked so spectacularly in France. One of the primary issues in the east was the lack of suitable roads. While this was a problem across the breadth of the front, it proved to be an especially intractable one for units operating in Army Group North, as its area of deployment was peppered with swamps and bogs. The following excerpts from the 8th Panzer Division's war diary highlight this obstacle to a blitz-type campaign.[11]

6.7.41: In addition to numerous smaller corduroy roads, an especially long corduroy road was built along the east bank [of the Ludza] that required some three to four thousand tree trunks that were cut down by the engineers from the outlying forests, had all the branches cut off, were cut into pieces, transported to the departure point and since they needed to be driven to the work site, were put on trucks that had been captured on the east bank and made drivable. Since the forest terrain was swampy, the engineers stood with water over their waists most of the time while dragging around the trunks. [...]

19.10.41: The extraordinarily difficult road conditions, the swampy terrain, with no room for the tactical manoeuvre of vehicles, and the slow movement of troops over the Volkhov bridges make only a very gradual advance of forces possible. Mine and tree obstacles allow for only a dismounted advance. All available forces must be deployed for road construction. [...]

31.10.41: The moors under the snow covering are only frozen a little bit and after each passing of only a few tanks, the road is completely impassable. [...]

Unlike France and its well-maintained and relatively dense road network, the Soviet Union's nearly non-existent system of roads precipitously slowed German armour and motorized divisions, frequently forcing them to wait for engineers to construct makeshift roads and bridges along the routes of advance.[12] The document also hints at the mounting tasks for soldiers, who were not only expected to fight the Red Army while advancing, but also found themselves labouring to make the advance possible.

Partially a result of these poor roads, but also due to stiff Soviet resistance, German armour divisions suffered heavy material losses during the opening months of the invasion. The following war diary entry from the XXXXVIIth Panzer Corps paints a troubling picture of those units that the success of the entire operation depended on.[13]

The following numbers are symptomatic of the present strength of the 18th Panzer Division:

From an authorized strength = 42 3.7cm and 9 5cm anti-tank guns are as of now 22 3.7cm and 8 5cm anti-tank guns combat-ready guns available. The 52nd Rifle Regiment alone has altogether 1,000 casualties from a combat strength of 2,359 men on 22.6.41, and what has to be considered here is that the disproportionally largest share of the casualties fall upon the dismounted elements that fight the battle. The division now has only 47 battle-worthy tanks against the 276 it had on 22.6. In addition, the division has a total loss of 1,300 vehicles. A further 1,000 vehicles are under repair, of which 500 can again be made operational. The French vehicles, with which the 18th Panzer Division is predominantly equipped, have proven to be cumbersome and therefore of limited use off-road.

The dramatic decrease in operational tanks significantly damaged the 18th Panzer Division's striking power, but the loss of vehicles should not be overlooked. Without the necessary trucks, cars, and motorcycles, the mobility of the division as a whole greatly suffered, as did its ability to bring much-needed supplies of food, ammunition and fuel to the front, an issue further discussed in chapter 4. So, even during the summer months when the Germans enjoyed some of their most spectacular successes of the war, the chances of German victory became increasingly fleeting as the panzer divisions' combat power slowly dissipated.

As the German attack lost momentum during the late summer due to heavy casualties (especially among officers and NCOs – a topic examined in chapter 2), supply difficulties and the attrition of armour strength, some units found themselves temporarily forced onto the defensive. This was especially true for infantry divisions operating in Army Group Centre during the battle for Smolensk. While German armour divisions were able to ensnare another large number of Soviet formations in a cauldron in this area, Red Army forces from outside of the pocket pounded the thin German cordon. As infantry divisions finally caught up to the exposed panzer divisions and replaced them in the line in hopes of the latter being able to refresh before the next stage of the advance, the war in the centre of the front temporarily shifted to positional warfare. While this was most pronounced during the fighting around the Yel'nya salient from late August through the end of September, Army Group Centre's panzer divisions had already been forced onto the defensive in early August. Due to the army's nearly exclusive emphasis on offensive warfare, it was not entirely prepared for fighting on the defensive and, as the following document relates, the commander of the 7th Infantry Division believed that his commanders needed to rethink how they approached this type of warfare.[14]

I reject the type of defence which is frequently carried out.

All depth is missing along the colossal breadth. Therefore, the defence was linear, which as we have learned, is incorrect. I can therefore not agree with the view that one or another commander had, who wouldn't or couldn't comply with my thought process and wishes – leading the battle out of strongpoints.

The linear deployment, without reserves behind it, must lead to critical situations, because no one was in the position to influence the battle in anyway. Solely because of this, a locally strong attack on one position had an effect on the breadth [of the line].[15]

Maintaining the initiative [*das Gesetzt des Handelns*] – active defence – can only be managed out of strongpoints. Actually, everywhere too much was done with men and too little with [the use of] weapons.

With the breadth of the front sections to be secured, our personnel weakness can only be bridged over through a well-considered use of weapons. The conduct of battle must therefore be led from strongpoints that can mutually support each other with flanking fire. The gaps between the individual strongpoints must not only be accepted, but rather they should be accepted since they are the only way to make possible the concentration of strength in an individual sector. Only in this way were the troops in the position to attack an attacking opponent on the flanks even if he had pushed through a gap and then throw them out again through the concentration of men on specific points. This is the only way that command of battle was possible, this is the only way that leaders could intervene and the individual man was not left all alone against the onrushing masses of men.

The 7th Infantry Division moved into the Yel'nya salient on 28 August and began its month-long participation in what, to all intents and purposes, developed into a battle of attrition, a type of combat antithetical to German goals in summer 1941. Developments in the centre of the front caused the first command crisis of the campaign for the army; while the OKH wanted to continue the drive on Moscow, which it believed was the strategic goal, Hitler was determined to seize the economically and ideologically important areas of Leningrad and Ukraine. The stalling of Army Group Centre only reinforced Hitler's proclivities and he detached the Army Group Centre's Panzer Groups and diverted them to the flanks. So, while the infantry forces of Army Group Centre fought defensive battles of attrition, its former Panzer Groups fanned out to the north and south. Simultaneous to the fighting in the Yel'nya salient, German forces, including Panzer Group 2, carried out a major encirclement at the battle of Kiev – one which 'utterly destroyed' the Soviet South-Western Front, with 'four Soviet armies and roughly three-quarters of a million men… removed from the Red Army's order of battle.'[16] This textbook example of mobile warfare existed in stark contrast to the 7th Infantry Division's experiences during the Yel'nya battle, as its after-action report on the battle clearly indicated.[17]

On 28 [August] the division was subordinated to the XXth Army Corps and brought forward for an intended deployment in the Yel'nya bend in the vicinity of Cholm. On 30.8., the division was supposed to continue its march in order to relieve a division in its position on the eastern bank of the Yel'nya bend in the night of 31.8. to 1.9. However, this did not take place, because the Russians broke through on 30.8. in the northern section and with tanks further in the south. The planned relief had to be abandoned for the time being.

1 September again brought a change. The Russians attacked the Yel'nya bend on its narrowest position simultaneously from the north and south in order to pinch it off.

Most exposed to these attacks were the left wing of Infantry Regiment 62 near Kukujewa and the adjacent division. Already in the early morning of 1.9., a recognized enemy assembly was smashed by artillery fire. At 8.20 the report arrived that the enemy had broken through in the northern Yel'nya bend. Infantry Regiment 61 was alerted. During the night, an important order was taken off a dead commissar from which could be gathered that an attack by one division was planned for on 1 September. 10:00 1 regiment against Kukujewa, 11:20 1 regiment against Stragina, 11:50 again 1 regiment against Kukujewa. The Russians attacked exactly according to the program and were caught and destroyed by our already waiting artillery. Since the situation in front of the neighbouring division on the left gradually became difficult, the I./Infantry Regiment 61 was subordinated to it and this battalion was deployed in the hot spot near Leonowa. Despite the bloody rebuff that the enemy got in the morning, he again attacked the left wing of Infantry Regiment 62 at Ssoliwenja and Kukujewa at 19:00, but was again repulsed. Since the continuation of the attack had to be expected and the left wing appeared to be threatened due to weak manning of the area, the division brought forward the III./Infantry Regiment 19 to the Barakssina area.

The battle continued. At 13:00 on 2.9., a platoon-strength enemy thrust near Ssolowenjka (in front of Infantry Regiment 62) was repulsed. At 15:00, III./Infantry Regiment 19 began its attack on Kukujewa from a south-westerly direction, found only minimal resistance and pushed into the town. Around 20:00, a Russian counterstroke took place, which forced a temporary clearing of the town. At 3:00, Kukujewa was again occupied by III. and II./Infantry Regiment 19 from the south and west.

On 3.9, the Russians attempted a breakthrough with all means. Day after day, they were attacking in vain. Now it was up to the tanks to create it. At 8:00 7 heavy tanks were reported in the direction of Leonowa, at 8:30 more than 20. Some of them were shot up by artillery, the rest remained stuck in the swamp. The tank attack in the southern part of the Yel'nya bend had failed!

At 10:45, the II./Infantry Regiment 61 was thrown against the enemy who had broken through in the north. Its brave commander, *Hauptmann* Freiherr von Meyern-Hohenberg, fell at the head of his battalion. At noon on 5.9., he was laid to rest in a dignified ceremony in Chaina in the midst of the then divisional command post.

3.9. had shown that the Russians wanted to spare neither men nor material in order to get a hold of the Yel'nya bend. Since the main point of emphasis for operations lay elsewhere for the time being, higher command decided to withdraw from the Yel'nya bend and to build a new front on the shortest line.[18] The rearward movement began on 5.9. and was for the most part completed on 6.9. The division took over the front of the combat sectors on the Strjana between Arshawez and Charin, with Infantry Regiment 19 and Infantry Regiment 61. Infantry Regiment 62 was withdrawn to the area Panjkowa-Barbarikin-Cholm as a reserve.

These movements did not remain hidden to the Russians for long. At first, they pursued on 5.9. but only tentatively. On 6.9., however, already during the course of the morning they sent out feelers from platoon to battalion strength of Infantry Regiment 61's combat outposts and the II./Infantry Regiment 19's positions by Kukujewa. Moreover, an only partially cloudy sky brought excellent flying weather so that the enemy reconnaissance aircraft and bombers appeared in large numbers and our fighters and flak could once again prove their ability with numerous kills.

Already on 6.9., the ordered defensive measures were carried out on all front sectors. The main combat line was set, combat outposts were assigned, mine fields laid, patrols reconnoitred. In the evening hours, the first prisoners were already brought in.

The now following days until 12.9. were completely marked by Russian attacks against the new main combat line. It was common for two to three thrusts per day, primarily against Infantry Regiment 61. Individual sections of the front fell under the enemy's heaviest artillery fire often for hours at a time. The Russian air force also frequently attacked with bombs and machine guns from the front to far into the hinterland.

On 7.9., the Russians planned a large attack against the positions of Infantry Regiment 62, which was already in the process of being relieved, on the right wing of the division. At 14:30, intensive assembly preparations were recognized in the Dubrowka area: 12 tanks, motorized artillery, and horse-drawn wagons. The enemy brought the attack forward for several hundred meters before he was stopped and repulsed by artillery, machine gun, and rifle fire.

The Russians also continued their attacks in the following days. It was always the same picture! Here they came in platoon strength, there in company to battalion strength. And again and again, our cannon and our infantry weapons shattered the brown-yellow masses, who tried to break through our positions in purposeless and aimless attacks. Enemy casualties were extraordinarily high. Prisoners spoke of more than 70% losses.

Meanwhile events occurred by our right neighbour that made us look with worry to the south. The enemy had broken into a section with tanks that our brave 62ers had held for a good 14 days against 11 enemy attacks. The division needed to widen the front sector to the right. On the evening of 11.9., the II./ Infantry Regiment 62 returned again to its old positions. The two other battalions were relieved later in the sector of Infantry Regiment 61, which had to suffer the most under enemy attacks.

On 13.9., the enemy discontinued his attacks. His infantry was utterly exhausted. Forays by Infantry Regiments 19 and 61 on 21.9. recently produced the confirmation through prisoner statements: the Russians were no longer capable on this front of bringing forward new attacks. Their strength was broken.

Our division, however, came out of this fighting to be sure weakened by casualties, but unbroken in combat power, again ready for great tasks.

In the fighting in the Yel'nya bend, the division took in 2,296 prisoners. The number of enemy dead is estimated at more than 3,000.

In consideration of the pronounced defensive character of this battle, seized goods are minimal. 5 tanks were destroyed, 3 blown up, numerous rifles and machine guns brought in.

The division's losses in the time period 23.8. until 24.9.41 amounted to:

Killed:	5 officers	144 NCOs and men
Wounded:	19	463
Missing:	1	11

A special supplement will report on the efforts of the supply organization. Signal Battalion 7 constructed a telephone wire net of 151km. The most important command positions were reachable by various means. Disruptions through enemy actions were extraordinarily frequent. For example, the central telephone in Panjokowa had 33, [in] Byki 63, [in] Karatajeka 72, [and in] Barbarikin-Cholm 98 disruptions to eliminate. Engineer Battalion 7 secured the position through the installation of 2,000 mines and through the construction of numerous obstacles and obstructions.

As this document makes clear, the German blitzkrieg had already sputtered to a stop in the Yel'nya bend by late August 1941; the Germans were clearly on the defensive and, in a campaign that was entirely constructed around the exploitation of speed and mobility, this was a real problem. The Red Army's seemingly endless supply of men and machines also emerges from this report; it is noteworthy that only Soviet tanks make an appearance, while German armour is entirely absent. Of course, Red Army numerical superiority was not enough to tilt the battle in its favour, as German tactical superiority was reflected in the casualty totals of the two armies. Finally, the report emphasized the division's fortitude. Despite being hammered continually by the Red Army, the 7th Infantry Division maintained both the necessary combat strength and morale to continue the offensive. This resilience in combat was indeed one of the strengths of the German army during the war on the eastern front and it would be tested time and again during the course of the conflict.

German fortunes in the campaign underwent a marked reversal at the end of the year. Despite major victories during the dual encirclement battles of Briansk and Via'zma in November 1941, the power of the Panzer Groups, as well as their accompanying infantry armies, had been ground down in their struggle against the Red Army and the elements.[19] The tenuousness of German success first made itself apparent on the southern section of the front, as the following entries from the 14th Panzer Division's war diary make clear.[20] In the course of a single day, the division both celebrated its greatest achievement of the campaign, and prepared to defend the seizure of Rostov against a suddenly superior and resurgent Soviet force.

21.11.41: Therefore the 5-day fight to seize Rostov is essentially concluded. The important industrial and trading city is in German hands; the door to the Caucasus has been pushed open. The last effective rail connection for the Russians to the vitally important Caucasian oil is broken.

The achievements of the leaders and troops in combat and in enduring extraordinary hardships are exemplary and deserve to be especially emphasized. The severe strains of the last weeks of combat have been forgotten in these days. Everyone approached the last great task with an exemplary attack spirit, in order to achieve a decisive goal for the entire conduct of war. At the beginning of the attack, the Panzer Regiment had perhaps company strength [while] the combat strength of the rifle companies was generally not higher than that of a platoon. The missing of all winter clothing whatsoever made itself even more noticeable with the severe cold.

Nevertheless, a breakthrough of the deeply positioned, excellently constructed enemy positions south of the Tusloff [River] was achieved in the first onslaught, the decisive defensive victory against heavy counterattacks led with the support of the heaviest panzers on Bolschije Saly, and finally the taking of Rostov city and bridge after bitter urban combat.

However, the division learned for the first time that enemy attacks against XIVth [Motorized] Corps have become so strong, that a considerable pulling back of the front has taken place. In the area given up, there are numerous divisional vehicles, especially panzers, which during the breaking of the rain and the subsequent frost period could not be carried along due to damage. Since the division was unaware of the strong threats to the flanks, it is not possible to send more towing services than before in the area of Agrafenowka. The division must therefore consider further vehicles, which due to minor damage in the area of XIVth [Motorized] Corps, as complete write-offs.

For the division, there will unfortunately still not be the hoped for quiet that the troops so deserved after the difficult fighting on the offensive. Heavy enemy forces are on the northern flank of the deeply advanced IIIrd Panzer Corps and threaten the already won Rostov. Therefore new heavy fighting is imminent.

Within eight days, the situation had degenerated into one that the division viewed as critical:

29.11.41: This day was the most difficult for the division in the entire war against Russia. The situation is extremely *critical* because
1) the troops are *completely* exhausted, as they have been given no break since the beginning of the offensive against Rostov on 17.11. The men have been continually in the tremendous cold, almost exclusively in the open, partially without winter clothes and warm food,
2) the vehicle situation no longer allows for any large-scale movements for eventual counter-thrusts,
3) the individual battalions are so weakened through losses, that no reserves can be formed,
4) the high losses in weapons and equipment have considerably weakened the combat power,
5) the enemy continually introduces new forces and attacks in mass.

The 14th Panzer Division's complaints regarding the effects of weather on the troops and the scarcity of operational vehicles were echoed by other mechanized units. Far to the north in the Volkhov River area, the 10th Panzer Regiment – the primary armoured component of 8th Panzer Division – submitted a report detailing the unit's deficiencies.[21]

To the 8th Panzer Division Ia.,
On 7.12.41, I submitted a report about the possibility or impracticality of refreshing the regiment for wide-ranging movements under the prevailing weather conditions in the east. After taking a look at the yet again concentrated battalions of the regiment, I once more report that a refreshing and restoration of the

regiment's combat readiness, which is necessary for wide-ranging movements, is not possible due to shelter and weather conditions in this region. The regiment's equipment, especially the tanks, suffers so severely due to the cold that new equipment and equipment that has been recently repaired in the *Heimat* breaks down very quickly with great damage. It is a known fact that all metal-pieces lose their elasticity due to the strong effects of the cold and often break like glass, without being caused by intense stress. A temporary storage and shutting down of the equipment is not possible, as training and supply runs must be carried out. The bringing-up of the spare parts from Minsk would by itself strain to an intolerable extent all vehicles dedicated to this task. The experiences of the previous winter in Neuhammer and the refreshing in Bohemia have revealed that the number of trips far and away surpass the previously set number. I don't believe that the workshop is in the condition to do any of the essential things for the new revitalization, outside of the continual repairs that continually crop up due to the effects of the cold and snow. Even with its extensive experiences, it has already practically reached its capacity for vehicles that require repair. As already pointed out in the report from 7.12.41, combat strength is in the first place based upon a well-trained officer corps and properly trained crews. Due to the heavy casualties of the eastern campaign, which have amounted to 14 company commanders alone, such gaps have occurred that filling them with replacements trained in the *Heimat* is only possible numerically. One can no longer speak of this unit having a substantial combat strength. The regiment must be newly trained from the ground up. This must begin with the training of new drivers, the familiarizing of the crews with one another and their tasks, the schooling of commanders and radio operators; furthermore, the binding together of the companies to combat units through closely monitored training exercises and familiarizing each battalion's members with one another is absolutely necessary. Furthermore, new technical personnel must be trained; a large number of specialists (tank mechanics, tank radio repairmen, truck mechanics, etc.) are missing. One cannot master these tasks in snow and ice or filth and mud. For this purpose, one requires terrain and weather conditions that allow for it. Three full months is the minimum period of time required for this training. It should not be interrupted by periods of leave or else its success will be called into question. To this end, a barracks-like stay is again necessary so that through inner service, discipline can be solidified and renewed. The billeting must allow for the possibility of classroom instruction for platoons and companies. All of this is not possible in the local horse shanties.

I maintain that the refreshing and reestablishment of the regiment's combat readiness in material and personnel in the already cited period of time of 3 months is only possible in an area that permits an intensive training of personnel and the total work of the workshop and repair services during the entire time.

Only under these conditions will it be possible for the regiment to restore the old striking-power that it had on 22.6.41.

From the perspective of the regimental commander, Operation Barbarossa had shattered his unit's combat power in two ways. First, the deleterious effects of casualties – especially at the leadership level – resulted in tank crews who were neither well led nor well trained, an issue discussed in more detail in chapter 6.

Second, the constant combat and the inability to pull the unit out of the line for a necessary period of maintenance resulted in a vehicle park that possessed fewer operational vehicles by the day. Finally, the effects of the Russian winter only exacerbated the problems faced by the unit, as the lack of suitable shelter made it impossible to restore the unit's combat efficiency. His admission that the unit could no longer be compared to that which had invaded the Soviet Union on 22 June 1941 was one that could be extrapolated to the army as a whole. During the fighting of 1941, the German army that entered the conflict was transformed by the ferocious combat that it engaged in with the Red Army. When it finally emerged from the subsequent winter crisis in spring 1942, it was a much-changed force in terms of quality of leadership, material, and its relationship to the political authorities.

The Soviet offensive that erupted across the breadth of the front during the winter of 1941–42 forced the German army as a whole onto the defensive. The crisis this caused within the army is well-known; in addition to the cashiering of numerous Army Group, Army, and Panzer Group commanders and Hitler's taking control of the army by replacing *Generaloberst* Walther von Brauchitsch as Commander-in-Chief of the army, Hitler also issued his famous 'Halt order' on 16 December.[22] This order was disseminated by VIIth Army Corps on 3 January 1942 to its subordinate units informing them of the necessity of standing and fighting in place.[23]

2) Since there is not a rear area position, large sections of troops are not mobile due to a shortage of vehicles and fuel, and large areas behind the present front are not passable, every retreat means the loss of heavy equipment and sooner or later certain annihilation, quite apart from the operational and psychological consequences....

3) Thus, I order the following for the conduct of war:

a) the present lines are to be held and constructed as winter positions. Without exception, all occupied villages are without any consideration of the inhabitants to be established as strongpoints and are to be given up under no circumstances whether or not the garrisons expect to be bypassed.

Necessary improvements of positions are to be undertaken forward if possible. Every operational withdrawal is subject to my personal authorization.

b) [...]

Furthermore, the enemy's high casualties suffered due to our tenacious resistance, in combination with the expected snowfalls of mid-winter, will paralyse the Soviet-Russian attacks. Until this point in time, the order of the hour is that every village and town is to be firmly clung to, no yielding of one step, to defend one's self to the last bullet and grenade.

I expect that every officer, NCO, and man will commit themselves in this sense until the last breath. [...]

Only by such a means of combat and from no other will the success of this winter defensive battle and the victory of 1942 ripen.

Not only did Hitler's order challenge the army's traditional practice of allowing commanders to make operational and tactical decisions on the spot, but it also made clear that the German army had now shifted over to the defensive; the blitzkrieg that had been operating in fits and starts since 22 June had now finally ended. VIIth Corps then distributed its own order, emphasizing various elements of Hitler's order.[24]

> The *main combat zone* is to be held to the last man and without consideration of the changing situation of one's neighbour. By-passed, cut-off or encircled elements defend themselves in their *positions*.
>   [...]
>   The *town commanders* are responsible for the strengthening of their towns. To this end, *all* units billeted there are subordinated to him. No German soldier – it makes no difference which troop he belongs to – can be spared for the defence and its preparation.
>   The civilian population is to be used ruthlessly for this work.
>   [...]
>   A place is only to be given up when the last cartridge has been fired. Then everything that is useable is to be destroyed, the ovens are to be smashed and every house is to be set on fire. The taking of a town should give the enemy not the slightest possibility for shelter and relief.

Such orders not only encouraged the German army to act ruthlessly in order to ensure its own combat efficiency, but they also provided some certainty to units that had been caught between retreat and maintaining the line during the chaotic period of the winter crisis. For the 7th Infantry Division, these orders were simultaneously welcomed and questioned.[25]

> The order to finally hold here is welcomed with relief by the commander and the troops after the perpetual back and forth, now that the position of the 7th Division is suitably entrenched. Based on previous experiences, the division is not quite completely convinced that this is the *ultimate solution. But all the consequences have been drawn and all strength has been shifted to the construction and holding of the position!!*

This defensive fighting, however, made just as many demands on soldiers as the advance did in 1941. Two additional factors exacerbated the combat of early 1942, both essentially due to the belief that the invasion would require only three months at most to achieve victory. First, the German replacement system nearly broke down, as there simply were not enough trained men in the Reich to replace the severe casualties suffered by the Germans during the invasion. Second, due in part to an overly strained supply system, the accumulation and delivery of winter clothing was not nearly sufficient to meet the needs of the army and this led to an ever-increasing incidence of frostbite, which necessarily weakened the army's combat efficiency. The following entry from the 126th Infantry Division's war diary illustrates the problems afflicting the division during its deployment along the Volkhov River in January 1942.[26]

Our own situation is essentially defined by the high [number of] casualties and losses due to frostbite, which the division has suffered in the fighting for the Volkhov Position that has now continued for 10 days. The powers of resistance of the combat troops [who are fighting] with the utmost bravery have considerably decreased as a result of the unbroken pressure of a numerically superior enemy and one with a considerable superiority in heavy weapons, as well as due to the outsized exertions and unsatisfactory clothing and equipment for the present weather. Therefore, the division faces the shortly expected massive enemy attacks with great concern.

For the majority of Army Groups Centre and North, the fighting in 1942 degenerated into positional warfare, as the Germans attempted to hold their lines against various generally poorly coordinated Soviet offensives. On the southern portion of the front, however, the Germans concentrated their mechanized and motorized formations in preparation for another blitz campaign, Operation Blue. Here, the ultimate goal was the seizure of the Caucasian oil fields. The offensive that emerged, however, differed from that of 1941 in two important ways. First, it was much smaller than that of the previous year, as only one Army Group went on the attack. Second, German field commanders saw their control over their formations significantly decrease, as both the Army High Command (*Oberkommando des Heeres* or OKH) and Hitler looked to circumscribe their independence. One similarity that it shared with the Barbarossa campaign was the offensive's lack of a main point of emphasis. Just as in 1941 when the Germans were divided between a direct assault on Moscow and one that looked to the economically advantageous areas on the flanks, so too did Operation Blue suffer from a dispersion of force. As the campaign developed, Hitler placed increasing emphasis on what was initially seen as a subsidiary drive to Stalingrad to cover the flank of the drive on the Caucasus until it was given equal weight, thereby completely eliminating any notion of one overarching objective. By dissipating the strength of the southernmost advance, he ensured that neither could succeed.[27]

While the campaign started successfully enough in late June, by the end of September the familiar problem of stiffening Soviet resistance, over-extended supply lines and a diminishing combat strength advancing in divergent directions made it clear that the campaign had already failed. A meeting between *Generaloberst* Hermann Hoth, commanding general of Fourth Panzer Army, and the commander of XXXXVIIIth Panzer Corps in early September detailed the superiority of German tactics and practices in 1942, as well as the increasing emphasis on the notion of will in the face of German material weakness.[28]

Everywhere that the Panzer forces have been deployed narrowly concentrated and with force, the attack has been successful. The new redeployment of the corps will and must lead to success. It is clear that the enemy – compressed into a narrow area – will offer considerable resistance.

Just as the great King before the battle of Leuthen[29] took the decision to attack and defeat the enemy from an apparently hopeless position, so now all commanders and every man must be imbued with this idea, that the attack will be successful, because it must be successful for us!

Commanders who cannot guarantee the carrying out of this difficult task are to be replaced by others.

The German attack on the city of Stalingrad – the culmination of the 1942 German summer offensive – was severely hindered from the outset by supply and manpower shortages; it also is rightfully seen as one of the important turning points, both militarily and psychologically, of the Second World War. Manpower deficiencies proved extremely detrimental to German attacks on the city. Most units that fought in Stalingrad had not reached their full complement of men even before the German summer offensive began at the end of June. By mid-September, the majority of the units had fought without respite for nearly two months and had received few replacements, and this manpower situation considerably worsened due to heavy combat within the city. The 71st Infantry Division, an experienced first-class infantry unit that carried out the primary thrust into the centre of the city, reported the following strength of its infantry units on 19 September 1942:[30]

Infantry Regiment 191		Infantry Regiment 194		Infantry Regiment 211	
1st Comp.	25 men	1st Comp.	12 men	1st Comp.	24 men
2nd Comp.	17 men	2nd Comp.	22 men	2nd Comp.	disbanded
3rd Comp.	20 men	3rd Comp.	14 men	3rd Comp.	disbanded
4th Comp.	32 men	4th Comp.	23 men	4th Comp.	28 men
Staff Ist Bat.	7 men	Staff Ist Bat.	20 men	Staff Ist Bat.	disbanded
5th Comp.	10 men	5th Comp.	7 men	5th Comp.	27 men
6th Comp.	13 men	6th Comp.	13 men	6th Comp.	22 men
7th Comp.	12 men	7th Comp.	10 men	7th Comp.	disbanded
8th Comp.	40 men	8th Comp.	23 men	8th Comp.	43 men
Staff IInd Bat.	17 men	Staff IInd Bat.	6 men	Staff IInd Bat.	31 men
9th Comp.	7 men	9th Comp.	8 men	9th Comp.	disbanded
10th Comp.	13 men	10th Comp.	9 men	10th Comp.	44 men
11th Comp.	19 men	11th Comp.	13 men	11th Comp.	disbanded
12th Comp.	35 men	12th Comp.	27 men	12th Comp.	38 men
Staff IIIrd Bat.	7 men	Staff IIIrd Bat.	20 men	Staff IIIrd Bat.	17 men
13th Comp.	53 men	13th Comp.	50 men	13th Comp.	61 men
14th Comp.	50 men	14th Comp.	40 men	14th Comp.	57 men

Regimental Staff 72 men   Regimental Staff 96 men   Regimental Staff 80 men

The combat strength of a full rifle company was around 150 men; most companies were therefore reduced to between 10 to 30 per cent of their original combat strength. It is also clear that, even within the infantry, the risk of being killed varied widely. The companies normally not involved in close combat (the 4th, 8th and 12th with heavy machine guns and mortars, the 13th with infantry guns, and the 14th with anti-tank guns) suffered smaller losses than normal riflemen companies.

In the upcoming weeks, Stalingrad became a proper meat-grinder for both sides. In the second half of September alone the Soviets threw some 100,000 men over the Volga into the city. But even with these reinforcements, the defending 62nd Army had fewer men at hand at the end of the month than it had only two weeks prior.[31] The lack of men and material forced German forces to try to conquer Stalingrad piece by piece, with time-consuming breaks taken for regrouping and the building up of available stocks. In October, there were frequent breaks of up to one week between German attacks; clearly the German summer offensive had petered out in the ruins of Stalingrad. For every further attack, additional units needed to be scraped together, but every unit sent to Stalingrad was found only by weakening Sixth Army's flanks. The practical meaning for the units there is clearly portrayed in a report of the XIth Army Corps, subordinated to Sixth Army and defending the area around the Soviet Don bridgehead by Kremenskaia.[32]

Through the use of all available strength, the troops work to build a continuous main battle line, an artillery protection position and blocking positions. [...] Every man in the XIth Corps is aware that the main battle line has to be held to the outmost.

But I feel myself obliged to point out, that the demands in the order could not be completely fulfilled at this time in the area of XIth Corps.

I report in detail:

1) The front area of the Corps on 27.9. amounts to 77km, consisting in part of extremely confusing terrain, that provides the enemy with the ability to easily approach [our lines]. In this section are 3 weak and worn-out divisions with 22 battalions deployed at the front (5 strong, 3 medium-strength, 7 average, 7 weak). The artillery consists of 18 light batteries (64 guns), 9 heavy batteries (30 guns), 4 *Nebelwerfer* batteries (21 launchers). Additionally, 3 engineer battalions (1 strong, 2 weak), 3 anti-tank battalions (7 companies), 1 reconnaissance battalion, 1 flak battalion with 6 flak-machine guns set for land battle, and 2 weak construction battalions are available. A continuous manning of the practically 80km main battle line to stop the penetration of the enemy is impossible with these forces. [...] It should be noted that the combat strength decreases daily. Over 600 men fell out of the 384th Infantry Division in just the time from 18.-22.9.1942.

2) The corps has absolutely no reserves, they are available to divisions only in an inadequate form. Generally, even in minor enemy combat operations, the valuable engineers must be used immediately. [...]. The shifting of reserves on the long frontline is hindered; the corps has only one divisional reconnaissance battalion at hand that has the mobility to reach an endangered position in time. Once this unit is in action, infantry reserves must be shifted, and they often arrive too late. The availability of vehicles is hindered by the high demands for supplies and by the lack of fuel. Therefore, the demand for a swift counterthrust can only be rarely fulfilled.

3) The construction of the main battle line, the blocking positions, the artillery protection position and the absolutely necessary quarters have

run into major difficulties and can only be completed before the beginning of the winter, if a *considerable* amount of labour, wood, construction material, and obstacles is delivered shortly. The troops are so weakened by the preceding tasks and through constant combat, and additionally by the continuous sentry duty, insufficient meals, inadequate quarters and hygienic shortcomings, that their work performance falls far below the normal rate.

4) The division's level of training is extremely low. Due to the continuous fighting and the necessity of building positions, the carrying out of a training program is neither possible at this time, nor in the foreseeable future. An intensive, systematic training phase would be inevitably required, since the troops completely lack suitable junior leaders, the most recently arrived replacements are absolutely insufficiently trained and, in general, the front-line troops are heavily reinforced with less aggressive men drawn from the baggage train, which has been combed out to the limits. These men consist nearly exclusively of *panje* drivers, who in crisis situations could become a burden for the [frontline] troops.

5) The will to hold out and the recognition of the need to persevere fully exists for all higher and middle leaders. Physical and mental exhaustion, however, cannot be ignored and it causes some concern. It requires the particular influence of the higher leadership, to inspire the appreciation for the demands of the *Führererlass*.[33] A large section of the younger officers lack any combat experience, or understanding of the officer's outlook and the handling of men. It is scarcely possible to change this situation in the foreseeable time. The NCO corps is severely decimated. It seems necessary to take accelerated and effective measures for its reconstruction. The men's mental attitude has suffered from the considerable strain and the temporarily scarce provisions. The thin manning [of the frontline] that is visible even to him and the feeling that he is insufficiently trained impairs his will to fight. Worries about the *Heimat* threatened by bombing trouble him. Only a long period of quiet and training could restore the necessary fighting power.

I am aware that the worries of the XIth Corps must step back behind the decisive operations of the army in Stalingrad. On the other hand, I regard it as my duty to describe the corps' actual situation and to propose means for relief before it is too late.

Even under these circumstances, Sixth Army tried desperately to fulfil Hitler's will to completely conquer Stalingrad. But what did the fighting inside the city look like? This can be seen in an after-action report of one of the final attacks launched by German forces in Stalingrad. On 11 November 1942, Engineer Battalion 179 tried to take Hall 4 of the steel works 'Red October', one of the last Soviet strongholds on the western bank of the Volga river.[34]

The 79th Infantry Division carried out an attack against the northwest section of the open hearth furnace hall (Hall 4) as a preparation for the final defeat of Red October. Engineer Battalion 179, reinforced by the 3./Panzer Engineer

Battalion 40, was deployed in the following echelon: on the right 3./Panzer Engineer Battalion 40, in the centre 1./Engineers 179 (in the hall itself), on the left 2./Engineer Battalion 179, with the 3. (motorized)/Engineer Battalion 179, in reserve in the centre. The combined strength was 120 men, which attacked as assault groups in four wedges with the support of heavy weapons against Hall 4. The objective was the seizure of the broad part of Hall 4.

The companies reached their jumping-off area between 1 and 2a.m. at the railway line eastward of Hall 4. At 2.50a.m. the formation of the spearheads was completed. At 3.55a.m., our heavy weapons first opened up on the hall, beginning on the centre of the north-western section of Hall 4. Despite the range being known, the original intention to direct this opening fire on the front side of the hall had to be given up, due to the danger of shots falling short because of the guns' cold barrels.

Immediately after the first fire strikes of our own weapons, the enemy started to return fire. His artillery fire partly targeted our jumping-off area. On our side, the first severe losses occurred even before we had even started the attack. The spearhead group of wedge III that was lying behind a pile of stones on the railway line received a direct hit. One man died, four were severely wounded, including the leader of the spearhead. Due to another hit on the second assault group of the second wedge (behind the house on the railway embankment), a group leader and four men fell out of the fighting. Weakened in leaders and enlisted men in this way, the spearheads attacked.

Wedge I: Advanced from Hall 3, it worked forward by several rushes, but was stopped at the locomotive shed by violent machine-gun fire from Hall 4 and took a defensive position with a front towards Hall 4.

Wedge II: Under cover of early morning darkness, the assault group advanced over craters and rubble to the right front corner of Hall 4. Suppressed by concentrated defensive fire (close combat arms), the spearhead could not push into the hall from here as planned. An advance on the right external wall seemed the only possibility. Extremely heavy machine gun fire from the first right entry blocked the further advance of *Feldwebel* Fetzer's spearhead. *Feldwebel* Fetzer knocked out that machine gun with a satchel charge, ordered a part of his group to get in and then led the mass of his unit forward to the second side door. Our own machine gun provided the necessary covering fire. Shot at by enemy snipers firing through hatches, openings and hidden nooks, the spearhead penetrated into the hall from the side. The inextricable mess of iron parts, debris from the wall, destroyed machines, twisted beams and rubble demanded the highest concentration and decisively delayed the advance. The men were dazed by the chaos before their eyes. It was impossible to take a secure step, as there was no footing in the jumble of iron pieces. Inevitably, attention was therefore kept off the enemy. At once, concentrated enemy defensive fire from all directions opened up after the penetration. Satchel charges, hand grenades, and submachine gun salvos hindered all further advances to main Hall 4. The enemy was surprisingly strong. It was a matter of massed forces, which included in addition to the well camouflaged defensive units, behind steel parapets and iron containers, riflemen in open positions. It was determined, among other things, that fire came from numerous thick-walled iron tanks with small fire openings. The walls of these tanks were around 15cm thick and they could withstand even satchel charges. In many cases these tanks were piled upon one another and this allowed a skilful flanking fire. With the utmost effort and satchel charges, as well as hand grenades, the group – after penetrating 30-40m into the hall – secured the side wall as rear cover. After the loss of its best soldiers, it worked back to door 1, very well supported from the squad left back there, and retreated to the locomotive hall.

Wedge III: Due to preliminary losses that left it severely weakened, the assault wedge reached the front side of the hall. The assault group leader already was lost. The spearhead blasted the wire-blocked entrance with satchel charges and penetrated a few meters into the hall. The enemy's uncontrollable defensive fire, partly from nearby, brought further losses. The enormous chaos inside the hall prevented any observation. A further penetration was not possible.

Wedge IV: Despite the loss of the leader, who was severely wounded after a few minutes, and many men, the assault wedge worked quickly forward on the left outside wall and penetrated under cover of the dawn along the freight cars up to 30-40m in front of Hall 4. Heavy fire from the rear and from openings of the side wall opened up at sunrise, causing many losses. An attempt to create a connection to the right was made by blasting the side wall of the hall. This intention failed. In the process, the deputy commander of the assault wedge fell, as he received a shot to his heart while bandaging an arm wound. The remaining men had to retreat.

All wedges suffered further losses, including among others two wounded artillery spotters due to hidden sniper fire, and through artillery and mortars. The difficult rescue of the wounded claimed numerous victims.

The enemy's concentrated and surprisingly heavy defensive fire, as well as the quick readiness of the artillery raises suspicions that our attack was carried out against an enemy who was prepared for a major attack. From this point of view, our defeated attack should be marked as a success for the defence.

Losses: [...] Total: 1/6 dead, 12/26 wounded, 0/4 missing, 0/5 frostbite [NCOs/enlisted men].

Such losses meant that no less than 50 per cent of the units' initial strength was lost in a single attack, one that achieved no gains. It was therefore no surprise that the commander of the battalion justified his unit's failure in the last sentence of the report. Obviously command and control proved very difficult to achieve on such a chaotic and fragmented battle site. These types of combat situations led German forces to rely on commanders leading their troops from the front, consequently resulting in high losses among junior officers. This command practice is why no lost officers were mentioned in the attack above – by this stage of the battle, the battalion commander was the only remaining officer in the entire unit! German infantry tactics typically utilized assault groups in platoon, or even sometimes smaller, size. The units would push forward to a given line, while reserves would then 'clean-up' the overrun area. These assault groups normally included a mix of weapons, relying heavily on automatic weapons (e.g. submachine guns) and were lightly equipped. The next wave of forces could rely on heavier weapons, such as ATGs (anti-tank guns) and infantry guns, single artillery pieces or heavy flak guns, including the famous 88mm gun, to reduce strongholds. Realizing that their preparatory fire only hindered their mission by creating more rubble and alerting the Soviet defender to an oncoming attack, the Germans limited the duration of their initial bombardments.

After being ground down by such urban fighting, the German Sixth Army was encircled and destroyed by Red Army forces, finally surrendering on 2 February 1943. Unlike the defeat in front of Moscow in 1941, which forced the Germans back several hundred kilometres but which failed to remove large formations from the German order of battle, the destruction of Sixth Army and the loss of four Axis armies completely unhinged German forces in the southern part of the Soviet Union. Due to the shift in initiative across the entire front as result of the battle of Stalingrad, scorched earth retreats became part of the German army's arsenal on the battlefield. In spring 1943, two nearly simultaneous retreats of this nature took place. In late February/early March, elements of Army Group North's Sixteenth Army cleared the Demiansk Pocket, while Army Group Centre's Ninth Army carried out a similar retreat from the Rzhev salient.[35] The following order from IXth Army Corps provides a glimpse at how such retreats were understood and planned for by the German army in early 1943.[36]

I. *In General*
   1) Every opportunity to do harm to the enemy, to slow down his movement, [and] to disrupt his supply is to be exploited.

   The divisions are responsible for the destruction in their movement corridors.

   The engineer commanders are commissioned for the scouting, preparation and carrying out.
   2) *The carrying-out of the destruction* is to be arranged according to an exact *plan of destruction.*
   3) All destruction is to be brought into harmony with the troop's tactical movements.

   Preparations for the destruction on the highway, rail road, and the Via'zma area takes place through the corps. The commander of Engineer Regimental Staff 517 is tasked with its preparation (Special Order).

   The *carrying-out* of the destruction occurs on the order of the troop commander, in general the rear-guard (rear-guards) commander.

   Orders for the demolition of especially important objects are to be given in writing to the explosive groups.
II. *Destruction in the Main Defensive Area and in the Movement Corridors*
   1) With the beginning of the movement, the existing gaps in the obstacles in the *main defensive area* are to be closed, and the communication trenches and supply roads are to be blocked.

   As long as they cannot be inconspicuously mined, pillboxes and combat installations are to be strewn with booby traps and mines.
   2) To be destroyed in the *movement corridors*:
       a) fountains
       b) all larger and important bridging objects, especially those vitally important for supply traffic of the enemy in the muddy time. [...]
       c) heated halls, garages for vehicles, workshops.

d) command posts and troop camps, especially in the vicinity of the rail stations [...]

e) supply installations including equipment and vehicles

f) other objects important for combat (hospitals, warehouses, etc)

Mines need to be scattered on all bridge by-passes of demolition objects and on all fords against tanks and trucks. [...]

3) *Destruction of Shelters*

It begins with the withdrawal from the Ia-Line and is to be correspondingly carried out with the march movements.

The still remaining civilian population is to be consolidated into individual houses; that which is necessary for life is to be left for them.

Special commandos (ski troops off the street) are to be assigned for the carrying out of this destruction. The troops are to be correspondingly equipped with the necessary materials (matches, Molotov cocktails, etc). That is to be organized now.

4) *Destruction of Material and Supply Goods*

No weapon, no equipment, no supply goods can fall in the hands of the enemy.

The first principle is that all weapons (including captured weapons), all ammunition, especially scare munitions, are to be saved and sent away.

As long as ammunition cannot be evacuated, it is to be shot-off on enemy artillery, previously known assembly areas, etc. beginning immediately or to be used for the demolition of objects in the main defensive area.

As long as food stocks, fodder, etc. cannot be evacuated, a timely destruction is to be *guaranteed* (open potato clamps).

Ovens and stove pipes as well as windows are to be saved and delivered to the new position. There will be no new deliveries. [...]

III. *Destruction in front of 'Buffalo'*

A 15km deep desert zone is to be created forward of the 'Buffalo' position.

The population necessary for keeping the roads clear is to be consolidated in towns and villages during the course of the march. All remaining towns and villages are to be destroyed, beginning now (windows and wood for bunker construction). The burning down can be carried out with the beginning of the movement. The failure to do so in order that the troops marching through can secure shelter *is forbidden.*

The commanders of the fortification construction staffs are responsible for the destruction. They are to personally report in writing the complete destruction (with maps). [...]

As the order indicated, scorched earth retreats were based on the notion of military necessity or, in other words, trying to ensure that the German army remained superior in the field to its Soviet counterpart. Anything that could benefit the on-coming Red Army was either to be destroyed – such as shelters, bridges, or installations – or dragged to the rear – such as weapons, food, and ammunition. Of particular note, the order made no mention of forcibly evacuating the civilian population, which later became an important component of scorched earth retreats; instead, it explicitly stated that civilians were to be left with enough food to live. How this was enforced is of course an entirely different issue, and depended on how the officer or NCO in charge interpreted how much food was needed for civilians' survival and how much was required by the army for its tasks and even its perceived survival.

The defensive and positional warfare posture adopted by the army in the northern and central sections of the front is well captured by an entry in the 126th Infantry Division's war diary from March 1943.[37]

I visited the 5th, 6th, 7th, 8th, and sections of the 13th and 14th companies of [Infantry Regiment] 426 and the deployed battalions of the 1st and 2nd [Mobile Battalion], the mounted rifle platoon 426, flak and the reconnaissance squadron. The combat position here lies in the middle of a swamp. With every step, one breaks through the thin covering of ice up to the knee. Elements of the men have absolutely no shelter and, wrapped in blankets, sleep during the day next to the machine gun as long as they do not have fatigue duty. At any moment, one must be prepared for a heavy artillery attack, which has repeatedly come on previous days. The battalion, which has repelled heavy Russian attacks and is well supported with anti-tank weapons, confidently looks forward to the coming weeks. The spring sun gives a new optimism despite the difficult circumstances.

Important elements of the German combat experience in the east are found in this passage. Soviet artillery superiority was a fact of life for much, if not all, of the German army from 1942 on, and the experiences of the 126th Infantry Division certainly fell into this general trend. The introduction of new weapons – such as the MG 42 or the 7.5cm ATG 40 – allowed the under-manned German infantry to even the odds against its Soviet opponent and this, in combination with the fact that Red Army attacks had been repeatedly repulsed over the course of two years on this section of the front, fed into the German army's still meaningful confidence on the battlefield. Issues of terrain, however, had yet to be solved, and these plagued the army throughout the entirety of the campaign.

This defensive mind-set was even applied to the panzer divisions that had served as the foundation for Germany's string of victories based on mobility and manoeuvre between 1939 and 1941. While his division was situated in the Polotsk-Vitebsk area, the 8th Panzer Division's commander explained to his officers the unit's role in early summer 1943:[38]

I. The *situation* of the army is clear. The army must hold its present position at all costs. The Russian has a particularly favourable spring board near us in order to achieve success. We cannot move back to the west under any circumstances. The *Eastern Wall* of our army must hold out against everything.

We need an Eastern Wall of men and it must be built to the utmost. [...]

Every man must be clear and unambiguous about this understanding of the Eastern Wall.

The wall must be held at all costs by weak forces.

[...]

II. Much has already been written and spoken, but it has not yet been translated
   into action such as the army must demand. Many orders of the army have been
   perceived as meddling.
   This is not as it should be.
   The will is to be translated into action that is decisive.
   A side effect of positional warfare is that details need to be ordered [from
above]. Unfortunately, there are still commands in which the necessary vigour
does not prevail.
   Guidelines for all commanders to emphatically do this. Especially the weak
ones must be exhorted to this end.
   Carelessness will not be tolerated, for that reason alone we are poor [in men
and equipment].
   Positional warfare brings the danger that a slackening occurs too easily. This
danger must be universally combated.
   First and foremost, the troops' spirit of the attack and their feelings of
superiority towards the Russians need to be promoted.
   The will for action and for work must be emphasized, when necessary through
a hard grip. Other than that, recognition in any form.

The very fact that a panzer commander spoke about the need to maintain a
'wall' spoke volumes about conditions on the northern and central sectors of
the Eastern front; clearly the German approach to combat was in a state of
transformation. This emerged from the statement on 'meddling'. What was once
seen as interfering with a commander's prerogative on the battlefield was now
seen as a necessity, due both to the larger context of the war in the east and to the
loss of experienced commanders who had been replaced by 'weak ones'. Finally,
the commander's emphasis on the importance of will reflected a larger trend
within the army that looked to balance out the Red Army's growing quantitative
and in some cases qualitative superiority with the supremacy of the individual
German soldier, an issue further addressed in chapter 7.
   In addition to its primary mission of fighting the Red Army on the battlefield, the
army also found itself increasingly engaged in combat in the rear area, fighting an
ever-burgeoning partisan movement.[39] This insurgency proved especially intractable
in the centre of the front, as the large forests and swamps offered numerous areas for
partisan bands to regroup and hide. German anti-partisan policy evolved by 1943
into one in which large operations had become the standard response. Involving
various formations – including front-line panzer and infantry divisions – these were
true military operations that looked to encircle and destroy insurgent groups.[40] The
following report concerning the outcome of Operation 'Gypsy Baron' provides a
look at the partisan threat facing the army and the Germans' response to it.[41]

   1) Operation 'Gypsy Baron' is concluded except for Group Bornemann's cleansing
      out of the corner Ssov-Nerusea on 6.6.43. In combat against a devious enemy
      with tremendous terrain difficulties in a swampy, heavily-mined forest area, the
      troops succeeded through considerable exertions in annihilating the majority
      of the gangs[42] in the area south of Briansk, destroying their shelters and seizing
      a large amount of goods.

[...]
8) Enemy losses and seized goods during Operation 'Gypsy Baron':

1,525 prisoners

869 deserters

1,536 enemy dead, the number of dead in reality will be substantially higher as it has been determined that the gangs buried their dead immediately after battle

15,801 evacuated civilians

201 destroyed camps

2,915 destroyed bunkers and battle positions

9 pistols [...]

1,093 rifles, of which 175 were [semi-]automatic, 26 gun barrels

87 machine pistols

123 machine guns, outside of numerous machine gun mounts and drums [...]

55 mortars

14 anti-tank guns, 2 anti-tank gun barrels [...]

9 light guns

12 heavy guns

3 tanks, including 1 T-34

2 armoured scout cars

2 planes, including one with telephone and radio equipment [...]

165,720 rounds of rifle ammunition

Around 30,000 rounds of machine gun ammunition

11,000 rounds of heavy machine gun ammunition [...]

183 sleds

316 horses

380 cows

717 panje wagons

Clothing and equipment for some 500 men

The complexity of the partisan war emerges clearly from this document. On the one hand, the partisan movement possessed the military means to threaten German lines of communication and supply, as well as the troops themselves. In addition to large numbers of small arms, machine guns, and considerable quantities of ammunition, German troops seized artillery pieces, tanks, armoured cars and even two planes (of course whether any of the latter were operational was left unsaid). On the other hand, German losses for the operation were quite small, suggesting that it was not characterized by pitched battles.[43] In contrast, Soviet casualties of over 1,500 dead suggest that the army's pacification policies frequently degenerated into arbitrary murder of civilians. The economic aspect of the operation also clearly emerges as cows, horses, wagons, and, most importantly, nearly 16,000 civilians were deported to the German rear for their use. This report therefore demonstrated the ways in which German military and economic goals – influenced by Nazi ideological beliefs – were inextricably entwined on the Eastern front. It also illustrated the various tasks that an increasingly strained and under-manned German army was being called on to complete. Since the army found it extremely difficult to adequately train its men for the multiplicity of these missions, violence frequently became the foundation of those – such as anti-partisan policy – which were deemed secondary to its primary task of combat.

July 1943 witnessed the last gasp of German offensive warfare during the Battle of Kursk. The scaling down of German goals for this offensive clearly indicated that the army had severely bled during the preceding years of war. Instead of an offensive designed to destroy the entirety of the Red Army and Soviet state, as in 1941, or one predicated on seizing the Caucasus oil fields and hopefully smashing the remaining Soviet power sent to defend the southern wing in 1942, the objective in 1943 was much more modest. It centred on ironing out a Soviet bulge in the line and destroying Soviet offensive capabilities, thus freeing German troops for use as a reserve both in the East and for deployment in other threatened theatres. Postponed several times due to the desire to introduce the Panther and Tiger tanks to the battlefield, the Germans lost any element of surprise and the battle closely resembled the attritional warfare of the First World War, albeit fought with the primary weapons of the Second World War – tanks, planes in the role of tank hunters, and ATGs.⁴⁴ While the decisive engagement of the battle was fought on the southern wing, it was the failure of Ninth Army's attack on the northern wing that ultimately doomed the offensive. The 7th Infantry Division, located on the far left shoulder of Ninth Army's advance, went onto the attack on 5 July and, though it reached its goals on the first day, subsequent attacks in the following days made very limited progress; by 16 July, the division had been withdrawn from the offensive in order to meet a major Soviet counterattack launched against the Orel bulge. For the next three and a half weeks, the division participated in costly defensive fighting against the Red Army until it took up positions in the Hagen Line in mid-August. The following monthly status divisional report was sent to its superior corps on 1 August 1943 and details the effects of such heavy fighting on the unit and its combat efficiency.⁴⁵

1. Personnel Situation on cut-off date of report: 1.8.43
   a) Missing ranks: 95 officers (of which 14 are medics, 3 veterinarians, 9 officials)
      492 NCOs
      2,822 Men
      180 Hiwi⁴⁶
   b) casualties and other departures in the reporting period from 1.7.43 to 31.7.43
      officers: 23 dead, 100 wounded, 3 missing, 4 sick, 6 left for other reasons
      NCOs and men: 518 dead, 2,997 wounded, 165 missing, 194 sick, 111 left for other reasons
   c) replacements who arrived during the reporting period
      officers: 11 replacements, 4 convalescents
      NCOs and men: 780 replacements, 196 convalescents. [...]
      3. Value Judgement of the Commander
   1) Combat Value
      The division has been in large-scale fighting for one month. The hard fighting during Operation Citadel, the extremely difficult actions of the

division in defending the enemy's major offensive and the beginnings of the Hagen-movement carried out under the most difficult combat conditions with the highest physical and mental stress for the combatants have considerably reduced the division's high combat value. The division has suffered very high numbers of casualties and an extraordinary number of weapon and equipment losses.

The troops, who can scarcely get any rest, are completely exhausted physically, have reached the edge of their effectiveness and are no longer capable of offensive actions.

On the defensive, the front only holds when the artillery is the decided bearer of the defence and the man in the trench knows that tanks or a mobile panzer defence is behind him. The troops can only move forward for counter-thrusts through extraordinarily spirited leaders under the accompaniment of tanks or assault guns. The high losses of precisely the best leaders and soldiers have left hardly any such leaders. In case of enemy breakthroughs, continual crisis situations are the result. The ceaseless large-scale combat, without any possibility for sufficient sleep or the necessary quiet and care, has taken its toll on the troops so that even the strongest wills can no longer muster the strength to resist or for the simplest tasks of daily life. A long period of rest is urgently required for refreshment and training in order to cover the missing leaders, NCOs and specialists and to train the replacements (partially older year age group, men rated as indispensible, men from Alsace) who are in no way sufficient for the demands of the war in the east.

The loss of artillery observers, signal personnel of all units and drivers and medical personnel is threatening. Therefore, crisis situations that arose could only be mastered through the mobilization of all strength. It must again be started here through systematic training.

In line with the high casualties are the division's losses of weapons. Without assault guns, panzer security is no longer available due to the very high losses of weapons in the anti-tank battalion and the 14th Companies. The equipping of the division with self-propelled ATGs has proven itself to be absolutely necessary [...]

Mobility:

Due to the high losses in horses and vehicles, mobility has considerably sunk from that of the previous month.

Infantry is on average 75% mobile.

Artillery with the light battalions is about 60%, with the heavy battalion, 55%.

During a march movement, numerous vehicles can only move in shuttle traffic.

Mobility of the heavy ATGs have sunk to 50% due to the losses of towing vehicles.

2) Morale and Mood

With its deprivations and stresses, the large-scale battle depressed the attitudes of the overburdened troops, without leading one to characterize their attitude as bad.

Political events, the continual attacks on the cities of the *Heimat* shake the heart and mind of the soldiers. All of these events together cripple the confident mood.

When the soldiers can again properly rest and sleep, the attitude will quickly reach its old high level. [...]

Concluding Judgement:

Due to its present combat strength, the condition of each individual soldier, [and] the weapon and equipment outfitting, the division is *not* capable of an attack. With support from assault guns or tanks, after the feeding of the necessary number of officers, and when it is freshly rested, it can defend a sector appropriate to its strength.

The various issues that afflicted German combat efficiency during the war in the east all emerge in this document. Heavy casualties were simply not made up for by newly arriving replacements and, perhaps even more importantly, those killed and wounded were the experienced officers, NCOs and veterans of the rank and file desperately required by the unit during a period of such high-intensity combat. Losses of specialists were similarly detrimental to the divisions as the incoming soldiers from the rear did not possess the necessary training to fill these vital roles. Material deficiencies – ranging from shortages of horses and vehicles to ATGs and assault guns – significantly limited both the division's mobility and its defensive capabilities against Soviet armour. Finally, the battle itself cannot be separated from the larger context of the war: while the men struggled against a more powerful and mobile foe, they were also aware of the bombing of their homes and the developing situation in Italy. Morale in 1943 increasingly became an issue that worried German authorities. In sum, these various issues led to the formation – a first-wave, elite infantry division – being classified as not only incapable of attack, but also able to mount a strong defence only after certain conditions had been met. This exemplified the 'infantry crisis' that plagued the German army from mid-1943 on, one further discussed in chapters 3 and 6.

Following the defeat at Kursk, the pendulum of war permanently swung in favour of the Red Army, as it maintained the initiative for the remainder of the conflict. While the Soviet offensive to the north of the Kursk salient sparked the end of Operation Citadel, it was the counter-offensives to the south in the second half of 1943 that put real pressure on the German army in the east. The following report issued by the 306th Infantry Division highlighted the experiences of a German unit during this period of combat and retreat.[47]

1) The attached report of an experienced regimental commander proven in heavy fighting accurately portrays the condition of the troops known to me for weeks.

Under strictest application of Führer order No.6 with pistol in the hand, *Oberstleutnant* Wittmüss had [again] personally led companies to the front, whose officers had fallen. He has again proven the necessary hardness for large-scale, intensive fighting.

He has been instructed by me, that an extraction of the 306th Infantry Division or even parts of it seems impossible in the actual operational and tactical situation.

2) After consultation with the divisional doctor, I report on the health condition of the fighting troops:

   a) All cases of non-communicable diseases remain with the troops.

   b) Since the troops had no opportunity for bathing or washing for 2½ months, they are completely full of lice.

   c) 60% suffered from scabies, 20% have lower-leg ulcers or extensive periarthritis.

   d) Under normal circumstances, around 25% of the fighting troops had to be treated for 3-4 weeks in a military hospital.

   e) The combat power suffers from complete physical exhaustion. It was found several times that individual soldiers were no longer responsive or that their will to survive had fully disappeared.

Appendix: Grenadier-Regiment[48] 579/Cdr., Value judgement on the combat power of the regiment, 1.12.43

In its current condition, the regiment as a unit cannot cope with offensive or defensive tasks.

Through uninterrupted action lasting for weeks, combat morale and the state of training have decreased to a point, which can only be termed as deficient.

Its causes lay in the following:

1) A welding together of the *Kampfgemeinschaft* has been largely hampered by disproportionately numerous changes in command and fluctuations of rank and file through casualties. For example the I. battalion has changed its battalion leader ten times since the last Mius battle. In the period from the beginning of October until now, 28 company and battalion leaders have been withdrawn due to injuries, with an average of 6 companies in action. In the same period, while 48 NCOs were sent as replacements, 76 NCOs were wounded, and with 525 men sent as replacements, 586 fell out. The balance between replacements and losses has been covered by the combing-out of the baggage train. Losses were nearly completely men from the [regiment's] combat strength.

2) The physical demands of officers, NCOs and rank and file have reached a dimension in the last weeks that exceed the soldiers' strength. The rank and file's state of exhaustion, which leads to indifference towards all events and disinterest in one's own fate, has up to now been balanced out only to a certain percentage by the unparalleled example and ruthless severity of officers and the few remaining NCOs, who in many cases forced the will to resist in the frontline with pistols in hand.

3) The increase of demands in the last 3 weeks combined with the losses of 30.11. (from 7 [officers]:28 [NCOs]:201 [men] attacking soldiers, 6:6:61 have become casualties, which means 60 per cent of officers, 20 per cent of NCOs and 30 per cent of the men) has caused the troops' resistance power to drop to the minimum, especially since the designated and urgently needed authorized day of rest on 11.11. as well as on 26.11. could not be

executed, but rather in its place a night movement under most difficult road conditions had to be carried out. Alertness at night could only be achieved by forcing the soldiers to stand next to their foxholes. Lack of trust in themselves and in their ability to use their weapons is widespread and this is caused by the fact that machine guns generally only fire, when a NCO or an offices himself mans the weapon.

Despite the circumstances described above, I believe the troops to be good in their substance and the condition is caused by overstrain, and is not a phenomenon of the fifth war year. A short period of relaxation is necessary, in which NCOs and officers could again influence their men; raising of morale and physical refreshment are inevitable. Then, in a short time, the will to resist will increase, the combat power will strengthen and the value of the troops which had proven itself many times in numerous hard fights in the past again will be achieved.

As this report notes, continual Soviet offensives had an extremely deleterious effect on the German army's combat efficiency. As pointed or in previous documents, the losses of experienced commanders and men fell disproportionately on the combat units and, while their numbers could at least be partially made up for by putting rear-area soldiers into the front lines, their training, knowledge and abilities were simply lost. Constant combat meant that soldiers had no time to tend to their hygienic needs and this inevitably resulted in lice infestation and a series of debilitating diseases. The combination of sickness, a leadership vacuum and simple physical and mental exhaustion culminated in a situation in which a frontline German infantry regiment was assessed as incapable of mounting either a successful offensive or defensive operation. According to the regimental commander, only a period of sustained rest would allow for the unit to return to its previous state; for the German army in late 1943, however, the scarcity of reserves meant that rest was a luxury it could not afford.

The infantry crisis that permeated the German army in 1943 and 1944 was starkly described in the following letter sent by the first general staff officer (Ia) in the elite *Grossdeutschland* Division to a superior in December 1943.[49]

I used today's thick fog to somewhat more closely inspect the present main combat line and to speak with the regimental commanders, the battalion leaders and the NCOs leading the companies. The following brief description comes out of this information.

1) The present main combat line (or MCL) is even significantly less favourable than it appears on the map; nearly the entire section of the Fusilier Regiment can be seen from a long distance on all sides and therefore it receives extraordinarily high casualties through enemy fire. The enemy himself has his numerous ATGs so superbly built into his line that in general, they have not been detected and combated by our Panzers. A shifting of the MCL into the prepared line on both sides of Wyssokij would therefore be especially desirable.

2) I myself looked at the just brought-in prisoners of the newly deployed independent 31st Guard Panzer Brigade, namely of the Motorized Rifle Battalion. They were again for the most part briefly trained Ukrainians, who, however, made a good impression. The sending in of this brigade shows that the enemy still has his main point of emphasis in this sector and therefore will again pursue his goal of a breakthrough in the next few days. This will give us no quiet in the next few days.

3) The following is to be said about our own troops:

Such a degree of exhaustion, which cannot be exceeded, has now occurred in all parts [of the regiments] up to the regimental staffs. As far as I know, we are indeed the sole division that has been constantly deployed at the point of emphasis and almost daily in combat without a day's rest since the beginning of July (start of [Operation] Citadel). The result of this constant combat is that the greater part of the officers and almost all NCOs have become casualties and also a cadre of veteran men no longer exists. The few remaining officers found at the front are the only ones who can master the situation that now exists there, but they are no longer supported by NCOs because they are no longer available. Almost all of the men are apathetic to such an extent, that they are fully indifferent to being shot dead by their own officers or by the Russians. It is already sufficient for the Russians to stand up in their trenches and shout 'Hurra' to prompt everyone getting up out of our fox holes and retreating. This is the moment when even the most able officer no longer has any influence over the troops. The retreating men don't even react to threats made with weapons any more. Any art of persuasion or appealing to their honour is likewise fruitless. One therefore needs to take into consideration that the men of these battalions are the best that there are in the German army because they constitute a carefully chosen group of replacements from the entirety of the Reich. The recruits, the majority of which unfortunately have already fallen, of course first and foremost look to the veterans and they retreat just as older men do, when they see the poor example. I have had details described to me on the spot that I will spare you, but which are really sad enough. That we are still successful in holding a position and ironing out smaller mishaps is either that sometimes an officer is successful in utterly forcing it through or the carefully maintained 16-man assault detachment of the regimental commander is thrown into the hot spot and will take those retreating forward again.

All in all, it's a picture that cannot be thought of more unpleasantly and one expects of all the men considerably more than each man can normally physically and mentally fulfil.

The limit of effectiveness is far exceeded here. It is completely unclear to me how we should hold our present or other defensive positions under the expected further attacks. One must hope that the situation can once again be repaired through the use of tanks, assault guns and the artillery. I believe, however, that this game cannot be continued for much longer. It is now so that everything is now brought down to a common denominator: the battle can only be led through the artillery, tanks, and assault guns and these are there to prevent all deployed infantry from running away at the same time. When one succeeds in keeping a part of the men stay in the line through the action of these heavy weapons, then one can hope that the situation can once again be rectified at the difficult spot.

4) Measures against this complete physical and moral deterioration are difficult to find. Any and all spiritual vitamin shots are useless; but other measures, such as a summary court martial, death sentence, immediate weapon use by officers, etc., no longer is of any use. It means nothing to a man from a group when it is shared with him that *Gefreite* X has been shot because of cowardice when he doesn't know this *Gefreite* X at all because everything is completely mixed up. Moreover, *Gefreite* X is missing the next day in the fox hole in which he might have been taken back to.

5) The real *Grabenstärke* [trench strength – a special form of combat strength] and therefore the men who are really deployed in the trenches, is so low that a man deployed [in the line] frequently cannot see his neighbour from his fox-hole. Through the constant casualties, this situation worsens hourly and daily. The battalions assembled out of many units are hardly manageable. The following were deployed from one of our strongest battalions, the I./Grenadier-Regiment, in the frontline this morning: 4 NCOs and 17 men from different branches of the service (from the supply leader's alarm units, the artillery and so on).[50] 2 NCOs and 18 men from the reconnaissance battalion, the engineer battalion of the division with a strength of 2 NCOs and 22 men. Altogether, it's called the I./ Grenadier-Regiment G.D. [*Grossdeutschland*] and it has to hold a frontline of 2.3km with its 8 NCOs and 57 men. Any comment is superfluous.

I write this to you to illustrate to you once again from a fresh experience the tremendous difficulties which we fight under and know at the same time that these difficulties are known by you as well as all other staff officers [of LVIIth Panzer Corps]. You can rest assured that we also will still do everything to hold the present positions. And what is in some way humanly possible will be done. As it has worked so far, it will again barely work. And when you help us with a delivery of a few NCOs and men, we will somehow hold out as long as necessary until another greater solution is once more due.

By the end of 1943, even elite units (or perhaps especially elite formations due to their frequent use in countering Soviet attacks across the front) were clearly suffering from the infantry crisis that permeated the German army. The heavy and near continuous fighting in the Soviet Union had, to all intents and purposes, decimated and degraded the German army to such an extent that it no longer resembled the institution that had initiated Operation Barbarossa three years previously.

Chapter 2

Command and Leadership in the *Ostheer*

Significant increase of the supply of trained officers and NCOs. Those officers drawn from all branches and retrained in short courses and those NCOs that are freed in comb-out actions in the homeland do not even meet the lowest demands of a calm positional front. The fighting has shown again that the attack and defence power of the infantry is decisively dependent on the availability of experienced, well trained leaders and NCOs.[1]

German military leadership was one of the key factors, if not the primary one, in the tactical and operational successes of the German *Ostheer*, even if the latter levels of command increasingly suffered from the interventions of Hitler and the General Staff. German leadership on the ground played an important role in the tremendous gains during the first long year of the war in the east (22 June 1941–end of September 1942), but also in stemming the marked Soviet superiority in men and material for two and a half bloody years. Vital in enduring the already discussed hardships in the east, leadership was important in creating a deep cohesion within units and giving the ordinary soldier an example of officers who endured the same hardships side by side with their men and who generated combat motivation among the ranks. But losses in command personnel were extremely high and the demands of the front could never be satisfied, not even with the infusion of officers from rear units. When the German army suffered its worst defeats in summer 1944, marking the start of the final phase of the war in Europe, the key factor for German success had been severely weakened by three years of attrition.

Military command is too often, even in military history studies, reduced to a few famous generals and their decisions. Of course, men like Fedor von Bock and Erich von Manstein, or Heinz Guderian and Walter Model, are essential to understanding the war in the east. But they were in need of a command staff to implement their decisions, they required lieutenants to fulfil their plans skilfully, sub-leaders on the spot to react adequately to surprising developments and finally communication equipment for transmitting orders and, in turn, to obtain an image of the situation at the front. This chapter will discuss the German ideas about command, such as the famous *Auftragstaktik* (generally translated as mission command) and see how these were practiced in the campaign against the Soviet Union. Furthermore, it will be discussed how losses in troop leaders were replaced. Finally, three mid-level commanders will be presented to give a face to that command level.

Professional German military understanding of leadership was based on an image of war founded, respectively, by Clausewitz and Moltke the Elder. War was seen as a phenomenon of contingency, in which chaos, coincidence and friction reigned, as well as an arena of moral powers, in which the character of the general and the military spirit of the army were vital factors. To command in the uncertain field of war and battle, virtues such as boldness and tenacity were an absolute necessity for a leader. Only those who had a strong will and an eye for the situation could influence battle by using the elusive chances of the moment. As the modern battle had become very complex, it was not possible for a commander to overview and control all things and actions – decentralizing responsibility of command and initiative were seen as appropriate ways to reduce this complexity. This was accompanied by the conviction that the value of an army depended on the ability of individual soldiers and the initiative of low-level leaders and even enlisted men. Staffs – not an idea of German origin, but strongly emphasized by the German military between the mid-nineteenth century and the Second World War – to support the commanders and thus free them from more technical aspects of command were another path to reduce complexity.

Based on the views and convictions described above, the German military developed over the decades an idea of command that is not easily grasped and which is too often misleadingly termed *Auftragstaktik*. Mission command is popularly described as a superior ordering a mission, allocating forces and defining boundaries, but then leaving the subordinate free as how to fulfil his mission. By examining German regulations, discussions and training papers, Marco Sigg has shown that mission command was part of German understanding of leadership, but it was embedded in a wider understanding than is often portrayed in the literature. The resulting system of command was founded on seven elements. The key factor – based on the image of war presented above – was a commander's character, which must include determination, courage, boldness, drive, and willingness to accept responsibility. Closely connected as a second foundation was offensive thinking; attacking would keep the *Gesetz des Handelns*, or initiative, on one's own side and thus force the enemy to react to it. Likewise, troops on the offensive were seen as the force possessing the stronger combat morale. Offensive thinking was accompanied by independence, the most controversial part of German command as it included initiative, but this could also develop into arbitrary acts on the part of the commander. A closer look at regulations and training papers reveals that independent action should happen mainly within the framework of a given mission and only against a given mission order in a clearly defined exception, i.e., when the fulfilling of the mission was endangered or an opportunity was seen, but urgent necessity or lack of communication with superior command levels did not allow for consultation. But while this is the very heart of German *Auftragstaktik* – the leader on the spot decides and possibly even against orders from his superior – training documents indicate that this was viewed as a rare occurrence. The Replacement Army's Chief of Training Issues noted in a leaflet on command in 1944: 'Deviate from mission 5%, hold on: 95%.'[2] Regulating independent action and initiative were the fourth and fifth elements of German command: obedience and discipline, which were important components of the unity of action, or Moltke's *ordre de bataille*. The latter meant the coordination and cooperation of arms and branches as a whole. This was achieved by tight command and functioning communication. The ability to judge – the sixth element – describes the creative part of leadership. This included the need to evaluate situations, but also the ability to not be fatalistically locked into any schema in command, such as rigid battle plans. Content was always more important than form. Finally, the German command system included the 'command process', which consisted of evaluating the situation, formulating a decision and giving orders. This also included formulating the intention of the commander and the mission for the subordinate. Mission command in the German understanding would only work if these elements were brought together and balanced situationally. To be clear: success was by no means something built into the definition of *Auftragstaktik*. Many German successes were achieved by arbitrary acts, and German mission command inherently contained the idea of failure, as one of the central German norms was that inactivity was worse than acting incorrectly. Such a complex model of leadership could only work with leaders well trained and educated to follow intuitively the norms and values inherent to the system.

Many of the issues discussed above can be seen in the following account of *Oberst* Richard Wolf, CO of Infantry Regiment 208, 79th Infantry Division, describing the first attack of that regiment on the Red October complex in Stalingrad, including loss of control by the higher command levels, problems in coordinating the different arms, or delays in tactical communication:

> Then [1.30pm] the well-known crisis of the attack occurred. No message at all came from the front. [...] One heard only sporadic small arms fire and the detonation of hand grenades and satchel charges from the attack area. [...] All communication lines to the front were broken. All wires were shot up. An elimination of the jamming was nearly impossible. Both radio lines failed. The ultra-high frequency radio was still working, but the station received no new messages. Only by going through significant trouble was it possible to communicate by messengers after hours. [...] These were anxious hours for the command. The higher levels of command demanded new situation reports nearly every half an hour. The liaison officers of the heavy weapons asked for new missions. Minutes passed incredibly slowly, they became torturous hours. It was not easy to stay calm. [...] Then, around 4pm, came the liberating message [that the Volga was reached].

A clear mission, independent action, and initiative should allow frontline units to act even without any further orders from the superior command levels to keep the attack flowing. What this meant in practice could be seen from the after-action report from 7./Infantry Regiment 211, 71st Infantry Division, as it approached Kiev from the west in August 1941.[3] It indicated how much could be achieved by educating the last soldier to maintain the initiative:

> 8.8.41: The night has been calm. In pouring rain at 10 o'clock we attack again after a short artillery preparation. A Russian machine gun group at the edge of the forest offered considerable resistance. A part of the company attacked that machine gun in a spirited advance. The company commander, *Oberleutnant* Westphal, fell at the head of the company. *Obergefreiter* Weber, leader of the

company troop, took the command of the company on his own initiative without any specific order, and carried the attack forward and destroyed the machine gun. In this way, he created the prerequisite for the company's further advance. The company now had the mission to comb through the very dense municipal woods of Kiev and to reach the northern edge. It encountered considerable resistance, essentially from the right flank where all contact with the 3rd battalion was lost.

The battalion's adjutant, *Leutnant* Pastor, now took command of the company. During a violent surprise artillery attack, however, he found the hero's death after only leading the company for half an hour. Again the company troop leader took command of the company on his own initiative. A fortified and occupied *kolkhoz* blocked the further advance of the company. Now a short halt occurred. The company had now to repel some strong counterattacks out of the open right flank. Through ruthless action, these were repelled and the *kolkhoz* overrun.

Now, *Leutnant* Lüttich took command of the company. The municipal woods were pushed through and the company went over to the defensive on the northern edge of the municipal woods.

It was by no means logical for Weber to take command, considering the presence of several higher ranking platoon and group leaders. And each platoon leader should have been as well informed on the company's attack plan as Weber. But Weber did not hesitate and took command. What is even more striking is the fact that he did it twice that day and achieved a considerable tactical success. As Weber had already earned both Iron Crosses, he received the Knight's Cross for that action, an award given for deeds that influenced the course of combat decisively.

As previously mentioned, there was a thin line between independent action and arbitrary acts, and this was always in discussion within the German military leadership. For example, in the winter crisis of 1941/42, Hitler and the OKH tightened the strings of command with the following order,[4] as they feared a loss of control over the local commanders in the east would cause an uncontrolled retreat.

1) The higher command institutions (OKH, army groups and armies) have to manage the leadership more tightly. The principle of just giving the mission to the subordinate authorities and giving them full freedom in the execution of the mission has led on various occasions to the fact that the execution of the ordering command institution's intention was jeopardized and serious disadvantages arose for the overall situation. Clear, unambiguous orders must be used again. The superior commanding institution must not hesitate to intervene ruthlessly in details in order to achieve the intended purpose. It bears the responsibility for the success, it has the right to ensure the execution of its intentions also by arranging individual measures. The duty of soldierly obedience leaves no room for the sensitivities of subordinate command institutions; instead, it requires the fastest and best execution in the sense of the commander's original order.

The struggle for balance was also discussed in combat experience reports one year into the campaign, as the following source shows:[5]

1. Leadership

1) the German principle of issuing combat missions remains. The leadership, however, must not hesitate to intervene ruthlessly by order, if the nature of the execution endangers the fulfilment of the mission.

2) Particular care must be taken by the leadership to keep the troops in a tight grip when deployed in large areas, particularly during movement. Flexible leadership with short radio orders is particularly important.

On lower levels, especially with the panzer troops, there had been previous clashes over freedom of action, as the following order by the commander of IIIrd Motorized Corps indicates:

The events of recent days with their changing situations have placed very high demands on the physical capabilities of troops as well as on the flexibility of the leadership at all levels.

The troops should be persuaded that they will be ordered as little as possible by IIIrd Corps Headquarters; as mobile troops of a fast unit, they need to be clear about this. With such units and in vast areas with uncovered flanks, the situation frequently changes in the course of a day, sometimes from the ground up, and therefore new orders *must* be issued when opportunities would otherwise be missed and one would then have to pay with blood when it is cheaper to pay with sweat — or when the previous mission has become completely pointless. As long as the enemy still has his own will, not everything will work as scheduled. [...]

Grumbling is psychological digestion and among us soldiers, no one finds it a problem. One can also rant freely and straight from the heart about frequent and changing orders that possibly bring the troops to the boundaries of their capabilities, or a demanded arduous counter-march, as long as one is clear that the justification of a new order can only be overseen by the commanding superior himself, not the subordinate who received it, who can only be aware of his limited sector. The subordinate must not lose sight of the fact that his superior is also a subordinate, who must cope with a new order and follow it.

All officers must be or become clear that the command of fast units demands a completely different tempo of command from infantry units.

While clearly pointing out that the extremely fluid combat situation of mobile units made independent command necessary, the commander also stressed the necessity for obedience from the point when orders were given. Together with the next source, this document also indicates that room for independent action was a question of the combat situation. Mobile warfare, especially by fast units at high tempo and over long distances, created many more situations for independent action than positional warfare. Therefore the switch from one form of the combat to the other demanded a rethinking of the balance between tight command and initiative, but also of the command process as a whole, as the following order by Fourth Army from January 1942 indicates:[6]

F) Giving orders

The immobility of the leaders and their staffs means that rapid decisions during the battle are rarely made and have an effect. The leaders of motorized units trained during the summer in rapid decision-making and the brief giving of commands have to relearn. It is necessary to think through all possibilities of the offensive action with imagination and to weigh up advantages and disadvantages. All leaders must be instructed in detail before the attack begins, if possible on the previous day, about the intended conduct of battle and the expected and possible combat crises. The leaders in charge must know what measures and actions are expected from them in each combat phase.

One important point to make here concerns the quality of the German officer and NCO corps. As previously stated, the German command system required a thoroughly trained and educated leadership to work smoothly. The homogeneity and quality of the German officer corps had decreased significantly in the rearmament period due to the need for thousands of new officers to staff the rapidly expanding armed forces. When the war began, the German army could field some 90,000 officers. Losses in the early campaigns were relatively high, but at the same time, the officer corps gained much combat experience and further time for training. Probably the high point of quality was achieved in the summer months of 1941, before the mass losses of officers and NCOs in the east again decreased the quality. Measures taken, such as field training for leaders, did not stop this trend, but considerably slowed it until summer 1944, when the German army began to collapse due to the Allied double strike in Normandy and Belarus. While this is a general observation, there were great differences between theatres and units, depending on combat intensity, periods of refreshment, and, of course, unit leadership interest in training and educating leaders.

The following document is a collection of guidelines for training based on combat experiences from mid-1942. While giving an idea about leadership training issues, it also reveals deficiencies in the German low-level leadership.[7]

1) With the broad front sectors and vastness of the *Ostraum*, every leader must be educated to fight independently, to secure his flank and rear, and to fulfil his combat mission in the sense of the whole. A much more flexible training of the entire low-level leadership is therefore necessary. [...]

3) The great carelessness, which manifests itself in the advance in concentrated clusters, in reckless movements at open points, lack of camouflage, rattling with equipment, loud chattering, etc., must be combated again and again, especially by the responsible leaders.

    There is a need to put more emphasis on this - this is mainly the responsibility of the company commander - that the troops on the battlefield are not concentrated but moving in open order. If breaks occur, every man must necessarily take cover or lie down. Everything must be done to ensure that unnecessary losses are not caused by negligence and a certain amount of herd instinct.

Particularly the officer must here act as an example through warlike behaviour, coupled with a willingness to take responsibility and the drive of his own initiative.

4) [...] The young company leaders lack a thorough training in leadership. This defect cannot be replaced by combat experience. Therefore, it is necessary for the company leaders to learn: a) tactical principles on the basis of manuals and based on the experience of the war, b) estimate of the situation and terrain c) formulation of decision and giving of commands, d) cooperation with heavy weapons, artillery and tanks, e) training of leaders for reconnaissance patrols and assault detachments f) organization, armament, equipment and training of reconnaissance patrols and assault detachments. [...]

5) It has repeatedly been shown that the mass of officers and NCOs is not able to train properly when units are withdrawn for refreshment behind the front. [...]

9) In the training of the officers, close combat training (with rifle, pistol, submachine gun, hand grenade and satchel charge), in conjunction with the training of reconnaissance patrols and assault detachments must be more stressed. The leader and subleader must learn to recognize each weakness of the opponent on the battlefield, and be educated to trigger the corresponding counter-measure in a flash-like manner. [...]

24) The leader and the NCO must have a certain ability to acquaint themselves quickly with captured weapons and to get the most out of this weapon for battle. The officer must take a certain pleasure in dealing with weapons of all kinds and their capabilities. The officer and the NCO must be able to use all the weapons of his branch. Where there are gaps, they would have to be closed if applicable in combat. In officer training, it must be expressed that it is no shame if even the officer is not familiar with individual weapons, but the greater his effort must be to close such gaps in training. [...]

25) The reports on the enemy and the situation must be formulated in such a way as to give a clear picture of the situation to the superior command level. Reports of the enemy must pay more attention to the impression of the enemy that the troops in the front have; therefore a critical assessment of the report and a corresponding forwarding. Education to check out the situation oneself as often as possible.

The directive demanded more care in preventing losses, better training in close combat and weapons handling, and an improvement in clarity and precision of messages. In addition, the order addressed issues typical to the German command system, such as an eye for the situation, independent command, and the will to take responsibility. The stress in point 5 on the general lack of command abilities of young company commanders is quite striking. A sufficient training of the low-level leadership was never fully achieved in the war, and the longer the war endured, the more low-level leaders became simple one-dimensional fighters, who electrified their men on the battlefield, but were not full-fledged leaders in the German sense. They still often matched their opponents in quality, but could not fully reach German leadership standards. This was also recognized by the German army and had organizational consequences, as discussed here in a presentation of Army Group South's propositions to raise the combat power of the infantry in 1943:

> Furthermore, it proved that the company leader was not able to orderly lead a strong company with numerous attached weapons, since he had increasingly transformed from a tactical leader to a standard-bearer as the war progressed. The tactical leadership fell to the battalion commander. Accordingly in some Panzer divisions even organizationally attached medium mortars and heavy machine guns were deployed by the battalion. However, due to the large width [of the company sectors], the machine guns must be again placed at the disposal of the companies in the defence.[8]

The problem was that the losses in the higher ranks made it necessary to promote neither fully-formed nor fully-prepared officers to the battalion and regimental levels. While special courses – including ones for divisional commanders beginning in 1943 – should have helped them, quality nonetheless suffered even with elite units, as a training order from Panzer Grenadier Division '*Grossdeutschland*' in May 1943 reveals:

> The proper conduct of combat: battalion commanders, company leaders, platoon leaders must be educated to fight with the most economical use of men and under the maximum use of machines. The favourite scheme of most battalion commanders with 1st company right, 2nd company left, and 3rd company in the centre behind must yield to a more intellectual approach.
>
> In this context, one cannot emphasize enough a good training, with sufficient time, of low-level leaders of all ranks, particularly the lower ones. Special arrangements of training are necessary. With them, the troops stand and fall.[9]

The source also points out again the importance of low-level leadership for the combat power of the troops, but also the need for training of those leaders behind the front line. What would such training look like?

The following order originates from the 58th Infantry Division, whose commander, *Generalmajor* Friedrich Altrichter, one of Germany's most prolific writers on military psychology and officer training, gives an idea about leadership training of frontline units.[10]

1) Objective of the leadership training

The training of the officers and NCOs is of decisive importance for the fighting power of the troops. The training of the officers and NCOs has the objective of raising their professional skills, strengthening their authority, providing them with uniform perceptions and convictions.

It is frequently noted that in front of their men, officers and NCOs stand their ground before the enemy, but are not capable of acting as tactical leaders, instructors, and educators of their men. In order to master these tasks, a certain amount of knowledge and insight is necessary, which can only be gained through proper special training.

2) Organization of Leadership Training
    Leadership training is divided into:
    A) Commander's Course
    B) Training of officers by regimental and battalion commanders
    C) Training of NCOs
    D) Map exercises
3) Execution of leadership training in detail
    To point 2) A Commanders' Course
        Purpose: Instruction on the tasks as battalion commander, to deepen the
    knowledge of the service, to teach the principles of education and training of
    officers, uniform approach to the handling and organization of the individual
    service issues.
        Head: Division commander
        [...]
        Participants: the regimental and battalion commanders as well as their
    deputies.
    On 2) B Training of the officers by regimental and battalion commanders
        Purpose: To provide guidance on the attitude and concept of being an
    officer, to teach about the principles of education and training, to train as
    a tactical leader of their unit, to guide the handling of routine service in a
    company (battery).
        Head: In the present tactical conditions, the officers' training rests mainly
    in the hands of the battalion commanders. It is their most important task
    during the pause in operations.
        [...] Time: In December 2-3 times weekly (main focus of this time to lay the
    foundation). From January once weekly.
        [...] Duration: the whole winter
        Participants: all officers, platoon leaders and officer's candidates of the
    battalions.
    To 2) C Training of NCOs
        It is divided into: a) The training of NCOs by the company commanders
    and b) The regiments' NCO candidate courses.
    To a) NCO training by the company (battery) commanders
        Purpose: instruction in the treatment and education of subordinates,
    direction as an instructor, training as a leader, strengthening of their position
    as a superior by developing [the necessary] personality and acquiring
    increased professional knowledge and skills.
        [...] Participants: all NCOs and NCO candidates of the companies.
    To b) Regimental NCO candidates courses
        Purpose: To instruct on NCOs' duties, to provide the service knowledge,
    to provide guidance in handling the practical service, to train as a leader of a
    detachment, to strengthen the military conception and attitude. In the case of
    NCO candidates, check for suitability to become NCO.
        Leader: 1 experienced officer by order of the regiments
        Course duration: 14 days
        [...] Participants: All NCO candidates as well as young NCOs by order of
    the regiments

To D) Map exercises

Purpose: Clarification of tactical questions and terms, training in decision-making, exercise in the giving of orders, instruction in the interaction of the different weapons, guidance in the leading of one's own and the next higher unit.

Head: Regimental commanders

Beginning: January 1942. The number of map exercises is left to the regiments.

Participants: The officers of the regiments according to instructions of the regimental commanders. In infantry map exercises, officers of the artillery, engineers, anti-tank and signal units are to be principally involved as well as infantry and engineer officers in map exercises of the artillery. [...]

4) It is envisaged to set up a divisional company leaders' course. The final decision on this question [will be taken], as soon as it becomes clear whether and which company leader training courses take place in the army or in the *Heimat*. The divisional company leader course could not be established before February 1942.

Leadership training was understood as a key factor of combat power. The training was carried out level by level. The divisional commander gathered his regimental and battalion commanders in the commander's course not only to lay the foundation for leadership training, but also to achieve a unified understanding among his officers. The regimental and battalion commanders would then train and educate their officers, the NCOs of their units. To train and mould the younger NCOs and NCO candidates, special courses were carried out in each regiment. The same was intended for new or designated company leaders. While not mentioned here, battalion commanders' courses were also soon ordered (normally at army or army group level due to the need for an instruction troop of several companies), as were staff officer courses. Finally, to provide advanced tactical training, but also again to unify understanding, the army held map exercises.

Looking at its subject matter, the order included as much on tactical themes as it did on daily services and the issue of leading men. Also important was the education of officer values. This is more clearly indicated in the annex to the order:[11]

I. Guidelines and aspects for carrying out leadership training

1) Basic principles

The training of the leaders and NCOs is divided into the following areas:

a) Instruction as an educator, b) Instruction as an trainer, c) Training as a leader

A major error, which is to be found again and again, consists in too much one-sidedness in leadership training. It is often found that it [training] is exhausted only in tactical discussions, map exercises and war games, that is training only as a leader. In addition to training as a leader, the areas of guidance to trainers and educators with their questions of treating and leading human beings, the handling and arrangement of the service as well as spiritual and mental care have the same importance.

2) Reasons for the inadequacy of the sub-leader training

   a) Local difficulties, wide dispersion to villages, lack of rooms. These difficulties must be overcome.

   b) Lack of insight of the commander in the necessity of training leaders and NCOs. Idea that it is not worthwhile to start within a short or indeterminate longer rest period. Through a fresh start, much can be achieved in a short time.

   c) Commander's doubts about what to do, how to do it, and when to do it. These doubts will be solved by the commanders' course.

3) Carrying out sub-leader training

   A) Instruction as an educator

   These include:

   a) Instruction of proper treatment of people. No swearwords, no ridicule of the awkward. Irony is always wrong. Individual treatment. Identify the men's performance limits and properly assess their readiness. Release men early who have worked particularly hard or are have the ability to work in a special field. Always insert dexterity exercises to keep the mind fresh. Bring people to the realization that the entire training is done only for their own benefit. (Superiority as a soldier and as a fighter opposite the opponent).

   b) Discussion of the great questions and the meaning of this war. Education for fighting spirit and the will to win. (See leaflet on national political education).

   c) Design the class on the duties of the soldier. Hereby making clear: the moral values, the spiritual backgrounds, and the tasks of being a soldier. Position of the soldier in the state. (See the knapsack brochure: 'The nature of the soldierly education').

   d) Handling the disciplinary authority. Briefing on soldierly concept and conduct. Violations and infractions.

   e) Handling the teaching on the Military Criminal Code, on offenses and crimes. (To d) and e) see the knapsack brochure: 'The nature of the soldierly education').

   f) Arrangement of the topic 'Behaviour in public'. [...]

   g) Instruction in the execution of spiritual care. [...]

   B) Instruction as a trainer

   The instruction covers:

   a) Teaching of the content of the relevant regulations [...].The individual sections are to be gone through one after the other and hereby the recognition of errors and their correction by the proper means is to be discussed. The instructor must be able to master the content of the regulations, but must not rattle it down by heart. Opposition of incorrect and correct is most instructive.

   b) Ensure a uniform view of contentious issues or open questions. Experience has shown that certain activities are carried out differently by the instructors as a result of different interpretations of the regulations. Uniformity within the battalions is necessary. For more important questions, ask the regiment's decision.

c) Instruction in the teaching. Principle: To teach the subject matter in the easiest and most comfortable way. The NCOs tend to make the easiest things appear difficult and to teach them in such a way that the motivation to serve suffers as a result. Always give people something new! Variety! No time to kill. Short, instructive, and tight! Mistakes observed again and again: To harp on things long mastered ('do the same again'). Well-trained soldiers with beginners in the same training detachment, rather than separating them in high performer and training classes.

d) Guidance in the handling and arrangement of the different service areas. Instruction on that in the commanders' course.

e) Principles for the establishment of training plans. The leader must learn how to organize the different training issues by subject matter and in time. The frequently observed idle time of training is mainly due to the fact that the NCOs are not able to do this. Pyramid-like training process, i.e. from the parts to the whole. Gradually increase the difficulty of the exercise and the speed of its execution.

C) Training as a leader

The training is divided into: map exercises (map 1:25,000 as a field substitute), tactical walks, instruction demonstrations, officer classes for firing at the artillery arm.

Leadership training must always be carried out by means of practical tasks. Purely theoretical instructions are pointless. The theory is to be deduced from practice. The resulting knowledge will finally be proven in the regulations.

Carrying out of the map exercises and tactical walks:

Mistakes in the map exercises and tactical walks: Unit level too high. Principle: Train leaders in the command of their units. Gain certainty here first, then the next higher level.

Mistake in artillery map exercises: too much firing technique, too little artillery tactics.

The tasks have to be introduced straightforwardly into the situation, which must be as simple as possible. Principle: the tactical framework is the next higher unit level. Everything superfluous in the situation is to be omitted.

The tasks must include the subject areas of our 'daily bread', i.e.:

a) Advance of the reinforced platoon that has already deployed into a skirmishing line (reinforced company). (Select terrain which causes change of the formation).

b) Behaviour of the reinforced platoon (reinforced company) when deploying into a skirmish line and receiving enemy artillery fire or machine-gun fire from long distances,

c) Advance of the reinforced platoon (reinforced company) under covering fire of light and heavy weapons (especially to practice: precise orders for mortars and subordinate heavy machine guns and ATGs)

d) Deployment of the reinforced platoon (reinforced company) behind a cover aa) for the further advance, bb) for the assault

e) Break-in and fight in the depth of the enemy's zone. To be practiced in conjunction with this: taking nests by pincer attack, advance past flanking nests, either with the whole reinforced platoon (reinforced company), or only with parts, as other parts must suppress the nest. (Procedure depends on position and condition [of the nest].) Combating flanking nests, which block further progress with fire, defence against enemy counterattacks in own sector or neighbouring sector, behaviour after taking a nest. All these tasks are to be practiced as decision-making tasks.

f) Agility tasks: quick occupation of a height, rapid deployment on the flank, rapid deployment to defend against a surprise attack.

g) Defence against enemy tanks. Proper and rapid use of the anti-tank rifle and ATG, conduct of the weapons firing armour-piercing bullets, of the other riflemen.

h) Orders to subordinate heavy machine-gun groups for the covering of deployment (when to open fire?), support of the attack (always indicate clear targets. When to open fire?)

i) Orders to subordinate mortar groups to support the attack (when to open fire?).

Procedure of training

The instructor must fight the inclination of the leaders to tell what they would do. Right from the beginning pay attention to command language. This is facilitated by integrating persons to which the commands actually are directed. [...]

4) Indications for the external form of the leadership training:

Outer form informal. As little as possible military drill-like. Smoking, coffee-drinking etc. No harshness of the superior. Frank discussions. The commander and his officers must look forward to it in the same way.

The training of German command personnel aimed to create a leader who could carry out three roles: to be an educator of his subordinates, an instructor, and a tactical leader. As a rule, all officers and NCOs had to carry out all three tasks. The emphasis on the areas of educator and instructor became especially necessary under the conditions of war in the East. The education of soldiers – which included stressing the duties of soldiers, infusing the will to win, spiritual care, and creating a combat community – played an important role in keeping German units fighting even under the most unfavourable circumstances and even after a string of defeats. During the course of the war, many of those educational issues were increasingly understood from a National Socialist perspective, so that the lines demarcating traditional army education and National Socialist indoctrination frequently blurred.[12] On the flip side, instructor abilities were necessary as training became an essential task for the field units due to the permanence of the war, as well as with the need to adapt to geographical regions and Soviet combat methods. As chapter 6 will show, the field training of German troops was an essential factor for the high combat power of German units. But this required officers and NCOs to be able to train troops effectively.

Looking at the training of tactical leadership, it aimed at basic forms of attack – and exclusively attack. Even in the defensive situation of 1941/42, German troops tended to train offensively. This was an expression of the already mentioned traditional conviction that only the offensive will bring a decision, but it also reflected the long-standing experience that attack is the more difficult tactical form. But the lack of defensive training, especially when it came to positional warfare, proved to be a problem that the army never fully solved.

Altrichter's recommendations on training are rather surprising, as they do not correspond to the common perception that the German army consisted of disciplined and stalwart officers in perfect uniforms. But the point here was about creating an *esprit de corps*, which was essential for the German command system, and which needed a unified understanding, as well as mutual confidence between superiors and subordinates, to work smoothly. This could be created by frank discussions in free and light-hearted situations. The German officer's mess, or the *Kasino*, had the same aim, as described in another document written by the 58th Infantry Division's commander:[13]

> Kasino: Necessary institution to educate the [officers] community. Place for the exchange of thoughts, education for the care of camaraderie, of training. Model for the kasino [were] English clubs. Only introduced since the beginning of the 18th century. Food is service. No cliques.

A last thing to stress from this order was the position of the NCO in the German army, which differed from most armies of the time. Since the turn of the century, and in accordance with the idea of decentralized command, NCOs formed an essential part of German low-level leadership, normally leading platoons, groups, and individual heavy weapons. This is clearly pointed out in the 'Guidelines for the training of the NCOs at the Field NCO Schools':[14]

> The modern method of combat has increased the importance of the NCOs. The fragmented combat method in the attack, the holding of wide sections by group-wise deployment, by strongpoints and nests, as well as by detachments kept ready for the immediate counter-thrust against an intruding enemy, places high demands on bold decision-making power and leadership. The cooperation of different weapons in a combat group requires tactical understanding and high practical abilities of the NCO.
>
> The self-reliant NCO must be aware of his responsibility and the trust placed in him, and resolutely and deliberately carry out his mission.

Training and education were tightly connected in the German understanding of forming leaders (and soldiers too). While training should result in military competencies such as weapons handling or tactical understanding, education should infuse soldierly values in order for soldiers and officers to act intuitively in situations according to the common principles of the German army, without which the German command system would not function. In other words, education was the training of character. To give an idea what this meant for NCOs and how education should work, a further section of the Guidelines for the training of NCOs at the Field NCO Schools follows:[15]

> The aim of the education is: a) Clear and serious concept of duty and profession, sense of responsibility and reliability. b) Confident and decided appearance as the basis for the teaching and leadership qualification. c) Crispness, determination and flexibility. d) Care for the subordinates. e) Good manners, tactful behaviour.
>
> Means of education are: a) Tightly handled service. b) Accuracy in the performance of the service. c) Order and cleanliness. d) Cultivate good manners and comradeship in comradeship rooms and at dinner.

The high losses in leaders, however, made German efforts to provide leadership training increasingly futile. A few numbers should give an idea of the extent of these casualties: Losses on all fronts from autumn 1941–1944 totalled more than 54,000 army officers, of which the great majority occurred on the Eastern front. A further 7,000 army officers were lost in these years due to illness, accidents, suicides or death sentences.[16] The 18th Panzer Division entered the Soviet Union in June 1941 with 401 officers – at the end of July it had already lost 153. When the same division was sent into action on 11 July 1943 against the Soviet offensive to crack the Orel salient, it only had 157 officers available. After twelve days of intense fighting, only thirty officers were ready for duty. The 12th Infantry Division marched into the Soviet Union with 336 officers. In May 1942, cumulative loss of officers had risen to 341, as many as the division had possessed at the beginning of the invasion.[17]

In addition to the lack of officers and NCOs, a main problem of command was the means of communication. In the 1930s, Germany was among the world's leaders in the use of radio equipment for the command of fast-moving motorized and armoured units. But the stocks of such equipment could not keep up with the massive expansion of the German army in the late 1930s and early 1940s. Following the doubling of armoured units in 1940/41 for the campaign in the east, the supply of radio equipment became a significant issue. Materials for the more conventional telephone communications were also lacking, especially cable. The production of communications material was always in competition with other items, be it for the use of rare raw materials such as copper, or for the special workers used for producing other electronic goods (radar equipment, searchlights for night air defence). The worker question also became important for the troops, since signal units needed specialists for operating and maintaining the radios and telephones. One has to keep in mind that electronic devices were not nearly as common then as today and the broad mass of the German population was unfamiliar with them. Exacerbating the lack of electronic equipment for communications were the shortages of men and vehicles for the signal troops. They were in need of all-terrain vehicles of military origin, specially designed to carry their communications equipment. Since there were never enough of these vehicles, be they half-tracks or wheeled, the communications troops had to rely more and more on improvised trucks that simply were not robust enough for the terrain in the east. This led to a vicious circle, as fewer and fewer operational communications vehicles were available. Even the spearhead Panzer divisions suffered from such shortages, as a late 1943 report by the divisional signal officer, typically the commander of the divisional signal battalion, from 8th Panzer Division indicates:[18]

[Divisional] Signal troops:
A) Telephony company

Authorized strength	actual strength:
8 large telephone-construction teams	3 large telephone-construction teams
6 small telephone-construction teams	3 small telephone-construction teams
2 [telephone]operations teams	2 [telephone]operations teams

Of these, two are in repair on average.
Cable length: authorized: 182 lengths; actual: 68 lengths

Considering the motor vehicle and cable situation, the company is still limited operationally. The requirements of the tactical leadership concerning telephone communication in the current organization of the division can still be essentially met. In limited attacks, the company is still capable of establishing and maintaining telephone communications to one battle group.

Main difficulties of the company: Motor vehicle situation, cable stock.
B) Radio company:

Authorized strength	actual strength:
1 medium command tank	7 medium radio teams type b
3 [light] command tanks	3 medium radio teams type a
2 [special-purpose motor vehicle] 267 (half-track)	1 small radio teams type c
1 [special-purpose motor vehicle] 268 (half-track)	
10 medium radio teams type a	
6 medium radio teams type a / f	
5 medium radio teams type b	
2 small radio teams type c	

By establishing the radio communications exclusively in 'star' traffic[19], the company has until now been able to meet the requirements of the tactical leadership. The company does not have any reserves which allow for the establishment of new traffic connections during changes in the situation. A tactical connection must be cancelled if a radio station fails. Since there are no armoured radio stations available, the required intercommunication cannot be made. Main difficulty of the company: Motor vehicle situation and the obtaining of spare parts for electric generators (GG 400).

2) [Panzer] Grenadier Regiments
  a) Telephone communication
      With the grenadier regiments, only wire connections from the regiments to the battalions can be built due to lack of personnel and equipment. When the regiments change position, it is not possible at to dismantle and at the same time to connect both battalions by wire again. In the event of a further loss of personnel, the telephone connections to the battalions will also be called into question.
  b) Radio communication
      An overlay of the telephone connections from the regiments to the battalions cannot be made at the moment. Radio connections to the companies can no longer be made due to the losses of the pack radio sets. The repair of the pack radio sets takes a very long time because of difficulty in obtaining spare parts, and often cannot be carried out. Frequently occurring malfunctions on the G device do not guarantee secure connections.

Personnel vacancies:
Panzer Grenadier Regiment 8

Radio operators:	Authorized 59	Telephone operators:	Authorized 54
	Actual 37		Actual 32

Panzer Grenadier Regiment 28

Radio operators:	Authorized 43	Telephone operators:	Authorized 37
	Actual 15		Actual 21

3) Reconnaissance battalion
  At the moment, radio communication of the battalion is still ensured. Difficulties arise from the fact that the battalion has to take over the radio communications made by the tank signal battalion, i.e. from the divisional commander to the [reconnaissance] battalion, and from the [reconnaissance] battalion to the regiments instructed to cooperate. Due to a total failure of a radio station, the battalion had to send one radio station to the third company.

Personnel vacancies:

Radio operators:	Authorized 38	Telephone operators:	Authorized 6
	Actual 25		Actual 4

4) Tank battalion
  Radio connection within the battalion is ensured. The only command vehicle is in need of repair, every day failure is expected. If this vehicle fails, the battalion is no longer connected to the division and to the supply trains. The remote station at the battalion cannot be set by the tank signal battalion, since it has no command tank.

Personnel vacancies:

Radio operators:	Authorized 6	Telephone operators:	Authorized 8
	Actual 6		Actual 4

5) Artillery
Telephone connections
   At distances up to 3 kilometres from the regiment to the battalions and from the battalions to the batteries, the required telephone connections can still be ensured at the moment. If the battalions are positioned beyond these distances, the construction of the telephone connections to the battalions poses considerable difficulties due to lack of cable. Due to the failure of motor vehicles, the regiment can only make radio connections to one battalion. For the same reasons and through the loss of G-devices, the battalion cannot establish a radio connection to the deployed batteries. The equipment of the battalions was handed over to the batteries in order to ensure fire direction. There are great difficulties with the artillery support of the armoured group, since the regiment currently has only two armoured observation vehicles. The observer may therefore have to direct fire of several batteries at the same time, which runs into considerable radio-technical difficulties. As a result of a lack of personnel, the radio stations can only be occupied by one radio operator, and with his loss, the device also fails.

Personnel vacancies:
Radio operators: Authorized 230   Telephone operators: Authorized 152
                   Actual 105   Actual 115

6) Engineer battalion
   Of five pack radio sets,[20] two are still operational. Radio communication is therefore conditionally ensured.

Personnel vacancies:
Radio operators: Authorized 40   Telephone operators: Authorized 21
                   Actual 12   Actual 6

7) Army anti-aircraft battalion
   Telephone connections and radio communication are ensured. Due to the loss of electric generators (GG 400), difficulties arise in the field of the supply of power sources.

Personel vacancies:
Radio operators: Authorized 68   Telephone operators: Authorized 68
                   Actual 37   Actual 45

8) Anti-tank battalion
   Radio communication to the division can no longer be established due to the losses of motor vehicles and equipment. An improvised establishment of a radio link to the deployed platoons can only be achieved with great difficulty. The radios are loaded on the self-propelled anti-tank guns, but since the space is used for the gun crew and ammunition, radioing is not possible in combat.

Personnel vacancies:
Radio operators: Authorized 24   Telephone operators: Authorized 2
                   Actual 17   Actual 2

Overall vacancies of unit signal soldiers:

Radio operators:	Authorized 508	Telephone operators:	Authorized 349
	Actual 254		Actual 229
	[Difference]: 254		120

Total vacancies of the unit's signal soldiers: 374 NCOs and men = in total 35%.

As this report notes, all of the division's units suffered from a lack of both radio and telephone equipment. It should be kept in mind here that both radio and telephone communications are systems, which require several devices and expendable materials such as cable or storage batteries. A shortage of one device could hamper the whole system, as was the case with electric generators for the 8th Panzer Division. Shortages and a general lack of communications equipment did not allow all units to connect with each other or with higher and lower levels, not to mention having reserve lines or being able to back up telephone lines with radio communication. Furthermore, the lack of equipment reduced tactical flexibility, i.e. positioning batteries outside of a rather small area or the simultaneous dismantling and the construction of telephone lines for the Panzer Grenadier units. The lack of motor vehicles – as will be discussed in chapter 4, a problem that plagued the German army for most of the war in the east – reduced the troops' mobility and did not allow them to carry much material. Especially problematic was the situation with armoured command or observation vehicles, as their scarcity made communication during attack difficult. The production of these special-purpose vehicles was always in competition with combat vehicles, as they drew from the same production resources. A final issue that can be seen from the report and was especially stressed in the artillery section was the lack of trained personnel. The shortage of adequately trained signal personnel led to higher losses in equipment due to careless use and poor maintenance, but also in longer interruptions in communication until deficiencies could be identified. For radio operators, ciphering was also an issue, and the frequency of openly sent messages increased as training standards declined.

To overcome shortages in communication equipment, and a lack of training at the lower leadership level, and also to influence the course of battles and operations, German commanders were often present at or near the front. By conferring with subordinates on the spot, they had a better understanding of the actual situation. Finally, the presence of divisional, corps and army commanders at the front line had a positive psychological effect on frontline troops. Even the commander of Sixth Army in 1942, *General der Panzertruppen* (later *Generaloberst*) Friedrich Paulus, often ill-reputed as a 'desktop general', regularly visited his subordinates and troops. The so-called 'front tours' were documented and provide good insight into that part of command practice. This is the report of the front tour of 15 October 1942:[21]

At night, elements of the 14th Panzer Division were able to advance through the Tractor Factory to the Volga River.

8.30am: The army commander presented to *Major* Knetsch, Commander Infantry Regiment 545 (389th Infantry Division) the Knight's Cross, as well as the

German Cross in Gold at his command post. At the same time, he also presented the German Cross in Gold to *Oberst* Schuster-Woldan, commander Artillery Regiment 389.

Further forces of the 14th Panzer Division and 305th Infantry Division have reached the Volga.

9.00am: In a meeting with [the] commanding general LIst Army Corps, commander 389th Infantry Division, 305th Infantry Division, and 14th Panzer Division, the army commander decided on the plan for the further attack.

The 305th Infantry Division and the 14th Panzer Division will attack on both sides of the railroad south of the Tractor Factory along the Volga. Elements of the 24th Panzer Division and the 14th Panzer Division should tie down their opponents on the flank by attacks from the west.

10.00am: The army chief reports to the army commander for verbal report and consultation on the forward command post.

11.30am–12.30pm: Ride accompanied by the commander 14th Panzer Division to the regimental command post of Panzer Grenadier Regiment 103 in a shelter west of Barrikady. The commanders of Panzer Grenadier Regiment 103 and Panzer Regiment 36 report on the breakthrough to the Volga.

14.00: Meeting with commanding general LIst Army Corps, commander 14th Panzer Division and the Chief [of Staff of] Sixth Army. Commanding general LIst Army Corps has concerns about an immediate attack without regrouping.

The army commander ordered: The attack south of the Tractor Factory will be continued early on 16 October.

Around 16.00 hrs. Return to quarters at the 389th Infantry Division's command post.

The advance by Panzer Grenadier Regiment 103 to the Volga, one of the most successful German attacks in Stalingrad, created a new situation for Sixth Army. Paulus visited the front sector the day after the attack and conferred with the commanders present there – not only his direct subordinate, *General der Artillerie* Walther von Seydlitz-Kurzbach, commander of LIst Army Corps, but also with divisional and even regimental commanders. After getting a clearer picture of the situation on the ground, he decided on the follow-up attack on 16 October. In addition to that, but no less important, was his personal handing-over of high awards to two commanders, underlining his recognition of their achievements, and thereby strengthening the *esprit de corps*. The same can be seen in his front tour on 29 October, this time visiting XIVth Panzer Corps, which was primarily fighting on Sixth Army's northern flank.[22]

13.00: Drive to the command post of the XIVth Panzer Corps in the ravine Dessyat north-west Gorodishche. The army commander congratulated the commanding general on his promotion to *General der Panzertruppen* and on his birthday, and at the command post he speaks to the divisional commanders and artillery commanders of the corps who were present there. (14.00 departure)

Other aspects of such tours focused on inter-service cooperation and understanding the capabilities of new weapons, as the tour report of 1 November indicates:[23]

7:45am: Take-off accompanied by the Chief of Staff to the advanced landing field of the VIIIth Air Corps [at] Station Rasguljajewka.
8.30am: Arrival at the advanced command post of the VIIIth Air Corps at the brickyard Rasguljajewka. The commanding general and chief of the LIst Army Corps are present. A short time later, the commander of the Air Fleet 4 and the commanding general of the VIIIth Air Corps arrived. After a long discussion
11.15am: Drive to Assault Gun Battalion 244 southeast of Gumrak Station.
The newly arrived self-propelled heavy infantry guns are demonstrated to the army commander. The battery leader points out various deficiencies. In his opinion, the gun is a makeshift solution which is not yet fully developed. Poor sight for the driver and gunner, low extent of traverse and vulnerability do not allow the use in the manner of the assault guns.
Continuation to the divisional command post of the 295th Infantry Division and discussion with divisional commander.
1pm: Arrival at the command post of the LIst Army Corps [at] Station Gumrak at the same time with the returning *Generaloberst* von Richthofen. The army commander has a second conversation with him.
14.00: The commanding general of the XIVth Panzer Corps and the commander of the 305th Infantry Division arrive for a verbal report and consultation with the army commander-in-chief and commanding general.
3pm: Return flight to Army Headquarters.

Similar events occurred at all levels of the army, as the following notes of the commander of 205th Infantry Division, *Generalmajor* Paul Seyffardt, during a visit to the front positions of his troops in Velizh, reveal:[24]

I a: Inadequate entrenchment, especially in the eastern section: the main combat line is not yet continuous everywhere, confusing foreground without wire entanglements and mines. Individual masts and so on offer the enemy good target points. The trenches are generally flat, there are no masks from the sections that could be seen by the enemy (Velizh creek ravine). No sap blocks. Poor bunkers without splinter-proof ceilings. Combat positions without side limitation of the firing field and sufficient splinter protection. Machine guns can partly not shoot over the ditch border.
Only one trench mirror per company. Telescopic sights are haphazardly passed around instead of remaining in the hands of a good rifleman.
There is a lack of tight time and work organization, which is often left at discretion of individual group leaders. Therefore, no sufficient sleep breaks. A rifleman stood as a sentry for 9 hours.
The forward [artillery] observer in the hospital did not have a signal pistol and flares, and explained that not he but the company commander was responsible for the triggering of the barrage. In the trenches of the east section cans, etc., lay

strewn around. Usually the trenches were not stabilized with planks. Ammunition not properly stored. Insufficient and dirty maps and plans.

The divisional commander intends to have the officers of the Infantry Regiment 353 view model positions at the other regiments and to demand deadlines for further entrenchment.

I b: Fountains!

Torn clothes, missing shoulder straps (regimental paymaster has to report on 6.10. at 12.00 at the division commander). Cold-resistant oil is supposedly already stored in the eastern section.

Weapons and equipment officer: weapon maintenance and storage leave something to be desired. Collect cartridges! There is a lack of German hand grenades and rifle grenades.

Engineer officer: There is a lack of wire, mine plans (supposedly there are still unrecorded minefields of the Infantry Regiment 257, of which nobody knows). Also desired are detonating fuses, gallery cases, electric fuses.

II a: Officers and men often unshaven, negligent uniforms (rolled-up long trousers). Misuse of awards. Think of proven NCOs and men!

IV b: The sick room in the hospital was unfriendly and unclean. Each soldier should be deloused at least once a month.

Seyffardt noted many details that required improvement through the efforts of his staff officers. They included tactical aspects, but also many disciplinary issues. He also had an eye for leadership deficiencies, such as leaving men on guard duty for too long, or unclean rooms in the field hospital, which had negative effects on both combat morale and the health of the troops.

Finally, there will be a closer examination of the men commanding at the mid-level of the German army in the east, that is battalion to corps level, exemplified by the career of three officers.

The most prestigious group of commanders in the German army were the Panzer leaders, both during the war and in historiography. While the men of the *Blitzkrieg* phase were well known, in their shadow grew up their successors, dominating higher army field commands and Panzer commands in the second half of the war.

One of these under-researched men was Traugott Herr, whose career culminated in leading the Tenth Army in Italy in 1945.[25] Born in 1890, he became an infantry officer before the First World War, in which he served both at the front and in staffs, exclusively on the Western Front. He was then taken into the *Reichswehr* and in late 1925, he took several training courses in the newly formed motorized troops, which were at this time merely termed 'logistical units' for camouflage purposes. As was usual in the different versions of the German army that existed before 1933, his rise was slow. When Hitler started his campaign to become Germany's *Führer* in 1933, Herr was still – at the age of 43 – a *Hauptmann*. The hasty and massive expansion of the German armed forces in the years that followed was a driver for his career (and those of most German officers). He rose to *Oberst* before the war, led both a battalion and a regiment and served as tactics instructor at the officers' academy (*Kriegsschule*) in Dresden. In France in 1940, he led the 13th Motorized Infantry Division's 66th Rifle Regiment, receiving the Iron Cross 1st Class. When the division was transformed into a Panzer division in October 1940, Herr received command of the newly formed Rifle Brigade 13, a command staff for both rifle regiments. He distinguished himself in the battle for Dnipropetrovsk in August and September 1941, with an independent decision to create a bridgehead over the Dnieper, for which he received the Knight's Cross. When the division commander was ordered into the Leader Reserve of the OKH in November 1941, Herr was commissioned to lead the 13th Panzer Division. His superiors, *General der Infanterie* Gustav von Wietersheim and *Generaloberst* Ewald von Kleist, both proven Panzer leaders, proposed an earlier promotion in March 1942 to make him full leader of the division. On 1 April 1942, Herr was promoted to *Generalmajor*. The evaluation by von Wietersheim reads as follows:

> Valuable leader personality. Clear and resolute. Very good brigade commander. Leads confidently and deliberately. Commits himself personally. He has proven himself particularly successful in the same way as divisional leader during the current heavy defensive battles. Fills this position very well.

A few months later, in mid-1942, *General der Panzertruppen* Friedrich Kirchner, commander of LVIIth Panzer Corps, to which Herr's division was attached, evaluated Herr in the following words: 'Possesses good tactical and operational understanding; energetic leader, clear and purposeful, is optimistic at all times.'

In the fighting north of the Caucasus, Herr drove over a mine on 25 September 1942. This interrupted his career, as a screw penetrated his skull. He also suffered from jaundice, probably a souvenir from his deployment in the Caucasus. When he was again ready for field operations in mid-June 1943, the preparations for Operation Citadel were already completed and all command positions filled. Due to the loss of the Axis position in North Africa and the danger of an Allied landing in Italy, the Germans moved troops to the south and were in need of commanders. Herr, now *General der Panzertruppen*, would lead the LXXVIth Panzer Corps there for the remainder of 1943 and 1944, before rising to Army commander as mentioned above. This saved him from Soviet captivity.

Herr's career was typical for professional soldiers in speed and scope. He profited from solid training and enough time between promotions to fully master the demands of each step. The evaluations of Herr also give examples of the qualities demanded by the German military: tactical understanding, determination, strength of will and confident leadership. By late 1942, National Socialist attitudes became part of the leadership criteria and these ideas were later too often attached to able leaders even without them being convinced National Socialists. One should keep in mind that many German soldiers' primary virtues of the time were congruent with National Socialist values, such as courage, aggressiveness, determination and so on.[26]

Karl von Oven[27] witnessed a somewhat different, maybe even more 'normal' Eastern front career. Born in 1888, he entered the army in 1908 as a *Fähnrich* with the Prussian Guards. He also saw service exclusively on the Western Front in the First World War, serving in the IIIrd Army Corps staff for a long period of time (possibly with Herr, who was also in this unit in late 1916/early 1917) and finally rising to the rank of *Hauptmann*. After the war, he left the army and entered police service in Prussia, where amongst other tasks he trained police officers and wrote manuals for police deployment during riots in cities. The great need for officers due to German rearmament led to a transfer of no fewer than 2,500 police officers in 1935 to the German Army (a massive impact on the officer corps considering that the Reichswehr only had a total of 4,000 officers). He was released as an *Oberst* from the police, but the army categorized him only as *Oberstleutnant*. In October 1935, he was promoted to *Oberst*. Until the beginning of the Second World War, he commanded a battalion and a regiment, which allowed him to strengthen his command abilities. Promoted to *Generalmajor* in June 1939, he did not receive a divisional command until May 1940, and then only for the briefly existing third class 393rd Infantry Division. After several short service periods, von Oven was commissioned as commander of the 56th Infantry Division in November 1940. He would lead this division for the next two years in the campaign in the Soviet Union, first advancing with Sixth Army on Kiev, then being transferred to Army Group Centre, where the division was deployed in different sectors during late 1941 and 1942. An assessment by his superiors from spring 1942 reads as follows:

5.4.42, [*General der Infanterie* Erich-Heinrich] Clössner [Commander LIIIrd Army Corps]: Character difficult to judge. Very ambitious, very sure of himself. Good military talents. Leads division hard, skilfully and flexibly. In difficult situations quiet and confident. Intolerant representation of his view sometimes complicates cooperation with neighbours. Fills his position very well.

[*Generaloberst* Rudolf] Schmidt [Commander Second Army]: Very energetic, as a subordinate, [his] personality is not easy to take. Fully proven as a division commander even in the most difficult situations. Commanding General

5.5.42, [*Generalfeldmarschall* Günther] von Kluge [Commander Army Group Centre]: Has always been a difficult personality. In the present time, a particularly suitable leader due to his energy and hardness, also as a commanding general.

While all three of von Oven's superiors praised his military leadership qualities, including hardness, they also agreed on his difficult personality, which made cooperation with him difficult. But it seems that this could be corrected, as his next assessment in January 1943 showed:

18.1.43, [*General der Infanterie* Lothar] Rendulic [Commander XXXVth Army Corps]: Active, confident personality, shows purposefulness and firmness. In leadership, can also be hard where the situation requires, good tactical abilities. He is infused with the National Socialist ideology, which he also represents. Combines the look for the whole picture with the interest for important details. The representation of his intolerant views and the friction with neighbours listed in previous evaluations have never appeared under my command. If these defects have actually existed, they are corrected. Good average. Commanding general of an army corps.

Schmidt: In all battles as a division commander fully proven. Stopped the Russian onslaught at Werchowije in December 41, leading in the frontline, and held up despite the most unfavourable conditions. In the following defensive and attacking battles of his division, he again led well and confidently. Fully suitable as commanding general of an army corps. No incidents of incompatibility occurred.

Again, von Oven was assessed as an above-average commander with a good tactical view and a confident leadership style. According to the new rules of the Army Personnel Bureau from late 1942, National Socialist attitudes were now part of the evaluation, with the problems for historical interpretation as mentioned above.

As suggested in all of his assessments, von Oven was commissioned to lead the XXXXIIIrd Army Corps in the area west of Velikiye Luki on 28 January 1943. Promoted to *General der Infanterie* on 1 April 1943, he became full commander of that Army Corps. The notion of incompatibility again arose, as a note from July 1943 by his new superior, *Generaloberst* Hans-Georg Reinhardt, Commander Third Panzer Army, indicated:

Again significant friction. If this doesn't stop, it is not acceptable for him to continue to remain as a commanding general.

Once again, it seems as it was possible to reduce these frictions, since Reinhardt's next evaluation on 22 September 1943 was very positive, even proposing that von Oven could rise another step in command:

Commands with a firm hand, good tactical eye and with the commitment of the whole personality. As far as I have known him in the time of the positional war, he will be able to gain the suitability as army commander.

Army Group Centre's Commander, von Kluge, did not fully agree:

Cannot be considered an army commander. As commanding general in a quiet sector fully proved, he will stand his ground, also – as in his time as divisional leader – in crisis situations.

Due to shifting of sector boundaries between Third Panzer Army (Army Group Centre) and Sixteenth Army (Army Group North), von Oven and his corps fell under a new chain of command in late-August 1943 (this being the reason for the belated assessment by Reinhardt and von Kluge mentioned above), which was more critical of von Oven's leadership. It seems that the battles around Nevel and later in the Narva bridgehead wore on von Oven. His new superior, *General der Artillerie* Christian Hansen, wanted to release von Oven, a decision supported by *Generalfeldmarschall* Walter Model in March 1944: 'No longer possesses the freshness and resilience needed for the leadership of a corps in the East. I therefore propose to use *General der Infanterie* von Oven after a period of rest in the *Heimat*.' His final assessment of von Oven was also rather negative:

Not a strong personality, who has his own views and represents them. Energy and resilience considerably affected. His leadership shows no decided flaws but little drive and strength, lack of freshness and hardness. Below average. Use in the *Heimat*.

Von Oven's career was typical for many German generals who did not climb up the ladder to the highest positions of command (even if one should keep in mind that von Oven's corps in the Narva area had five to six subordinated divisions, which was far more than usual and could be viewed as a small army). But more interestingly, it shed light on an often forgotten issue of German command in the East: many officers simply burned out under the burden of command, especially as the war dragged on and the German situation became critical and finally desperate. These men were in their fifties and conditions in the Soviet Union were demanding, especially as mid-level command staffs often had to choose Soviet village houses for command posts and quarters. Von Oven was relieved from his command in March 1944 and sent to Germany for a cure. He was then chosen to command *Feldjäger-Kommando II*, a staff with subordinated military police units, which had to combat signs of disintegration, collect stragglers and control rear-area units for combat-ready men without mission and forward those to the combat units. In case of emergency, these staffs were also to organize lines to catch unorganized retreating forces. Ironically, von Oven – termed by Hansen as lacking drive, freshness and hardness – was commissioned with leading the staff deployed in Belarus, which soon witnessed a major Soviet offensive that crushed Army Group Centre. It seems that he again stood his ground there, as his organization was essential in collecting soldiers in East Prussia and Poland to stabilize the German front there in autumn 1944 – a task that demanded all the qualities that Hansen believed von Oven no longer possessed.

A third person to look is one of the most highly decorated non-generals of the army, Werner Ziegler.[28] It is more difficult to reconstruct careers of the less well-known and documented men of field officer ranks (in Germany called staff officers). Ziegler was born in the middle of the First World War in April 1916. He grew up in the uncertain times of the Weimar Republic and the National Socialist 'seizure of power'. As usual for his age group, he served a six-month period in the Reich Labour Service in 1936 before joining the infantry as a volunteer – a rather rare case, as most volunteers choose prestigious arms like tank troops, aircraft pilots or the *Waffen-SS*. He was not directly chosen as an officer, but served for one year as a rifleman before becoming a reserve officer candidate. He then was successively a deputy group leader, group leader, and platoon leader and attended a platoon leader course at the infantry school in Döberitz. On 20 April 1939 he was commissioned *Leutnant der Reserve*. With the beginning of the Second World War, Ziegler was sent to the 186th Infantry Regiment (73rd Infantry Division), which would become his home for the next three years, and was additionally transferred into the active officer corps. He served with the regiment in all German major campaigns, starting with the invasion of Poland as platoon leader (but with only minor action, as the 73rd Infantry Division was in reserve and after its initial deployment sent to the Western front), the offensive against France (as battalion adjutant, winning the Iron Cross Second Class), the campaigns in the Balkans and against the Soviet Union (as company commander, winning the Iron Cross First Class in the Balkans, and both the Knight's Cross and the Infantry Assault Badge in the Soviet Union) before rising to the status of battalion leader in June 1942, while his division was engaged in the German summer offensive of 1942. But his rank lagged behind his status. He was only promoted to the rank of *Oberleutnant* in November 1941, and by this time he had already served for more than a year as company leader. It took nearly another year until he was promoted to *Hauptmann*, when he was already leading a battalion. And he did this with skill and courage, as the following episode shows, when Zielger was leading I./Infantry Regiment 186 in its assault of the Black Sea port Novorossiysk:[29]

At 2.30pm Infantry Regiment 186 approaches on the outskirts of Mefodiyevskiy. The place is heavily occupied by enemy. From all the houses and well entrenched positions on the outskirts of the village, it fires mortars, machine guns and sniper rifles.

The artillery defence, including naval guns of heavy calibre, increases, so the attack breaks down. A concentrated fire attack at 4.00pm from 3 [artillery] battalions on the outskirts brings relief. Closely behind the fire, the regiment advances on the houses. The Second Battalion succeeds at first in breaking in from northwest. Due to this thrust in the flank, the opponent has to give ground to the frontal pressure of the First Battalion and withdraws.

Independently of each other, both battalion leaders made the decision to take advantage of the momentary success and to push through to the harbour. Assault guns ahead, closely followed by the infantry, they push through from street to street. Second Battalion intercepts heavy counterattacks from the railway area at the west edge again and again, thereby shielding the right flank of the First Battalion, for which it become possible through this to reach the harbour in a bold thrust at 6.00pm. Through this bold penetration, all [enemy] elements west of the Tsemes were cut off and the defensive front around Novorossiysk collapsed. Now, however, success must be maintained. The battalions take up an all-around defensive position. Counterattacks, especially from the west, are always repelled, 4 guns are stormed. 1 anti-tank company and the Bicycle Company 173 are immediately thrown forward as reinforcements and Second Battalion of Infantry Regiment 213 is brought up to the town.

Ziegler not only led his battalion (with subordinated assault guns) at the mere rank of an *Oberleutnant*, but he also did this in especially demanding urban terain in the attack, a very difficult task. Furthermore, he took an independent decision that proved decisive in that battle, as it led to a temporarily collapse of the Soviet defences, which allowed the Germans to take one third of the city in a few hours, tore the defenders in two parts, and established an essential base for conquering the second third of the city in a few days. For this decisive action, Ziegler was the 121st soldier of the Wehrmacht (and 43rd of the Army, of whom most were generals) awarded the Oak Leaves to the Knight's Cross. He also successfully led his battalion through the winter 1942/43 in the Kuban bridgehead. He was then transferred to Vth Army Corps staff (to which 73rd Infantry Division was subordinated at the time), serving there a brief period as Deputy First General

Staff Officer and also was promoted to Major. In July 1943, he left his 'home' for the first time and was attached to 23rd Panzer Division for preliminary general staff training – he was soon thrown into the deep end, as the division had to first stem and then counterattack against the Soviet Donec-Mius-Offensive (17 July–2 August 1943). One month later, he was named commander of the Panzer Grenadier Regiment 128 for two months before joining the 11th General Staff Course at the reopened *Kriegsakademie* in Hirschberg. He returned in February 1944 to his 'home' Infantry Regiment 186, as its new and last commander. As most of the unit was destroyed in the Crimea in May 1944, Ziegler was free for a new task, which came when in summer 1944 dozens of *Volks-Grenadier*-Divisions were hastily formed, which were in need of experienced leaders. Promoted to *Oberstleutnant* on 1 June 1944, he was transferred to 558th *(Volks-)Grenadier* Division to command its *(Volks-) Grenadier*-Regiment 1123, attached to Fourth Army in the Suwalki area, where it was to help stabilize the front after the Soviet summer offensive of 1944. He was severely wounded there leading his regiment and did not recover before the end of the war. His leadership earned him the Swords to the Knight's Cross; he was the 102nd soldier in the whole Wehrmacht to receive the coveted decoration. After the war, he joined the newly formed *Bundeswehr* in 1956 and finally retired in 1968 as *Oberst* and commander of Panzergrenadier Brigade 19.

Ziegler's career raises two points. Firstly, even outstanding officers needed some time to rise through the ranks, but they could lead formations before having the necessary rank. Secondly, officers remained attached to the unit in which they made their career, normally returning to it after being wounded or after courses.

Leadership – even if decreasing in quality during the war – was essential to the German war effort in the east. At a lower level, leadership was part of a military system that also included tactics and small-unit techniques, weapons and equipment, and the organization of units. Only if these features were adjusted to each other could the system successfully function and tactical superiority be achieved. The next chapter will discuss the other three features besides leadership, with a special focus on the continuous adaptation process.

I met Werner Ziegler in 1969 – 1970 whilst carrying out Recce NCO duties with 23rd AAC and sought permission to land 6 helicopters in one of his fields S of Hamburg. I had many discussions with him in the 48 hours we were on his property, a really nice man!

Chapter 3

The German Army in the East as a Fighting Machine: Tactics, Weapons and Organization

The following after-action report describes a typical minor engagement fought by elements of a German reconnaissance battalion in the early stages of the war in the east:[1]

While the division pushed along the right and left of the railway further eastward on Dnipropetrovsk, the battalion had the order to secure – first on the western half and then with front southward - the pocket that was formed by the combat sectors of the 13th Panzer and 60th motorized Infantry Divisions.

The Russian had partly yielded, partly been pushed into the encirclement.

Around 15.00 hrs the battalion received the divisional order that the enemy identified in battalion strength on Hill 82.6 had to be destroyed by fire.

For this purpose, 1 light infantry gun under command of *Leutnant* Müller, the self-propelled anti-tank gun and the 2cm [gun] armoured car of armoured scout troop Oertel, and armoured scout troop Simon were subordinated to platoon Sassenberg, which was already in position on the hill southwest of Ozenowka. Mission for the platoon: destruction of the enemy on Hill 82.6 by fire. Since the armoured cars and the light infantry gun first had to be loaded, the heavy weapons under the command of adjutant *Leutnant* Wolff von der Sahl did not reach platoon Sassenberg until 1700 hrs. *Leutnant* Wolff von der Sahl delivered the order of the battalion commander about the approach of the operation to *Leutnant* Sassenberg. Meanwhile, it was determined by combat reconnaissance that the enemy had left Hill 82.6 and had escaped from the 60th [Motorized Infantry] Division's artillery fire in the direction of Mironowka. At the same time lively enemy movements on the hills eastward of Mironowka and in Mironowka itself were recognized. While platoon Sassenberg initially stayed in its old position, the 5 available armoured cars and the self-propelled gun were commanded to outflank the village on its right with the mission to break enemy resistance on the outskirts of the village in a tank-like advance and push into Mirkonowka.

While under enemy fire, *Leutnant* Müller and his men brought the light infantry gun into position in a spirited way, so that it could fire directly into the village and on the hills lying behind it. Even before the armoured cars could open fire, the light infantry gun made an effective surprise attack on an enemy grouping by the church. A short time afterwards, one heard lively fire from the cannons and machine guns of the armoured cars and flares indicated that the outskirts of the village had been taken and the armoured cars that had pushed out even further to the right had driven into the enemy's rear. Now *Leutnant* Sassenberg decided to attack the village with group *Unteroffizier* Blöde and group *Unteroffizier* Schütze also sweeping to the right, while group *Unteroffizier* Luderer was left behind for the security of the light infantry gun and flank protection.

Leutnant Müller had recognized a horse-drawn column at the northern edge of the village and immediately opened fire on it, whereupon all vehicles hastily tried to escape to the north under the protection of smoke. Likewise the armoured cars had recognized the worthwhile target and opened fire from all barrels at the column shrouded by smoke.

The smoke lost its effectiveness rapidly due to a favourable wind. In the shortest time, *Leutnant* Sassenberg reached the outskirts of the village with motorcycles and deployed both groups to comb through the eastern part of the village, in which the armoured cars had already broken the main resistance. Inspired by the attack signal sounded by the platoon's bugler, which obviously impressed the enemy from a morale perspective, both groups dashed further forward with fire support from the armoured cars.

The light infantry gun monitored the western part of the village and the hills behind the village and could effectively fire on the enemy fleeing from the village.

Feldwebel Oertel, who with his armoured car was receiving fire from 6 enemy machine guns on the main street, forced the enemy to yield and, while doing so, had 3 tyres destroyed and the rims penetrated by armour piercing rounds.

By 1930 hrs the situation was as follows:

The motorcycle groups had combed through the eastern part, while the armoured cars had already broken the main resistance of the enemy in the western part of the village. Meanwhile dusk was so advanced, that *Leutnant* Sassenberg decided to withdraw all units of the operation and to take up a position of all-around defence in Ozenowka and wait for new orders from the battalion, since the purpose of the attack – to throw back the enemy and to inflict losses – had full success with extremely low losses on our side.

Statements of that battalion's prisoners, who were taken the next day at a different place in the sector, confirmed that the enemy had left behind numerous wounded and dead men.

The operation again was executed by *Leutnant* Sassenberg in a calm, objective-focused and rousing manner. Our losses: 1 wounded.

This battle highlighted the most important facets of German tactical thinking and practice: speed, surprise, initiative on all levels, decisiveness, aggressiveness, combined arms action, the combination of manoeuvre and fire, flanking and leadership by example. Those terms applied to German tactics throughout the war.[2] But the way those words were carried out in practice did evolve over the course of the conflict. This was a consequence of the many challenges that arose in the eastern theatre, most of which were not closely examined or thought about before the war due to the expectation of a short *Blitzkrieg* campaign. On the tactical level, these challenges included terrain and weather conditions not previously experienced in the war by German troops, such as extremely cold winter weather, high-altitude mountain warfare, fighting in the endless primeval forests of north-western Russia, and urban warfare. Adaptation was also needed against the Soviet opponent, which injected its own will, its own ideas and, in some areas, superior weapons and huge quantities of men and material into battle. While the minimal research that exists on the topic suggests that the Red Army was slower to adapt on the tactical level than the German army, what Williamson Murray termed 'complex adaption' fits for both armies in the process of learning and adapting on the Eastern front, since both were in constant development.[3] Furthermore, as the war went differently than planned, the Germans needed to (re-)learn tactical practices that had been neglected up until this time, such as positional or anti-tank warfare, as well as defensive warfare in general. Tactical developments were strongly influenced by issues discussed in other chapters, such as the often critical supply situation, the continual warfare on the Eastern front, and the enormous losses in leaders and soldiers. Therefore, the following chapter focusses more on the dynamics, dependencies and development in the tactical area than specifically on tactics. Since tactics are closely related to weapons and organization structures, these will also be discussed here.

The German army had a long tradition of achieving high levels of professionalism in this area, allowing it to successfully attack and defend against much more numerous enemies. While recent research has supported the thesis that this tactical excellence was achieved at the cost of sound strategic expertise, the sources of this tactical excellence still require more research. This is all the more astonishing, because even though the German army continually suffered high losses from mid-1941 on, it maintained a relatively formidable level of tactical professionalism until summer 1944, when the massive double defeats in Normandy and Belarus profoundly changed the character of the army.

In looking at explanations for this tactical superiority, flexible guidelines that not only allowed for a commander to decide on the spot the best way to fulfil his mission, but actually demanded it, combined with a thoroughly trained and educated officer and NCO corps, were clearly important factors, as seen in chapter 2. Skilled, battle-oriented training by combat-experienced officers and NCOs, as well as further training behind the front for men and leaders, was another essential basic. This will be more closely examined in chapter 6. Finally, and what will be discussed here, is the impact of rapid learning. Experiences over long periods of time were distilled, learned, and applied by German units and their leaders much more quickly than by their opponents.

At the base of the learning process lay the will to learn and improve, and to do so in a systematic manner. The foundation of this practice could be found in the Napoleonic era and in the formation of the General Staff, but a massive impulse came after the Franco-Prussian War.[4] So the German army in the east had a well-established reporting system, which included special experience reports. On certain occasions, such reports were ordered by superior commands. In the following source, Sixth Army ordered such a set of reports by its subordinated units after the end of the German summer offensive 1942[5]:

In the near future, a specially commissioned officer of the 6th Army staff will be sent to the corps commands and to individual divisions for the purpose of compiling combat experiences of this year's summer campaign. Written experience reports are to be supplemented and deepened through personal debriefings.

The divisional and corps staffs now need to take a position on the following questions and prepare their oral answers:

1) Battle in the steppe (all corps): advance, attack, transition to the defence.
2) Special features of the battle in the Stalingrad fortress (only LIst Army Corps): Attack preparations, attack, deployment on the main battlefield located in the urban area.
3) Defence of massed tank attacks (only XIVth Panzer Corps).
4) The layout of, entrenchment and combat in this year's winter positions (without LIst Army Corps).

Points of view frame how experiences are written down:

A) Experiences of the leadership
B) Tactical combat experiences
C) Weapon technology experiences
D) Other experiences

The required reports covered issues new for the German army (such as fighting on the steppe), but also issues that were understood as becoming increasingly important (such as urban warfare or defence against massed tank attacks, both of which had already occurred in 1941 and early 1942, but were previously viewed as being the exception). The corps mentioned in the order did pass the demand for experience reports to their subordinate divisions (i.e. LIst Army Corps ordered 24th Panzer Division to report about urban warfare), and the divisions collected information from their organic and temporarily subordinated units. These analyses were then summarized into a final report and, together with selected reports of lower levels, sent back to the corps. The corps normally added its own observations, sometimes offering a contradicting view, to the division's report, or it compiled reports from several divisions. In the best case, this went back to the army's central institutions in Germany. What made the German system so effective, however, was that this was not a one-way network. Divisions and corps did not simply wait for regulations coming back from central institutions, i.e. official leaflets or even manuals, but immediately used their collected experiences, ordering changes in tactics, unit structure, weapons use, command style and training.[6] A closer look at the German army in the east reveals that it was in permanent evolution. This frequently included trial and error, as war is no exact science. Not all variations proved successful, and many lessons learned could not be implemented due to a lack of men and material.

The next source presents a different type of learning, one that focuses on weapons. One year after the invasion, a special mission of officers and officials of the First Department (Munitions and Ballistic) of the Army Ordnance Office's Group for Development and Testing was sent to Army Group North on a fact-finding mission. The small staff toured Army Group North's area from 10 June to 13 July 1942, visiting staff officers from all levels of the hierarchy, from the Army Group down to battalions, as well as units in the field of all kinds, including the often-forgotten army coastal artillery battalions. Rear-area installations, such as collection points for captured material and field workshops, were also visited. Additionally, the staff talked with individual soldiers, including specialists in anti-tank warfare, and interrogated captured Soviet officers. Their findings were summarized in the following report:[7]

The aim of the mission was to ascertain if the troops possessed sufficient weapons, equipment and munitions for the actual demands, as well as forwarding on the wishes, demands and suggestions of the troops in the quickest way to the department. [...]

The troops clearly recognized that the bureau had recently developed many good weapons; on the other hand, flaws and complaints were expressed openly and without reserve. Frequently voiced was: why doesn't the bureau give us this or that? Why do we get so little munitions? Why don't we get these weapons?

That the allocation of weapons and equipment is not the business of the bureau was often not known; many incorrect suspicions of the bureau could be dismissed.

Further, it was possible to establish a vibrant contact between the troops and the bureau, a direct connection which will persist beyond the posting. This appears to be even more necessary as the monthly condition reports of the divisions can contain only particular details and are cut considerably by the corps and armies.

Furthermore, it is not only practical, but urgently necessary, that officers of the bureau who have no idea about the war in the East personally receive an opportunity to see the terrain in which the troops fight. Especially the bog forest that predominates in large sections of Army Group North and which demands the most of men and material, is at its foremost unique in Europe.

Between Lakes Ilmen and Ladoga, countless battalions lay day and night in the swamp. The enemy shells with artillery and heavy mortars, constantly causing casualties. At the same time, our own field of fire is only 30 to 50m at the most. Connection from combat position to combat position consists only of duck boards, that sink again and again and that must be continually worked on.

Difficulties with food do not exist in the summer, water for washing is extremely scarce. The mosquito plague is considerable, especially at night. Nothing like relief is known, given that neither the divisions nor the army command possess even a single reserve company. Everything is permanently in the frontline.

The supply routes of many infantry regiments, the only connection between the main combat line and hinterland, were muddy to such an extent even in the month of June, that light, only partially loaded field wagons had to be drawn by 6 strong horses, who, literally in the mud up to the belly, could themselves only slowly work forward.

What the infantry, the forward parts of the artillery and anti-tank units suffer daily and hourly in that terrain – even under positional warfare conditions – cannot be overestimated.

The majority of the agencies had a great interest in weapons and ammunition; likewise, they were willing to report orally and in writing. During the mission, 3 preliminary reports with a rash of notes by the troops were submitted; meanwhile they have been sent to the responsible sections.

Attached to the final report are 36 troop reports:

SS Infantry Regiment 9, Infantry Regiments 151, 162, 176, 380, 390, 489, cycle battalion 402: Answers to the questionnaire: 'Infantry'.[8]

Artillery Commander 123, Artillery Regiments 110, 193, 215 (2x), 269: Suggestions for improvement, artillery pieces, munitions, optical equipment.

Infantry Regiment 490, 1st Infantry Division, 61st Infantry Division, Group Debes: Responses to questions of Fourth Department.[9]

Engineer battalions 1, 161, 193, 269: Answers to questions of Fifth Department.[10]

Anti-tank Battalion 193: modification suggestions.

Anti-tank Battalion 563: Experiences with the 5cm ATG 38 against T 34

Anti-tank Battalion 563, 269th Infantry Division: Experiences with the *Stielgranate* (stick shell) 41.[11]

Artillery Regiment 269: Experiences with 10cm shell 39 (red) hollow-charge.

12th Panzer Division: Experiences with self-propelled 7.62cm ATG.

Panzer Engineer Battalion 32: Experiences with heavy rocket launcher 40.

Infantry Regiment 24: Experiences with heavy Russian mortar.

III./SS Regiment 9: Safety of MP 38 and 40.

1st Infantry Division: Equipment, spare parts, [...]

Ist Army Corps: Munitions, adhesive [hollow] charge, vehicles, sleds.

Divisional Supply Commander 21: Sleds [...]

The report mentions an often forgotten fact; namely the relative ignorance of German central institutions about the demands at the sharp end of the Eastern front. Of course, over the years as personnel shifted from the central institutions to the Eastern front or vice-versa, this knowledge increased, but such unfamiliarity led to the development of weapons not entirely useful in Russian conditions. Some examples include the overlapping road wheels used by the Tiger and Panther tanks, or the heavy German ATG.

In summary, it is to say: the problem is anti-tank defence. Adhesive charges, *Stielgranate* and Russian ATG were thankfully welcomed everywhere; plenty of special requests and suggestions for improvement were reported and forwarded to the bureau in the preliminary reports.

Generalfeldmarschall von Küchler demanded, in reference to the *Stielgranate* 41, that a gun had to destroy more than 2 tanks, since they always appear in a wedge formation in threes, often in larger quantities. Many ATGs and light field howitzers have been overrun by tanks because they were attacked in too great numbers. The tank shock, however, has been overcome, especially after the introduction of the adhesive charge.

The *Generalfeldmarschall* then dealt with the wearing out of artillery barrels. He spoke about the scattering of shells up to 500m when firing on a medium distance, so that shelling could not happen as close to the infantry as necessary. [...]

Generalmajor Hasse, Chief of Staff of Army Group North, himself commented on the anti-tank defence as follows: *Stielgranate* good, but too delicate, range too small. The 3.7cm and also the 5cm ATG were usually powerless against the T-34, which was the predominant tank in the north. During the development of ATGs, one must strengthen their penetrative power as the armour of Russian tanks has become increasingly stronger.

He said that at the moment, anti-tank defence had reached its lowest point. This was countered by the development of the heavy ATG, which had been completed long ago. However, the new weapons are not yet available in such large quantities to equip all divisions with them. But the situation is improving from month to month. Meanwhile, General Hasse will have changed his negative point of view after the enormous successes of our anti-tank defence in the Volkhov cauldron and in the Volkhov bridgehead Kirishi.

The rifle (anti) tank grenade, while joyfully welcomed by the troops, had too small an effect. The destruction of tanks by hand is only a stopgap measure that one cannot afford in the long run; this objection must be agreed to.

While the mindful observer could already have recognized in the 1940 Western campaign that anti-tank defence was the Achilles' heel of the German army, this proved relatively unimportant, as the Germans' approach to the war rarely allowed for larger French or British tank actions to become dangerous. The invasion in the Soviet Union confronted German troops with even more modern tanks, such as the T-34 and the KV-1, but their tactically weak use and their relatively small numbers initially precluded a larger crisis on the German side. As their numbers rose and the German army was forced onto the defensive in the first winter, the weaknesses of German anti-tank defence became fully visible. The means presented (*Stielgranate*, hollow charges to be put on the tanks, use of captured ATGs) were improvisational and/or demanded high skills. The deployment of heavy ATGs helped anti-tank defences, but demanded towing vehicles that were also needed by artillery or supply units. Self-propelled guns of the *Marder* class were a more effective measure, but it predictably took time to bring them to the frontline units. Even after more useful weapons such as the *Panzerfaust*, the *Panzerschreck* and diverse tank destroyers were available, from 1943 on, these would not fully fill the gap. Anti-tank defence remained a German vulnerability and it was one of the main causes of the 'infantry crisis' discussed later.

Steep angle fire weapons have a special importance for Army Group North, since it must be reckoned that we will probably face a long period of positional warfare. The troops do not need many sorts of things, instead, only a few types of heavy mortars. 8, 12 and 15cm with substantial ammunition because the Russian always rapidly and effectively digs in and then can only be fought successfully with effective steep angle weapons.

Discussions with other agencies and units went similarly, which are not described here. The further one goes down, the more that details were naturally debated. The troops' interest in weapons was without exception great. This was especially true for the infantry regiments, which sensed through their losses that good weapons and ammunition are crucial for success.

The staffs, corps and divisions often had less interest, sometimes none at all. It was also noticed that even agencies that themselves need to pay attention to weapons effectiveness, not only failed to evaluate the weapons' effectiveness correctly, but that they also even completely lacked the goodwill to concern themselves with such things. This is an evil that viewed in the long run, has to be described as dangerous and which must be necessarily suppressed.

This last section emphasizes how different perceptions of the war in the East emerged within the army's hierarchy, depending on how close one was to the front line. Of course, soldiers in the front line would recognize deficiencies of weapons faster than army staffs or institutions in the *Reich*. This can be seen most obviously in the discussion about heavy mortars. Mortars were one of the primary weapons of the Eastern front and responsible for many losses. They were easier to produce and more often available to the troops than artillery, and were feared for their noiseless fire that allowed for effective surprise bombardments. With their excellent 12cm mortar, as well as with larger quantities of mortar shells, the Soviets had a distinct advantage. While there was, from late 1941 on, a strong demand for that weapon from the frontline troops who suffered from Soviet superiority in this area, central institutions occupied with that question did not seem to view it in the same urgent way. One should also be aware that the German stressing of 'will' as a key factor in battle success sometimes interfered with demands for better equipment, as that was seen as of secondary importance.

The following section of the report deals with artillery questions.

The effect of the [Soviet] 7.62cm [and] the 12.2cm guns and the 12cm mortar is judged as very good: the shells fragmented into many little splinters. The splinters of the 12cm mortar occasionally penetrate the German steel helmet and then cause light wounds. The shells of the heavy guns fragment less effectively, big splinters are frequent. All in all, the splinter effect of the Russian artillery is allegedly considerably better than in the [First] World War. The sensitivity of the fuses fully equals the requirements.

[...] While in the first months of the war the Russian often shelled only by batteries, he has now learned to concentrate the fire of a battalion or even several battalions. It has been observed in the Leningrad sector that Russian artillery surprisingly fired on one single target from positions in Leningrad, from the opposite coast, in Kronstadt and from the Oranienbaum [Lomonosov] cauldron. That is a noticeable achievement in terms of artillery and communications.

After the end of a year of war, Russian artillery also perfected the manoeuvrability of fire, the relocation of fire from one target to the other. Reconnaissance by sound [ranging] and subsequent combating of recognized fire positions is now the rule. The only thing the Russian has not yet mastered is fire by aerial observation.

With regard to mobility during the mission, the Russian artillery seems to be exemplary. It has often occurred that [Soviet] batteries that put our infantry and artillery under considerable fire were revealed by sound and air reconnaissance and then fired on by our own artillery. Immediately after fulfilling its mission, however, the Russian artillery had moved to an alternate firing position - as became apparent after the fact - and our fire hit an empty area. A Russian battery often had one main firing position and two alternate firing positions.

In contrast, our artillery is reproached for a lack of mobility. One Army Corps complained: 'Our artillery cannot be moved by any power of the Earth to change positions. In the style of *Erbhof* farmers, it persists in its positions, embracing the principle: "Here I fire, here I stay, here I live, here I die!"' The difficulties of the terrain, even those of the roads, as well as the lack of horses and other vehicles may partially, but not completely excuse that disinclination to move. This point is probably no longer stressed enough during training.

Almost all artillery regiments complained that the infantry approaches the artillery with all and every request concerning fire support and too little use is made of their own heavy weapons. Since the infantry, including the machine gun, infantry gun and ATG companies have higher losses than the artillery, in many cases there may exist a lack of appropriate low-level leaders. The artillery considers it possible to eliminate this dependence by subordinating the infantry's artillery weapons to the artillery's care.

Much is said about the guns in the individual reports. In summary, it will only be expressed here that the artillery on the whole is quite content with their weapons, even after a year in the Russian war. One often sees light field howitzer barrels that have fired far more than 10,000 shells and which hardly exceed the firing-table dispersion. On the other hand, barrels have worn out before they should have. Special esteem is enjoyed everywhere by the heavy infantry gun. The infantry regiments constantly regret that they can only have 2 guns at their disposal.

The terrain in most parts of Army Group North, especially in those areas where the bog forest predominates, is very difficult to navigate and this needs to be pointed out again and also within this context. Everywhere, the demand was made to convert completely the heavy field howitzer 18 to motorized towed vehicles. Strong horses are often missing; when they are really available, the marching speed of the horse-drawn artillery is so minimal, that it never catches up with the infantry. The same demand to convert to motorized towing vehicles was also made several times for the heavy infantry gun.

In the discussion of artillery, there was a clear recognition of the Soviet artillery's qualities, including it being more agile than German artillery, as well as having learned command techniques to concentrate more firepower. But the Germans still possessed advantages such as fire observation by plane. The competition between infantry and artillery over the command of various artillery segments also clearly emerged. While the artillery claimed superior leadership in using heavy weapons, the infantry demanded more support weapons under its command, since artillery units could not always maintain the pace of the advance and were therefore not always available when needed. This demand was made regarding the heavy infantry gun, but it was even more evident with the already mentioned heavy mortar, as can be seen in the document's next section:

All ATGs with a calibre 5cm or bigger are in their actual form too heavy for mobile warfare in the bog forest or even for positioning in the positional war. By request of the troops, those weapons should be easy to disassemble, in order to carry them in the way of mountain artillery pieces everywhere.

The interim report already pointed to the importance of the Russian heavy 12cm mortar. The troops are extremely appreciative that the bureau copied the mortar. One can hear again and again: 'Hopefully it will come soon in great numbers'. Infantry and artillery struggle in the same way for that weapon, which has proven always the same in attack and defence, in summer and winter.

Since we did not possess the capacities at the time, one had to reduce equally the programs for the light and heavy field howitzer. Today, every division prefers to take 4 heavy mortars instead of one light field howitzer, 6 mortars instead of one heavy field howitzer. This is one of the few points in which the requests of the troops conform. One should not disappoint the troops and do the utmost so that the mortar is built as fast as possible and in the highest possible number. If the troops receive 1,000 mortars, only 5 mortars are allotted to each division, and that is with a front sector often of 20-30km. Whether the infantry or the artillery will be equipped with the mortar, or if one organizes divisional mortar battalions, 3,000 mortars must be produced in 6 months, and at the cost of the light and heavy field howitzer and the light mortar, which was not used much in the winter due to the small effect of the light mortar rounds in the snow.

This demand on these grounds is especially important, since it gives the superiority of weapons back to the German infantryman, which, at the moment, is with the Russian side (semi-automatic rifles, rifles with telescopic sights). In addition it is emphasized again and again that the Russian digs-in in an unbelievably short time and can be contained only with a steep angle weapon.

From 1943 on, German units received the heavy 12cm mortar 42, an improved version of the Soviet mortar. Even more of a problem than the numbers of mortars produced was the availability of mortar shells, as enough failed to reach troops at the front. This was a consequence of the far too broad array of weapons in service and the resulting dispersion of production capacities. The report also mentioned infantry weapons:

Infantry weapons are only briefly addressed here. [...] Repeated here are the most urgent demands: Equipping of the troops with an explosive cartridge [...]. The troops do not understand why this cartridge is denied to them, but expect that they will be constantly shot with them by the Russians. The Russian explosive cartridge is not only morally damaging– especially in the woods! – it also causes such heavy wounds, that a full recovery from even apparently light wounds is extremely rare.

A likewise urgent demand is for rifles with telescopic sights. The infantry generally complain of bad training, especially the poor marksmanship training of the replacements. [...]

The infantry men fires little with the rifle, he relies on machine and heavy weapons. It is all the more important to arm the few good marksmen with a premium weapon, namely the rifle with a telescopic sight.

A higher SS commander has 'obtained' 300 rifles with telescopic sights through the *Reichsführer* SS. In each battalion, he equipped a sniper group with those weapons. An NCO continuously promoted the training of the riflemen, their operations come out of alternating positions. Their own losses are rare, in contrast some of those men have 'kill lists' of 30 or more opponents.

The cry for the rifle with telescopic sight is considerably stronger than the one for the [semi-] automatic rifle. This may be explained by the fact that the Russian semi-automatic rifle often fails in deep temperatures, and many an infantryman discarded his captured semi-automatic rifle in wintertime and again snatched up the German infantry rifle. In contrast, the Russian sight [on a normal rifle] has given [German soldiers] good experiences. [...] Our sight may have proven its worth over 150 years and in many wars – the Russian one is superior. [...] A rifleman is unquestionably easier and faster to train with the Russian sight than with the German one [...] In a comparison shooting in which soldiers of all grades participated, good results were achieved with the Russian rifle, despite the fact that all riflemen were trained with the German and not the Russian rifle. One should order a replacement battalion to train 100 recruits with both sights and then execute a comparison shooting.

The shortcomings of the German submachine gun and the superiority of the Russian one in some areas is also pointed out here [...]. It is generally complained that our submachine gun is more delicate than the robust Russian one; it continuously needs careful maintenance to remain ready for action. In addition, its low safety is accentuated again and again. The number of deadly accidents – officers alone – is frighteningly high. [...]

What can be said for the Russian submachine gun in terms of primitive construction in contrast to the German one also applies to other Russian weapons. For example, the Russian tank rifle is according to German standards 'thrown together'. One agency used the expression 'Woolworth goods'. But this W[oolworth] good is easy to produce, easy to use, needs little care, is immune to temperature, fires as well as the German one and frequently has a longer life. The troops themselves say: 'Each individual weapon of ours is a piece of good German handicraft work, but the Russian weapons are real mass-produced goods'.

This comparison does not apply for all weapons; anyway it gives food for thought. Since the weapon is in any case not kept very long due to the wearing out of weapons in the front line (i.e. MG) through enemy fire, defective care, a considerable lack of spare parts, our manufacturing engineers could probably adopt many Russian principles. This is also a demand that the Führer and the deceased *Reichsminister* Todt made again and again. The machine gun 42 constitutes a step forward in the identified direction.

An additional new experience for the German infantrymen in the fight against the Red Army was their inferiority in infantry weapons. While the main German rifle, the 98k, was not significantly better or worse than the Polish, British or French equivalent, the Germans had advantages in submachine and machine guns. The Red Army confronted the German with a technically comparable rifle, but one that required less training to use effectively, with a more reliable submachine gun that possessed more firepower due to its drum magazine, and with reliable semi-automatic rifles and rifles with telescopic sights in large numbers. The important advantage in machine guns rested with the German MG 34 and was expanded by the MG 42 with its higher rate of fire and limited maintenance needs.

Whatever gaps existed between German and Soviet weapons, German armaments could only be effective if they were operational. The climate conditions in Russia, the lack of maintenance due to the demands on the troops, and the lack of training, as well as the unexpected duration of service for German weapons, wore many of them out. Only a constant flow of replacement weapons and spare parts could fill this gap. But this was not the case and the capability to repair weapons simply did not exist, as the report shows:

> On the question of spare parts indicated above – which was already addressed in an interim report, must be pointed out again. A really frightening lack of spare parts exists everywhere with all infantry weapons and the artillery. One agency literally reported: One would rather receive a complete gun than some spare parts.
>
> For this reason, numerous guns of all kinds, infantry guns, ATGs and machine guns, as well as bicycles, have already fallen out by now and are continuing to fall out. Since scarcely any spare parts were in supply - there are unsatisfied demands for spare parts of 6 months and more - the troops cannibalize their weapons, i.e. they make 2 machine guns out 4 defective ones. The rest is carried along for a while at best and is then lost piece by piece. Why such a lack of spare parts exists is difficult to say. Either this crisis is not sufficiently known, or the 'Führer's demands', which refer only to new weapons, do not permit the production of spare parts to a sufficient extent, or the allocation of raw materials is inadequate.
>
> Last year, a huge campaign 'Panzer spare parts' went through the bureau. A similar campaign 'weapon spare parts' must be launched. With a fraction of the capacity required to produce new weapons, the same quantity of weapons could be restored by providing spare parts, thus restoring their readiness.
>
> The same shortage exists for all kinds of tools. If one were to help the field workshops and armourer platoons one-time in this respect, many defective weapons could be restored, which the troops are not now in the position due to the current tool situation [...]
>
> [...] New enemy weapons, tanks, guns and munitions are not to be expected for the time being. In addition to the T 34, particularly the heavy mortar and the so-called '*Stalinorgel*' [the German nickname for the Katyusha] have moral effects.
>
> [...] Assault guns are still demanded in as large a quantity as possible. A corps-commanding general remarked that assault guns and planes with machine guns and machine cannons had helped him most in attack. This is understandable inasmuch as we have for some time apparently held absolute air-superiority. In one section, 92 Russian airplanes were shot down in a single day without a single loss of our own.
>
> [...] The troops are aware that German industry is fully occupied and that the same lack of manpower dominates at home as at the front. Nevertheless, the soldier expects that his most urgent demands will be fulfilled – here the heavy mortar will come first – because the lack of suitable weapons costs his blood.

The call for assault guns was heavily driven by the anti-tank capacity of those vehicles, especially as the new long-barrelled version arrived at the front in spring 1942.[12] As with the heavy mortar, German industry never satisfied the frontline demands for this weapon. While this was due in part to industrial capacity, it was also a result of the artillery branch not being a priority (the assault gun was part of the artillery branch) for the High Command, which preferred offensive weapons such as tanks, and this preference continued even after Germany was definitively on the defensive. But even inside the artillery branch, the heaviest guns were preferred over the assault gun.[13] The lack of assault guns and later tank destroyers substantially decreased the defensive capabilities of German infantry units, as they lacked mobile anti-tank weapons with heavy firepower.

While some areas of German weaponry underwent major developments, other areas only experienced minor changes. Though already outdated by the beginning of Operation Barbarossa, Mark I and II tanks still constituted 28 per cent of the armour in the invasion. By summer 1944, the long-barrelled Mark IV was the main combat tank, but Panthers and Tigers had become available in larger numbers. And while assault guns and self-propelled ATGs were rather the exception in summer 1941, they surpassed the numbers of tanks in 1944. ATGs had risen in calibre from 3.7cm to 12.8cm, in weight from 435kg to over 10,000kg, thereby completely transforming the tactical idea of the ATG. In 1941, infantry units had oversized rifles of questionable value for anti-tank defence. In 1944, German infantry units could field the *Panzerschreck*, an improved copy of the US Bazooka, and the *Panzerfaust*, a cheap one-man single-use weapon. Both were highly effective against tanks, but were also valuable in other arenas as well, including urban warfare.

The changes were much smaller where artillery or infantry weapons were concerned. In fact, except for anti-tank weapons, few things changed for the ordinary infantry division between summer 1941 and 1944. Most notably, divisional artillery remained the same, with the exception of organically attached rocket launchers in a few divisions. The same was the case with infantry weapons. All attempts to replace the outdated rifle 98k failed due to a mixture of excessive demands on a new weapon, military conservatism, and finally, of course, a lack of production capability. The widespread use of a technically reliable individual weapon with more firepower, such as the semi-automatic rifle G43 or the revolutionary Assault Rifle 44, earlier in the war, would have had a strong tactical effect, but it failed to occur. The technology and structure of German heavy infantry weapons also experienced only minor changes. In contrast to the individual weapons, the machine gun 42 should have completely replaced the machine gun 34, but this never fully happened. Even worse, many newly formed units, as well as many rear area units, had to rely on captured machine guns or on old German First World War models such as the MG 08/15. While the light 5cm mortar was put out of service in 1942, generally replaced by the rifle grenade, the fire support combination of medium mortars and light and heavy infantry guns was never called into question. This combination allowed for a broad ability to respond to various tactical issues, but it also resulted in a lower production output as various weapons were produced instead of concentrating on one model, and it required differently trained crews and leaders to be able to use the combination effectively. Experiences with the Soviet-copied 12cm mortar offered an alternative that, however, was never seriously considered.

The introduction of new weapons under war-time conditions is a task often underestimated, as the following two sources indicate. Even when only parts of a weapons system were replaced, this proved problematic, as the following report from 1942 on the first use of heavy infantry guns on assault gun chassis – both proven systems – shows:[14]

> The following deficiencies were found after arrival of the assault guns with heavy infantry guns, with six of each sent to the Assault Gun Battalions 177 and 244:
> 1) Assault Gun Battalion 177
>   A) Guns
>   Old assault gun chassis with significant technical deficiencies which must be repaired before deployment: typical deterioration due to age of the chassis and engine (steering brakes, carburettor, fuel pump, track roller, tracks, etc.). No observation equipment for gun commander (the battery commander's telescope must be installed in a makeshift position). No ballistic tables and operating instructions available.
>   B) Staff
>   Of the 12 men sent, 7 are trained with horses as drivers for the wagon-driver's seat or on the saddle. These, as well as a further 3 men, are not trained on the heavy infantry gun. None of the men were briefed on the heavy infantry gun on the assault gun. All tank drivers without experience. Driving license exam was done the day before the departure.
> 2) Assault Gun Battalion 244
>   A) Guns
>   Operating instructions and ballistic tables are missing.
>   B) Staff
>   The men who were sent along had been commanded by the replacement battalion for three days in the factory where the guns were made. They are neither trained on driving the assault gun chassis nor on the gun.

The troops of the LIst Army Corps that fought their way through the rubble-filled streets in Stalingrad desperately awaited new weapons that combined high mobility and firepower, especially as their time for attack was running out in November 1942 due to the need to save troops to counter the expected Soviet winter offensives. An efficient deployment of those weapons was hindered by several issues, including the failure to properly maintain old chassis, crews that were either poorly trained in the use of the weapons or were inexperienced, and the lack of vital equipment. Even if they had arrived in early November, they could never have been a game-changer, as the larger context of the German attack on Stalingrad – and the Soviet response – did not allow for German victory at that time.

The introduction of completely new weapon systems under wartime conditions provided an even stiffer challenge to the military system. An excellent example of this phenomenon can be seen in the case of the '*Sturmgewehr*' (Assault Rifle) 44, which proved revolutionary in infantry armament as it combined the long-range precision of a rifle with the short-range firepower of the submachine gun. Hitler was opposed to such a weapon for a long time, but he was not alone, as is often claimed in literature. Many of the army's central agencies feared a loss of fire discipline, which would necessarily lead to a higher consumption of ammunition. The new weapon would result in the introduction of a new type of rifle ammunition, further complicating the supply system. Following early tests in 1943, the infantry branch urgently demanded that the weapon be put into production. Two waves of large combat tests were carried out in spring and autumn 1944, before the weapon was finally put in service in December 1944.[15] The following source is the evaluation report given by the 1st Infantry Division in autumn 1944. Typically, the evaluation report was written in response to a questionnaire:[16]

I) Structure

1) Has the concentration of the snipers in the company headquarters of the Grenadier companies proven itself? How was the deployment of the snipers carried out?

Concentration of the snipers in the submachine gun (SMG) company has fully proven itself. In the *defence*, the deployment of snipers (in each case a sniper and an observer) in the centre of gravity is advisable. Deployment by individual groups is a proven failure, since this often results in sentry service. The deployment of snipers inside the company sector must be *mobile*. In the attack, the sniper group remains with the company leader as a reserve for deployment at the appearance of enemy snipers and individual targets difficult to distinguish.

2) How effective has the merging of the light machine gun squad and the rifle grenade squad in *one* group of the platoon been: a) from the point of view of the platoon leader? b) from the point of view of the group leader?

To a) The merging of the light machine gun squad and the rifle grenade squad in *one group* under the command of the platoon leader has proven itself effective. In the attack, the group is with the platoon leader, the light machine gun follows during the attack behind the advancing SMG groups. When meeting fierce resistance and at the shift to defence, the light machine gun squad will be deployed by the platoon leader and strengthen the defensive power of the *SMG groups, which by then have frequently depleted their ammunition.*

The complete rifle grenade squad will also be tasked by the platoon leader against enemy targets under cover. It is easier for the rifle grenade riflemen to supply themselves from the following infantry cart when completely deployed than when individually attached to groups. It is advised that the leader of the machine gun and rifle grenade squad [should be] the deputy platoon leader.

To b) Such an arrangement is solely a relief for the *group leader*. The few available *good* group leaders were tasked with leading the mixed groups. For the average and poor group leaders, which are the majority, the leadership of a group which consists of only one [type of] weapon is simplified.

3) Has the structure of the SMG group proven itself? Did the firepower also suffice in the defence?

The structure of the SMG group has fully proven itself. Leadership and training with only one [type of] weapon is simplified. A SMG group is more

agile in counterthrusts than previous riflemen group. The firepower of a
SMG group is also sufficient in the defensive.

In what was typical for the German approach to warfare, the first questions
addressed did not concern technical points, but rather tactical ones, i.e. how to
structure the groups and platoons to most fully exploit the available firepower. This
also included the question of leadership, a pressing issue in the later war years, as
experienced and well-trained leaders on the lower levels were increasingly in short
supply. The central question above in structure and command was about how best
to integrate the fire elements (light machine gun, rifle grenade, snipers) into small
units. In the 1930s, the German rifle group used rifles, one or two submachine
guns, a light machine gun for fire support and an anti-tank rifle. This could be
handled by an NCO. This set of weapons rapidly expanded from 1942 on, as
rifle grenades, semi-automatic rifles, rifles with telescopic sights, and, eventually,
automatic rifles and the *Panzerfaust* were introduced. Captured weapons further
complicated the situation. A group with this set of weapons proved too difficult
to be effectively trained and commanded by NCOs, especially as the level of
training decreased during the course of the war. As a result, fire elements on the
platoon level were concentrated in one special group, while the regular infantry
was equipped as uniformly as possible, ideally with the Assault Rifle 44.[17]

II) Combat Power
  1) How is the gain of the infantry's combat power with the introduction of
     the SMG 44 evaluated?
     Combat power and *mobility* of the infantry was *substantially* enhanced
     by the refitting with SMG 44. Combat power does not suffer as much
     through the loss of an individual SMG 44 as by the corresponding loss of
     rifles in the old riflemen group.
     In the *defence*, the SMG ensured targeted single shots up to 600m and a
     dense fire curtain on close range. With only a medium use of ammunition,
     the SMG provides the particular counterthrust momentum through the
     extraordinary moral effect of full-automatic fire. The same is true for the
     attack of the SMG company.
     The SMG group has especially proven itself effective in the woods and
     bush terrain.
     The experiences of the recent battles in the south have shown that night
     attacks could be carried out with particular success and with few losses
     through the mass deployment of the SMG 44. These night attacks allowed
     for a relatively easy breakthroughs against strong enemy ATG and heavy
     weapons frontlines, against which attacks during the day seemed hopeless.
     [...]
  2) Should it be considered necessary to completely outfit the other units of the
     Grenadier regiment (except the Grenadier companies) with the SMG? For
     which units and [individual] soldiers would the arming with the rifle 98k
     suffice, when applying a sharp standard?
     It is considered necessary to equip at least the battalion staffs, the
     [regimental] engineer and bicycle platoons, and the machine gun companies

with the SMG 44. This is based on the experiences of the last battles, in which regimental and battalion staffs and machine gun companies were often involved in close combat, as were sometimes the crew of the heavy mortars and infantry guns, and had to be deployed for counterthrusts to eliminate penetrations due to lack of other reserves.

a) Due to considerations of the danger of gangs, the possibility of surprise attacks in the rear area, and of sudden breakthroughs, it is desired that all soldiers that, according to the table of organization, are equipped with the rifle are equipped with SMG 44, with the exception of snipers and rifle grenade. The baggage trains then would also have a greater self-protection.

b) When applying a sharp standard, the equipping of the baggage train with the SMG 44 could be omitted.

c) When applying an especially sharp standard on the equipping with the SMG 44, the crew of heavy mortars and infantry guns (without forward observer personnel) [could] also [be omitted. [...]

When the increase in combat power provided by this weapon is considered, it seems surprising that the German army took so long to introduce it. The assault rifle gave the German infantry a massive superiority in tactical encounters, as it combined firepower and mobility. For example, the addition of this weapon solved the problem that plagued German Panzer units in 1943 and 1944, namely massive ATG fronts. It also compensated for the German soldiers' numerical inferiority, a regular condition on the Eastern front. The introduction of this weapon did not come about in one sweep, and it actually never appeared in substantial numbers on the Eastern front. As there were never enough assault rifles, it was discussed which soldiers should receive it for the greatest effect, as the source above indicates. One has to add that for most German units on the Eastern front in September 1944, the issue of partisan warfare had disappeared as the frontline was rapidly reaching German and allied territory.

III) Training

Has the concentration of the light machine gun, the SMG, the snipers and the rifle grenade riflemen had a favourable effect in regard to training?

Until now, no difficulties have occurred in the training. But it is already necessary to train and equip the replacements in the Grenadier replacement and training battalions. The concentration of the light machine gun, the SMG, snipers and rifle grenade riflemen substantially simplify the training.

IV) Fire discipline

1) Was fire discipline maintained in such way that ammunition consumption had a favourable ratio to the necessities of the combat even after the loss of leaders and sub-leaders and in difficult combat situations?

With regular training, especially with replacements already [trained] at the attached replacement unit, there was no higher ammunition consumption. The last large combat actions have shown that it was possible to maintain fire discipline so that ammunition consumption stood in normal relation to the necessities of the combat even after loss of leaders and sub-leaders and in difficult combat actions.

What is the ratio between the ammunition consumption of the Grenadier company with experimental organization in comparison to a Grenadier company with the previous organization?

Ammunition consumption had not increased through the arming [with new weapons]. The now higher consumption rate of the SMG is fully compensated for by the previous higher consumption rate of machine gun ammunition.

In the end, field tests and later actual combat use proved those who feared a mushrooming ammunition consumption completely wrong. The advantages of the weapon, including the higher concentration of fire that quickly broke enemy resistance, the better chance of hitting the target due to the easier targeting process, and finally the above-mentioned lower ammunition consumption of machine guns caused this somewhat paradoxical result. Another virtue of the gun's use was that firepower was less concentrated on individual soldiers, which gave smaller units a higher sustainability in a fire fight.

V) Weapon-technological questions
  Larger defects of the SMG did not appear.
  The following smaller failures are pointed out:
  [...]
  b) The SMG 44 is often tilted due to the exceptionally high front-sight base
  c) The gas lever was partially jammed with brand-new SMG. Therefore the tightening was no longer perfect.
  d) On various occasions the barrel protection broke from the holding notching through falls, pushes and so on.
  [...]
  f) The butt holding bolt is too loose. When it's lost, the weapon is non-operational.
  g) The jamming of feeding cartridges and the expulsion of cases often occurs with new weapons. Good oiling largely eliminates these jams. After firing around 500 cartridges, the jams are eliminated by the loosening of the sliding parts.
  h) Other jamming did not occur. Merely when cramming the magazine with 30 rounds were light jams produced with the feeding of cartridges. Therefore the magazines must be filled with only 25 rounds.
    In order to avoid an early rusting, the black finishing of the weapon must be better. It is advisable to produce the magazine pouches of a basic soldier's material so that they have a longer life period.

VI) Ammunition supply
  [...]
  1) What was the effect of the introduction of a new type of ammunition on the infantry?
    The introduction of a new type of ammunition had no particular consequences.

As previously mentioned, one of the main fears of introducing the weapon was the burden on the supply system caused by a new type of ammunition. But as that report (and most others on the supply question) illustrates, it was not an issue.

What seems striking is how many technical details required improvement. But one should not be misled by the catalogue of complaints. A look at comparable files on proven weapons in service for years or even decades had similar lists of technical issues. The German military apparatus placed great value on the frontline's suggestions for improvement, and those often became something like a 'wish list' with any and all possible details mentioned. While this helped to continually improve weapons and equipment, it put an enormous burden on the military bureaucracy's decision-making process: which improvements were necessary and which were merely desired. Furthermore, due to so many changes in the details of a weapon system, its production numbers were negatively affected. A well-known case is the Junkers Ju 88 bomber which went through no less than 58,000 modifications during its period of production.[18]

The report shows all the questions that arose with a new system and highlights the importance placed on a full range of issues, as opposed to simple technical questions. Often tactical and organizational adaptations were needed to make a new system effective. Questions of training, command and supply also arose. The evaluation reports from the combat tests raised yet another issue: there were often contradictory observations and experiences taken from the tests. It was then up to the interpreting agency to decide what to do with the results. Even here, there were problems; while extensive combat tests may seem logical, they could compromise secrecy of a new weapon and allow the enemy to take defensive measures. As seen with the Assault Rifle 44, actual testing of the weapon was a time-consuming process, which was often not possible under wartime conditions. This resulted in numerous weapons going into action before they were fully operational. The Panther tank, which later evolved into Germany's best tank, was a complete disaster in its first use during Operation Citadel in summer 1943. Technical problems, as well as faulty organization – the Panther units were oversized and therefore very difficult to command – plagued the initial use of these tanks.[19]

New weapons therefore shaped the organization of the German army in the East, which seems to be a not overly surprising insight. What is underestimated by historians, however, is the other side of the coin; namely that slowly adapting organizational structures prevented the timely and effective use of new weapons.

As previously shown, the German army encountered many new types of terrain and fighting, which also demanded a learning process. Urban warfare, a now common issue in military practice, was relatively new during the Second World War.[20] There were a few battles on a smaller scale in 1939 and 1940, but the German army was confronted with urban warfare on a large scale from summer 1941 on. The most famous of these battles was the one for Stalingrad. By that time, the German army had learned many lessons about this type of combat. Units sent to Stalingrad summarized these lessons in information sheets for their commanders, such as the following issued by the 305th Infantry division:[21]

Combat in densely built-up areas is marked by the following characteristics:

Complexity, fragmentation of every combat situation into individual actions, thereby aggravating leadership even in lower-level units; a reduction of our own weapons' effectiveness; difficulty in recognizing the enemy's main battle line [and] strongpoints, danger of ambush; limited effect of our own local successes.

Command: Careful preparation, clear briefing on the local situation with maps (sketches), unambiguous designation of the – mostly limited – objectives of the attack and systematic coordination of the separate combat actions are the preconditions for success.

The sure recognition of the moment, in which one can deviate from the systematic advance after local successes and go over to deep breakthrough, is the art of command.

To guarantee permanent insight in the course of the combat actions and the crucial personal influence, all leaders have to be as close to the troops as their command tasks allow.

Combat in the formal deployment structure will be the exception, the formation of battle and combat groups of all branches will be the norm.

Most often, success depends on low-level commanders acting on their own initiative. It is therefore important to give them a detailed picture of the contexts of the planned combat actions beyond their own limited mission; this is the precondition not only for individual initiative, but also for appropriate conduct in the sense of the entire combat action.

Combat conduct: Combat will generally be fought from short and even shorter distances; it naturally disintegrates into a series of successive *assault detachment operations*. The number of the required assault detachments [and] their composition is the concern of the lower command; it arranges the timed sequence on the basis of exhaustive reconnaissance and planning.

Precise reconnaissance and detailed discussion of the combat plan is a prerequisite of success.

The combat mission and nature of the attack objective determine the composition and combat form of the battle groups.

The use of tanks, assault guns, heavy infantry weapons and individual guns in the frontline, as well as engineer assault detachments with flame throwers, is the rule. Guns are to be moved forward by the crew (muzzle forward, shell in the barrel).

When using assault guns, one has to keep in mind their weakness against fire from above.

Principle: Through their fire, the heavy weapons cover the assault detachments reaching the attack objective; in the conquered target areas, the assault detachments enable the forward move of the heavy weapons and their positioning for covering fire for the next push of the infantry (engineer) assault detachments.

Due to the difficulty in recognizing the enemy's resistance line (strongpoints, concealed weapons which hold their fire until the enemy has reached certain points), the build-up of a surveillance coverage fire is most important, in addition to covering fire against identified objectives. Shooting 'on suspicion' will be used frequently. Cellar rooms and rooms on the ground floor are generally to be neutralized by hand grenades. The feeding of reserves, who have a previously determined combat mission, are to shield the flanks of the territory won.

Special cleansing units are to be brought forward behind the battle groups. It is their task to destroy overlooked strongpoints and to put down any revived resistance behind the battlefront. Brutal hardness is necessary.

Riflemen on the roof are irritating, but not decisively dangerous; their zone of effectiveness is limited.

The conquered area is to be cleansed thoroughly by reserves ordered for this purpose after the end of every local combat action as well as after reaching daily objectives. Surprises are always to be expected. An opponent familiar with the location uses canals, subterranean tunnels, [and] roofs to emerge unexpectedly in the rear of our own troops.

The leaflet highlights German tactical practices, such as the importance of a combined arms team and decentralized leadership, both of which were very effective under urban conditions. It also emphasizes the assault group as the most important element of fighting in the city. While close combat was recognized as the rule, even under urban conditions German units tried to support their advancing troops with as much firepower as possible. The difference with other types of combat lay simply in increasing direct firepower, including providing assault troops with individual artillery guns for point-blank fire support. On the other side, one should be clear that German troops had no qualms about inflicting collateral damage on civilians present in the combat area. This was simply not an issue in the tactical guidelines.

An even larger theme for the German army in the east was the return of positional warfare. The German army went to war extremely offensive-minded and, as a consequence of the First World War, with a strong will to fight the war as a war of movement. When the Soviet counter-offensive in winter 1941/42 petered out, both sides lacked the power to resume the offensive along the whole length of the front. In the following years, a war of movement was an exception, limited in time and space, from the prevailing positional warfare. In summer 1942, the Germans attacked only on the southern wing of the Eastern front, with the sectors of Army Group Centre and North remaining static for the rest of the year. Soviet offensives directed at these sectors failed to dislodge German positions, with the exception of a few kilometres here and there. The German offensive bogged down in most sectors in September, gaining little space in October and November. The next phase of the war of movement was a Soviet one, reconquering most of the territory lost in the summer 1942, but it was also temporary and limited to the southern wing. The Soviet offensives in 1943/44 happened in phases and on individual sectors. While being significantly larger than before, there were still areas in which positional warfare predominated with consequently minor changes in the front line.

German troops in the east had to relearn positional warfare and adapt their procedures to evolving Soviet tactics and operations against defensive positions and fortifications. The remarks of the commanding general of the VIth Army Corps, *General der Infanterie* Hans Jordan, defending the western shoulder of the Rzhev bulge, highlight a few aspects of that learning process.[22] This time, learning did not happen by compiling and analyzing lower-level reports, but rather by a higher commander visiting his subordinated units at the front, a practice described in chapter 2. The close monitoring of the front through frequent visits by German commanders sped up the learning process.

My visit to the frontline positions prompts me to make the following remarks:

1) The troops in the main combat zone have to be richly equipped with close combat anti-tank devices (stun grenades, smoke grenades, Molotov cocktails, 5 or 10kg explosive charges, adhesive charges). The satchel charge of 6-7 hand grenades is ineffective against the tank.

2) The submachine gun is one of the most effective defensive weapons against assaults. It belongs in the main combat line and not as a private weapon for leaders of rear units. Ample ammunition is the prerequisite for effectiveness. A submachine gun requires 1,000 bullets. The rifle companies' platoon and company leaders must have assault troops, equipped with submachine guns and numerous hand grenades, at their personal disposal.

3) Heavy machine guns belong in the depth of the main combat zone. Flanking machine guns with ample ammunition firing in front of the main combat line are an effective protection for wire entanglements and mine fields with weak trench troops. Where the wire entanglements are incomplete, the use of heavy machine guns flanking the gaps is necessary. Against hostile skiers who approach the main battle line under protection of night and fog, single wires are already effective.

4) In the case of a large sector width and low [troop] strength, it is not appropriate to distribute the men individually or in twos over the whole section. The man feels lonely and fails during an enemy attack. Groupings of at least 4 or 5 [men], as well as ample equipment with hand grenades and submachine guns, give more security. If there is a danger that an enemy assault detachment can penetrate the trenches between 2 such posts, trap doors (simple wooden frames covered with barbed wire) in the trench will give flank protection to the posts.

5) Battalion and regimental command posts are to be urgently expanded to strongpoints. Such a strongpoint must be at least some 100m in diameter, and include anti-tank capabilities and artillery observation. Linkage with another strongpoint, i.e. battery positions, is advisable.

6) Each command post, including up to the divisional level, has to set up one or more observation points on the battlefield, with a view of the main combat line, so that it receives immediate reports about where the apparent hotspots of the battle are developing. At the divisional and regimental command posts, reconnaissance patrols led by officers have to be held ready, in order to be sent to the critical positions for immediate reporting. Waiting for reports from subordinate commands is incorrect.

7) Due to the extent of the [defence] sectors, in no case can one count on artillery protection by barrage fire. Unobserved firing of the artillery on fire areas and target points is a makeshift measure for night and fog. The task of artillery battalion commanders is to concentrate the fire of their battalion (group) on recognized targets and to strengthen [it] if possible by the fire of neighbouring batteries. If numerous targets are on the battlefield, he must, in close connection with the infantry, decide on the

order in which the objectives are to be combated with a concentrated fire. The fragmentation of fire by assigning targets to the individual batteries is erroneous. The rapid change of target by as many batteries as possible is to be constantly trained by the artillery leaders. Continual verification of this ability by the artillery leaders and by the sector commanders is required.

8) The scattering of individual batteries in the area is disadvantageous. It makes the fire concentrations more difficult, reduces the influence of artillery leaders; the signal communications are sensitive and require numerous personnel for their maintenance. If the enemy advances as far as the battery positions, the individual battery easily falls prey by the encirclement, especially since the crew is usually weak while in the fire positions.

9) Divisional boundaries must not be blinders for artillery. Artillery battalions located at these boundaries must possess their neighbour's radio information, so that the observation points can fire with the neighbouring batteries.

10) Heavy ATG belong in the main combat line only in exceptional cases. They easily become the victim of the enemy's fire preparations there. They are better positioned in the depth of the main combat zone. Each major fighting action proves the necessity of a grouped positioning of the ATGs. The influence of the platoon leader must be preserved. A reserve of men and ammunition must be found with the company leaders. The mobility of the ATGs must be ensured, so that concentration at threatened points is possible.

11) The rather middling enemy preparatory fire on 25.11. has caused individual divisions not inconsiderable losses. Once again, I point out the need to deepen the trenches in spite of the frost and to make as many foxholes as possible. In the splinter-covered foxhole, only a direct hit can cause damage to the man. The winter clothing allows the man to stay in the foxhole for a long time without any damage to his health.

These remarks cover many issues that were not commonly addressed in the German army due to the lack of comprehensive defensive manuals. But they also point to tactical weaknesses present in the army, such as a lack of awareness of boundaries or the correct positioning of the ATGs. At the same time, one can see the efforts to overcome such issues. Finally, positional warfare in the Soviet Union significantly differed in one way from German experience (and our picture of that kind of warfare stemming from the First World War Western Front), namely the enormous length of the front line, which neither allowed for an elaborate construction of field fortifications, nor for a strong occupation of the trenches. In many sectors, such as on the boundary of the Army Groups North and Centre in the area between Velikiye Luki and Demidov, there was not even a continuously manned line.

One of the tactical elements that the Germans had to relearn on the Eastern front, and especially under positional warfare conditions, was the use of snipers. For readers closely acquainted with the campaigns in Italy and northwest Europe, this sounds rather puzzling, as snipers there were a feared part of the

German defence. While the German army in the First World War achieved a high standard of sniping, most of that was lost in the late *Reichswehr* period and during the rearmament years. Few German divisions possessed telescopic sight rifles when entering the Soviet Union and special sniper training was more or less non-existent. The clash with Soviet snipers, the rise of positional warfare in large sections of the Eastern front, and the recognition of the need for precise fire on the smallest tactical level led to a renaissance in German sniping starting in 1942, but major progress was made in 1943 with expansion of training units and an increased production of weapons. The products of these efforts were the snipers encountered by the British and American troops in the west from 1943 on. Experiences for sniper training were gathered from the allied Finns, who had a particularly well-developed sniper branch and plenty of practical knowledge from the Winter War. The Soviet use of snipers was also closely observed. Before the start of systematic sniper training in the Replacement Army, the field units improvised training facilities themselves. For that purpose, leaflets were produced, such as the following one from XIIIth Army Corps, fighting in the Don area under 2nd Army:[23]

A) Leaflet for snipers
  1) Be proud of your weapon. There are many other weapons in the company, but only 4 telescopic sight rifles.
  2) Maintain your rifle carefully. Then you can always rely on the weapon.
  3) Be like the hunter! With perseverance, cunning, and calm blood, one hunts down game as well as the Bolsheviks.
  4) Commissars and red officers are the best trophies. You can recognize them by the binoculars, the map pouch and special behaviour.
  5) Lurk for the imprudent observer behind embrasured emplacements, on deploying enemy weapons, on vehicles, in cars; the latter often follow the same paths.
  6) Again and again, let observation posts and other sniper comrades call your attention to worthwhile goals. Examine the observation books and, above all, inform the observation posts about all your discoveries.
  7) Look for favourable positions to shoot, apart from other comrades. Often you will find a favourable fire position behind the front trench in covered places.
  8) Camouflage yourself well. With snow, wear a white headcap, white gloves, and paint your gun white.
  9) Always ensure that you have a firm rifle base. For this purpose, always carry a specially cut fork with you.
  10) Never fire more shots from the same spot, otherwise you will be subject to counter-fire. Watch carefully before the shot and immediately afterwards change place.
  11) Always remember that if you and your sniper comrades shoot only one Bolshevik daily, in a month with 4 snipers in the Grenadier Company, your regiment will face 1,080 fewer Russians.
  12) Read this leaflet again and again until you know it by heart and act and follow it in the trench – to the best of your comrades.

The language which equated sniping with hunting, thereby relegating Soviet soldiers to game, is noticeable. From a tactical point of view, the focus on Soviet leadership was clearly important. German reports from the east often mentioned the decline of fighting power in Soviet units after the loss of their leaders and especially after the loss of the commissars. While this is difficult to prove or refute, this was the German perception and it guided many German measures. Also highlighted in the leaflet was the pride of arms of snipers, as well as the care for weapons. While this was (and still is) an important issue for snipers, under the extremely demanding circumstances of the Eastern front, maintenance of weapons was even more important. Finally, the integration of snipers into the intelligence gathering network (point 6) was a very progressive concept.

Due to changing conditions, the use of German armoured units also had to adapt. After Operation Citadel, German armoured troops were rarely used in an operational manner; rather, they were most often employed in counter-strikes at Soviet breakthroughs. The divisions suffered heavily in men and material from being thrown from one crisis to the next with only minor breaks between fighting and movement, and they rarely approached anything comparable to divisional strength. Furthermore, the often hasty manner of the counter-strikes did not allow for full assembly of the units, so most attacks were conducted by battlegroups that although called divisions, often had the strength of a mere regiment. This, as well as Soviet tactical progress in intercepting German armoured attacks, i.e. by the already mentioned ATG fronts, forced the German army to adapt in its use of armoured units. The next source, a widely circulated experience report by XXXXVIIIth Panzer corps about its deployment in the Ukrainian fighting of late 1943/early 1944 – an especially grim one thus far under-researched – provides evidence of the evolution of German armoured operations:[24]

> The corps has always fought at the decisive point in the attack and on the defensive. A various number of army and Waffen-SS Panzer divisions and infantry divisions were subordinated to it.
>
> 1) Infantry divisions in the present form are no longer up to date. The assignment of an assault gun battalion can fundamentally remedy this ill and at one stroke make our infantry fully fit for action again. The light machine gun with its accessories is too heavy. The infantry is so scattered in all directions in today's Panzer war, that it will throw away its machine gun equipment due to physical exhaustion after a short time. Experiments with the new machine carbine (submachine gun 43) must seek the removal of the light machine gun. Towed anti-tank guns break down for the same reasons. The infantry requires self-propelled anti-tank guns. Close combat anti- tank weapons of the '*Faustpatrone*' [fist cartridge] type are required by every group. As a result of what was mentioned above, the structure of the infantry and motorized riflemen companies is as follows: 2 assault platoons with 3 groups each, group around 1/7.[25] Weapons: 5 machine carbine rifle men, 2 men with pistols, *Faustpatrone* and hand grenades. 1 heavy platoon, 2 heavy machine guns, 2 heavy mortars, 3 *Ofenrohr* [bazookas] [...]
>
> 3) Panzer divisions proven. Our tanks are absolutely materially superior to the Russian. Training: The corps owes a great part of its successes to the use of

the night, to the ruthless continuation of the attack by moonlight. The troops had to become accustomed to this kind of fighting. In particular, newly formed tanks units and army tank battalions believe that the tank is not be used by night and brusquely refuse its commitment by night. Training must remedy that. The Russian uses his tanks with full light (strong spotlights with blinding effects) against our retreating columns by night with good success. The training of all soldiers in the mine war that I demanded earlier has to be put into effect. […] Unfortunately, the decree of the General of the Engineers of 20 December 1943 for the relevant training and use of mines also includes too many obstructions. The low number of Russian tanks destroyed by and through mines may have the same cause. Losses through our own mines must be accepted by the troops, as well as losses through other [of our own] arms. The Russian throws entire ATG regiments and brigades against our tank attacks. The breaking of such ATG lines has proved especially difficult. Partly, the troops shrank from it more than tank combat. The use of terrain, night attack and above all the cooperation of all weapons, particularly the timely and skilled use of artillery, lead to success. Also the use of air force (tank hunters) was quite successful.

4) Blocking units. The German side could for the most part only throw alarm units against Russian tank formations that rapidly penetrated in depth. Their combat value was low. Following the Russian example (see above), ATG regiments seem necessary. To prevent the German addiction to over-organization and the therewith connected wastage of personal and material, it is recommended to take the Russian combat strength table[26] as a basis. The units can then win on handiness and agility. As a weapon for those units, there would only towed ATGs. Self-propelled guns don't have any operational mobility and [suffer] too many breakdowns during marches. […]

6) Command experiences. The cavalry use of Panzer divisions, which means the exploitation of their great mobility and the encirclement of the enemy, has been proven again and again and is above all cheaper than the frontal 'fighting through'. In this way, the corps managed a completely surprising push into the deep flank of the Soviet 60th Army which was carried forward during the day a further 30-40km into the enemy's rear, following a night march on the 5th/6th December 1943 from the Zhitomir area with an average achievement of 70 km per Panzer division. With only minor own losses, it succeeded in completely disarraying the enemy and inflicted heavy losses on him. The Russian immediately constructed such strong defensive lines around his breakthroughs and bridgeheads on the flanks that an attack against these fizzled out, likewise against the spearhead. In contrast, a diagonal attack from the side led to sweeping success. […] The 'Citadel'[27]experience repeated itself daily in miniature. The night must be exploited more than previously for the attack and pursuit. Marching with lights on must not be shied away from. Resistance of the troops to night marches must be broken. Tanks can attack by starlight and moonlight too. The troops must again learn how to use the compass.

If at all possible, the breakthrough of enemy positions must be carried out in a complete corps' attack as follows: first the entire artillery helps all tanks and assault guns of one division through, then the entire artillery shells the second divisional [attack] sector until it is ripe for attack, and the tanks that initially went on with the attack of the first division, break out of the second divisional [attack] sector from the flank or the rear. That procedure is particularly necessary due to the decreasing number of panzers during the course of a combat action. In defence, the armoured groups of the divisions have to be held in reserve and are to be centrally commanded by the corps. Their cooperation with the air force is to be secured.

The strongly decreasing number of tanks, assault guns and self-propelled guns are partly the consequence of the unsuitable deployment of workshop companies and maintenance services. In particular, army troops position themselves so clumsily, that 100% of their repairs break down on the long march to the front. In this way, many units were worn down without combat. Commander training courses must be expanded on in that area. Firm leadership and constant supervision of workshop and maintenance services through the corps and divisions is today more important than ever.

In its present organization, the artillery is very difficult to move, especially because the apparatus of staffs and supply units, which is constructed around the few barrels, is too extensive and complicated. In this way, a battalion staff, which today often commands no more than nine barrels, can just as well cope with three times that number. To achieve a mass effect and a destructive effect at the decisive point, an increase of mortars and [rocket] launchers at the expense of the [barrel] artillery is necessary. The Russian has moved in this direction for more than a year.

Since 1941, Soviet defences had become deeper and more stable, as well as better organized and led. This demanded a more thoroughly planned German breakthrough with heavy fire support as described above. The Red Army, recognizing that the Germans favoured flank attacks, strengthened these areas, forcing the Germans to look for new attack methods. German units also practised more night attacks in the second half of the war, as these allowed for surprise. Fire support and fire preparation became important parts of armoured attacks, issues that rarely surfaced in 1941 and 1942 attacks.

Whatever the value of armoured units in the German army, they were a distinct minority. The report shows that the mass of the army – infantry divisions – could no longer effectively fight, unless heavily reinforced by assault guns or tank hunters and infantry anti-tank weapons, and by becoming more mobile. The points concerning the infantry division in the report are part of a far larger discussion, arising from mid-1943 on, as the German military leadership recognized the decreasing combat power of their infantry units, terming it an 'infantry crisis'. In addition to the lack of mobility and anti-tank capabilities, this decrease was also the consequence of manpower shortages leading to exhaustion in the troops and thereby a diminishing of the will to resist. The infantry crisis was never properly solved, as the melting resources of the Third Reich did not allow for such a far-reaching transformation.

Chapter 4

Supplying the German Eastern Army

As seen in chapters 1 and 3, combat on the Eastern front involved an unprecedented level of men and material and reached a hitherto unheard of level of intensity. This was only possible when the German (and Soviet) armies could rely on a large network of rear units and received a continuous stream of supply goods.[1] Rear units performed numerous tasks to maintain the frontline troops' combat efficiency, including transporting men, as well as material and supply goods, the maintenance and repair of weapons and equipment, collecting food and preparing meals, and caring for horses. Other vital tasks included building, maintaining and securing lines of communications and necessary infrastructure such as depots, quarters, railway lines, streets, bridges and airports, and medical care for wounded as well as the prevention of illness. Finally numerous administrative tasks, such as promotions and awards, the ordering of goods and replacements, the regulation of leave, military justice, sending soldiers to training courses, and so on, also had to be completed.

The stream of goods needed by the German armies included most obviously ammunition, fuel and food. But there were many more, often forgotten goods: an army literally marching by foot deep into Soviet territory required shoes and replacement clothes. In addition to essential food rations, it was important for the morale of the troops to provide them with alcohol, tobacco and candies. Extra efforts could be achieved by using methamphetamines such as the widely distributed Pervitin. Articles of daily use such as toothbrushes, razor blades and soap also had to be supplied. All kinds of individual equipment had to be replaced due to wear or loss, such as helmets, pouches, spades and so on. The same was true for weapons, ranging from bayonets and hand guns to tanks, aircraft and guns. Larger non-combat equipment such as field kitchens, vehicles, radio sets and generators were much needed, as were consumable materials and equipment for special units, such as engineers and medical services. Wired communications, still essential for the German army, necessitated kilometres of cable and electrical tape, not to mention all the special equipment required to lay the wire. To keep all of these complex army systems working, many materials for their maintenance were needed, such as a broad array of lubricants. In case of breakdown, workshop units with many different tools and machines – that also needed replacement equipment – repaired those systems, but they obviously needed spare parts in huge quantities. And due to the lack of production and standardization, there were thousands of different spare parts in the supply system. This problem was significantly increased by the use of captured equipment, primarily motor vehicles, but also weapons.

Army Group Centre estimated at the end of 1941 that its sub-units were in need of over a million different spare parts. The massive use of horses also made fodder an extremely important commodity. Specialists responsible for ensuring that the horses remained healthy enough to work, such as blacksmiths and veterinarians, also needed many specific items. Harsh winter conditions demanded their own goods such as winter clothes, trench ovens and Hindenburg lights for the men and antifreeze agents and cold-resistant spare parts for guns and vehicles. Marching into climatically different areas also added demands, such as special medicaments and vaccines for the Germans who entered the Kuban area, a subtropical region. Other areas such as the relatively tree-less steppe west of Stalingrad required the supply of wood for the construction of defensive positions or shelters, the maintenance of streets and railroads or simply just for heating material. And finally, to keep this supply system working, many typewriters and phones, as well as a tremendous amount of paper, were necessary too.

The following source gives a rough overview of the different tasks demanded of a division's rear troops, as well as some numbers to consider, such as the distances to cover or the amount of material to be transported. It also shows once again the strain caused by prolonged heavy combat, such as urban warfare, on supplying troops. The source is a report on the achievements of the 7th Infantry Division's supply services during the one-week battle for Mogilev in July 1941:[2]

The fight for the enemy bridgehead at Mogilev brought increased burdens on all supply troops and, in part, lasting activity day and night. [...]

a) *Supply Services*

From 20.-26.7., altogether 508 tons of munitions were driven by the motorized supply columns, reinforced by vehicles from the supply company. While doing this, *31,055 kilometres were travelled in 3,111 driving hours*, in which every hour of driving averaged a 10km route.

From 20.-26.7., the munitions columns of the Division Supply Leader drove altogether 5 days and 8 hours. For the day, rest and vehicle maintenance accounted on average for only 5 and ¾ hours.

b) *Medical Service*

During the battle, the deployment of the medical service took on an especially busy and successful form.

It was managed – a record achievement – as a result of the especially favourable location of the main dressing station Ssofijewa, to give final treatment to the wounded of [Infantry] Regiment 19 as early as 1-2 hours after their wounding took place.

After the crossing of I[nfantry] R[egiment] 19 over the Dnieper [River], the 1st Platoon of Medical Company 1/7 was employed on the far side of the river for the first aid and rescue of the wounded. In recognition for carrying out their task while partially in range of direct enemy fire, it received 5 Iron Crosses.

At the main dressing area, 484 wounded and 111 sick, in addition to 107 wounded prisoners of war, were treated during these days.

Field hospital 7 utilized by the 23rd and 7th Divisions treated over 500 wounded during this mission.

Especially worth pointing out is the untiring activity day and night, partially under heavy enemy fire, of the ambulance platoons' crews.

c) *Workshop Company and Fuel Column*

The days of battle brought an increased loss of vehicles through direct enemy action, therefore the performance of the Workshop Company rose from a previous average of 80 vehicle repairs per day to *174 on 23.7. (a record day).*

The fuel column had especially great efforts to overcome during its path of advance from the [Fourth] Army fuel dump Krupka (one-way distance of 190 km) with dismal road conditions. The section of the fuel column that supplied I[nfantry] R[egiment] 61 during its Dnieper crossing was therefore directly involved in the course of combat.

d) *Administrative Service*

As a result of the high number of [Fourth] Army and Army troops[3] subordinated to the division, the demands made on the Administrative Service grew. Instead of 17,000 ration strength, a number for which Administrative Service was equipped for, *24,000 men* had to be supplied.

At the time in question, *Rations Department 7* provided, outside of meat and bread, some 20 tons of food and 56 tons of oats for each distribution (every 2 days), that had to be picked up from the 100km distant [Fourth] Army rations storage area Krupka.

In this time period, instead of the normal number of 60,000 loaves of bread, *Bakery Company 7* baked 82,500 and daily drove 170km with 22 tons storage space for the meal and bread transport.

During the same time, *Butcher Company 7* daily drove together a herd of 24 cattle, butchered and prepared altogether 165,000 portions of fresh meat. In addition to that, 7,000 portions of fresh sausage were produced daily by manual work (that means without a sausage machine).

The supply of the combat troops, above all the supply of munitions and the care for the wounded, took place under the most difficult circumstances, whose surmounting demanded the highest efforts. It *succeeded* thanks to the restless activities of the supply troops, who, in accordance with their strength, were all carried by the will to provide the material foundations for battle and victory to the fighting troops.

These numbers give an idea what quantities of goods were necessary and had to be transported to keep a single infantry division in combat for a week. As the German army in the east fielded some 150 divisions and numerous independent infantry units in summer 1941, one can estimate the enormous task to keep those forces supplied.

The first required commodity, especially in an industrialized war, was ammunition. The following source gives an idea of the scale of ammunition required by the German army during this conflict:[4]

Year	Month	Consumption		Consumption per year
		In tons	Trains	
1941	June	23,077	51	
	July	101,594	226	
	August	108,855	242	583,341 tons =
	September	107,670	240	1,297 trains
	October	90,563	201	
	November	68,035	151	
	December	83,547	186	
1942	January	69,165	154	
	February	92,270	205	
	March	114,771	255	
	April	69,451	154	
	May	71,254	158	
	June	106,708	237	1,234,218 tons =
	July	72,657	162	2,744 trains
	August	146,285	325	
	September	160,645	357	
	October	110,208	245	
	November	102,267	228	
	December	118,537	264	
1943	January	137,950	307	
	February	155,400	346	
	March	158,400	352	
	April	61,239	136	
	May	89,078	198	
	June	74,586	166	1,861,711 tons =
	July	232,621	518	4,137 trains
	August	254,648	566	
	September	205,196	456	
	October	185,712	413	
	November	151,921	337	
	December	155,260	345	
1944	January	195,701	435	
	February	161,764	359	
	March	181,745	404	
	April	117,612	261	
	May	81,892	182	[1,605,517 tons =
	June	140,150	311	3,567 trains]
	July	193,378	430	
	August	248,940	553	
	September	131,363	292	
	October	152,972	340	

Total consumption from June 1941 October 1944 (included) = 5,284,787 tons = 11,748 trains

Not only does this table indicate the enormous amount of ammunition spent by the German army in the east as a whole, but it also shows an increase over time. While the average monthly consumption in 1941 was under 94,000 tons, it rose slightly in 1942 to nearly 103,000 tons per month. For 1943 there was a striking jump to over 155,000 tons per month, an increase of nearly 50 per cent. This was strongly driven by the extremely high consumption during the period of July to September 1943, but also by a general increase in ammunition consumption in ten out of twelve months. The highest consumption in July/August 1943 was due to the German summer offensive, Operation Citadel, and the Soviet counteroffensive, which probably represented the culmination of combat intensity on the Eastern front. The enormous increase in 1943 starkly reflected the evolution in German war production from a limited war to a total war with an armaments industry now more thoroughly mobilized and more tightly controlled to achieve a much higher output. However, ammunition production had its major increase in late 1942/early 1943.[5] This explains in part the only slight growth in 1944 to somewhat over 160,000 tons/month. But it should also be kept in mind that by 1944, Germany was much more involved on other fronts than in previous years. There was a constant increase of German engagement in the Mediterranean theatre that accelerated from mid-1942 on and which drew considerable resources away from the east. Even more important for 1944 was the expectation of the Allied invasion in the west. While stocks were built up in France in the first half of 1944, from June 1944 there was a direct competition between the Third Reich's two primary theatres for all kinds of goods. Despite these circumstances – not to mention the effects of the Combined Bomber offensive – ammunition consumption in the East still increased.

What is also striking from the table was the seasonal pattern of consumption. There was a high consumption in summer (reflecting German offensive efforts and in 1944 a high-intensity defence along the whole Eastern front), a decrease in the autumn (except for 1942 reflecting German defensive action along large parts of the Eastern front) and a low point in late winter and spring. This decrease was often the consequence of winter weather or the subsequent muddy season that emerged during the thaw of spring. Weather, therefore, not only hindered combat, but also the supply of forward units.

In one regard, however, the above list is misleading. Munitions were not simply tons of materials sent to the East, but part of a complex logistical system, since that class of supply goods included hundreds of different items, from rounds for hand guns to heavy artillery shells, from explosives to signal flares. A regular infantry division in 1942 had two calibres for small arms infantry weapons (7.92mm and 9mm), two for mortars (5cm and 8cm), two calibres for infantry guns (7.5cm and 15cm), three for ATG (3.7cm, 5cm and 7.5cm), one for anti-aircraft guns (2cm) and two for artillery guns (10.5cm and 15cm). These were multiplied by different types of bullets (such as tracer or pointed steel-core armour-piercing) and shells (such as high-explosive, armour-piercing, high-explosive anti-tank, and smoke). To further complicate things, the same types of shells and rounds existed in different production versions.[6] In addition, a division had two types of hand grenades, signal rockets, smoke pots, flare cartridges in four colours and various types of explosives. In panzer divisions, the different types of ammunition increased due to the different shells for the tank cannon, and these were often of three or four different calibres. Further up in the command hierarchy, all kinds of army units with their special munitions had to be added, including heavy artillery units. Though it falls outside the bounds of the present volume it needs to be mentioned that the *Luftwaffe* and the few *Kriegsmarine* units in the East also needed munitions – and, just like their army counterparts, they also required different calibres and types, such as bombs and torpedoes. While maintaining the regular and orderly supply of German munitions by itself was very complex, it became even more difficult due to the extensive use of captured weapons, as well as the need to supply Allied armies, multiplying the types of required cartridges and shells. This can be illustrated by the situation of the Vth Army Corps in summer 1942. It commanded the German 9th, 73rd and 125th Infantry Divisions, as well as the 3rd Romanian Mountain Division. While all three German divisions needed those types of munitions mentioned above, each also possessed additional weapons. The 9th Infantry Division fielded several batteries of Light Field Howitzer 16, 10.5cm guns as the German standard gun Light Field Howitzer 18, but with different shells. The 125th Infantry Division had a few 4.7cm ATGs of Czech origin and 7.5cm ATG 38/97, the barrel of which was of French origin and needed different shells than the usual 7.5cm ATG 40. All three divisions had 7.65mm hand guns, which added a further type of ammunition to be delivered. The 3rd Romanian Mountain Division fielded few weapons compatible with German munitions, which meant dozens of additional types of ammunition were required. Furthermore, the Corps was responsible for supplying several subordinated army units. Those included two assault-gun battalions that had short and long-barrelled assault guns, each needing different shells even if they had the same 7.5cm calibre. It also included rotating heavy artillery units with 10cm Cannon 18, 15cm Cannon 18 and 21cm Heavy Howitzer 18 and captured Czech 10cm Cannon M35 and 15cm Howitzers M35, as well also two army artillery battalions for coastal defence with captured Norwegian 10.7cm cannon and Dutch 10cm cannon. So, the Vth Army Corps quartermaster staff had to manage the administration and distribution of far more than 100 types of ammunition and to ensure that the right type of shells reached the right gun in time. This demanded thorough planning, but also strained the means of transportation. The consequences of wrongly supplied shells can be seen in a report by the Artillery Regiment 89 (24th Panzer Division) from that time:[7]

During the previous deployment, the following deficiencies occurred in the ammunition supply:
A) Ammunition for light field howitzers
        In the time from 29.8.-5.10.42, too many shells with combination fuses were supplied, sometimes more often than shells with an impact fuse. The regiment was therefore forced to fire combination fuse [shells] as impact fuse [shells]. Therefore a remarkable number of duds were observed. Ricochet fire is not possible with combination fuse [shells], since the fuses have no delay. In addition, combination fuses are more versatile in their design, making the production more difficult and expensive.
        In the period from 14.10.-21.10.42, hollow charge [shells] had to be fired due to the lack of impact fuse [shells]. Ricochet fire is also not possible with these shells. The splinter effect of these shells is somewhat larger in

impact up to 20m wider to the sides than in the normal shell, since the hollow charge has thinner walls. After 20m, it remains considerably less effective than the normal shell. The cause is the directional detonation wave acting in the direction of the longitudinal axis. This shell is more difficult and expensive to produce.

B) Ammunition for 10cm cannon 18

Sometimes gaps occur in the supply of special cartridge bags. The combating of enemy batteries, which were far in the rear area, could not take place. On 20.10., 10cm shells 19 FES[8] were delivered for the first time without notice. These shells could not be fired at first because the necessary ballistic tables were missing. After a telephone conversation with all available commands, the regiment learned that a regular ballistic table, the only one in the army area, was available from the I./Artillery Regiment 430. After copying the changed values from this ballistic table, shells FES could be fired.

C) Ammunition for heavy field howitzer 18

There is also a shortage of special cartridge bags for the heavy field howitzers' ammunition. The range is thus limited to 9,775m. Batteries positioned at some distance cannot be combated, but [they] interfere with our own intentions unopposed. 15cm Grenade 19 with the designation o.M.[9] may be fired only up to the 5th charge (barrel bursts). The range is thus limited to 8,500m. Since the heavy field howitzer combats mostly [enemy] artillery at a great distance, such shells are useless. It would be better to completely pull them out of supply as they are only a burden.

On 2.9.42, 15cm Grenade 36 were delivered. Nothing was known about the firing of that shell from the heavy field howitzer. Higher commands were also unable to provide information. The shells were locked. At last on the 10.10.42, the regiment learned the set values for their firing. Due to the lack of impact fuse [shells], the heavy field howitzers also had to periodically fire shells with a combination fuse as an impact fuse [shells].

D) Ammunition for 12.2 cm Russian howitzers

As replacements for heavy field howitzers lost in the middle of September, 3 Russian 12.2cm calibre guns were deployed. These have a range up to 12,800m. The initially available 300 rounds were fired with good success. Further ammunition has not been found or supplied as yet. For 4 weeks, these guns have been without ammunition, hence worthless and only a burden. If the supply of 12.2cm ammunition remains hopeless, the regiment will be forced to give up the guns again.

E) Ammunition for 7.62cm guns

There are 3 7.62cm guns in the regiment. So far, all found captured munitions was fired. For a short period, the ammunition was supplied regularly. [...]

F) New introduction

Notice about the introduction of new ammunition partly did not come to the regiment at all, partly belatedly and stingily. The persons responsible are thus not in a position to provide detailed information on the newly introduced ammunition. It would be desirable if the introductory decrees with detailed descriptions would also be distributed to the regiments.

This report clearly shows the problems of the broad array of guns and shells in use, as well as the logistic difficulties that arose as a result. The document also addressed the information flow issue, which was an essential part of the logistic system. This included not only the timely forwarding of information on new types of shells, such as use, effect, and ballistic tables, but also the flow of information on the use of ammunition from frontline staffs through higher command staffs to the groups and central institutions in the Reich that regulated the production of munitions and the loading of supply trains for the Eastern Front. This was a very demanding and elaborate – and still under-researched – administrative process that produced a massive flood of papers that have subsequently become valuable sources for military historians.

All the shells that could not be used due to either missing information or ballistic tables were a waste of transport capacity and this was even more the case at the end of a 2,000-kilometre supply line, hampered by many bottlenecks and frictions, as was the case for the Sixth Army in the battle for Stalingrad. Even though this Army was the point of the main effort from September 1942 on, ammunition remained scarce. Already after only a single week of fighting inside the city, munitions became a major concern for the Germans, as a report of the OKH Forward Officer attached to Sixth Army shows:[10]

> Due to the especially heavy fighting inside Stalingrad, the troops suffer from an ammunition shortage. The 2nd Heavy Rocket Launcher Regiment that is especially useful for combat in an urban area has not been deployed due to a lack of munitions at LIst Corps, a situation that has existed for days. The supply of small quantities of munitions is not expected for 6-12 days.
>
> Similarly a whole 10cm canon battalion (II./64) had to be withdrawn by LIst Corps due to lack of munitions. There is also no further ammunition available for the other thirteen 10cm cannon batteries of the army.[11] The entire army will have 400 rounds available again in another six days.[12] Improvement is not to be expected for three weeks.
>
> Light and especially heavy field howitzer ammunition is continuously scarce due to its very high consumption inside the city and on the northern front.
>
> Assault gun ammunition (long barrelled gun) is also scarce. At the moment this shortage is especially noticeable, since around 50% of the assault guns are long barrelled. Their use is therefore considerably limited.

Due to the mentioned lack of ammunition, key combat systems for urban warfare such as assault guns and rocket launchers (in German: *Nebelwefer*) could not be deployed. The lack of artillery shells for the 10cm cannon 18 meant that the main artillery gun for counter-battery fire was not available, while the general lack of artillery shells impeded German defences north of Stalingrad. Combined with shortages of fuel and rations from September 1942 on, Sixth Army units were logistically not in a position to assault a city. These material problems were exacerbated by the German numerical manpower inferiority against a massively reinforced Soviet 62nd Army. Despite facing such obstacles, German troops were able to take nine tenths of the city, a credit to their superior tactics and low level command.[13]

Long and intensive combat frequently exhausted German ammunition stocks in a rapid manner, since the supply system could not cope with the German war machine's voracious ammunition consumption. The situation was somewhat different when possibilities existed to build up stocks, such as was the case with the last major German offensive in summer 1943, Operation Citadel. The Germans took advantage of a lull in the fighting to concentrate fighting power – both men and material – for nearly three months before the operation opened. This allowed the army to fire an enormous mass of ammunition, as already described in the introduction to this chapter. But such a build-up and subsequent consumption, especially in the second half of the war, when the German Reich was also under pressure from Western Allied forces on the ground and in the skies, could only be achieved by strict conservation measures in all secondary theatres, including large sectors of the Eastern Front itself such as Army Group North's area or the northern part of Army Group Centre, an often completely forgotten section of the line. The following order from the 87th Infantry Division, deployed in the Velizh area, gives an idea of such measures designed to save ammunition:[14]

Based on particular circumstances, which are thoroughly positive with reference to the larger situation, the use of ammunition must be even more keenly limited from now on than has so far been the case.

The following is ordered for the prevailing combat situation:

Infantry munitions:

1) Infantry munitions of every kind are preferably not to be used during the day.
2) ATG 3.7cm high explosive shells are only to be used in defence against enemy attacks. The munitions quantity approved for training remains the same.
3) The use of 8cm mortar shells is as of now only approved for the battle group Velizh (1st *Jäger*[15] Btl.) and even here only after daily query by the divisional quartermaster section for those [fired during] night to smash enemy attacks.
4) Fire on especially worthwhile targets is to be carried out with light infantry guns. Use of heavy infantry guns only with approval of the divisional Ia.

Artillery munitions:

1) Use of light field howitzer munitions only for identified enemy attack or deployment in at least platoon strength. (Indication: 30 shells).
2) Use of heavy field howitzer (French) munitions is only approved for individual night time harassing fire and enemy attacks above platoon strength.
3) Use of 15.2cm cannon (Russian) [munitions] in the next ten days only up to 15 shells daily, especially on rear area movements.
4) Counter battery fire only with approval of the division.

The principle must always be to use the available munitions primarily during the night.

Ammunition needed to be saved whenever possible to counter Soviet attacks, making the Germans more or less passive from an artillery perspective. Especially effective heavy infantry weapons such as the 8cm mortar or the heavy infantry gun faced such a shortage of ammunition, that these battalion or regimental weapons were allowed to fire only with divisional approval, eliminating the notion of decentralized command. Not even mentioned in the order are the so-called 'shortage munitions'; types of ammunition such as the *Panzergranate* 40 with its tungsten core, which was so scarce that it was perpetually in short supply. This phenomenon was not only restricted to special types of shells, but often extended to whole calibre categories, such as the 8cm mortar grenade or the 10cm K18 shells. The order further illustrates the diversity of equipment and weapons, including French and Soviet guns, in regular divisions. In many divisions, essential parts of the artillery regiments, as well as many of the army support units with heavy artillery, could not have been armed without French or Soviet guns, such as the artillery regiments of the ill-fated *Luftwaffen-Feld-Divisionen* (Air Force Field Divisions), many of which were deployed in late 1942 on the Eastern front. One last point of the order has to be highlighted: even under these circumstances, munitions were made available for training. This underlines the importance given to training by the German army, a point to be discussed in more detail in chapter 6.

While production of goods and the process of ascertaining needs and distributing materials were great challenges that often overwhelmed the German military apparatus and the other agencies involved, the real Achilles' heel of the German supply system in the east laid in its means of transportation or, more precisely, in the lack of an adequate means of transportation. The campaign in France in 1940 had already demonstrated strains in the logistic system due to transportation shortages, but the Soviet Union's vast distances and much poorer infrastructure would devastate the German system.

As previously mentioned, the Eastern theatre had enormous dimensions. This therefore required an enormous apparatus to bring men and material to the front (or, in case of wounded soldiers and material in need of a general overhaul, to the rear). A comparison of German and Soviet rail networks highlights this fact: The *Reichsbahn* ran 42,000km of railways in the occupied Soviet territories (compared to some 62,800 km in the German Reich) and therefore needed 112,000 German railway employees and 634,000 Soviet auxiliaries. Added to this were Wehrmacht security units, the German police and regionally recruited militia units, as well as technical troops under military command (*Eisenbahnpioniere*, railways engineer troops).

Due to the enormous distances, there only a thin transport network in the Soviet Union. Therefore, traffic junctions were of strategic importance, an issue underestimated in German operational planning. For the *Blitzkrieg* campaign to be successful, these traffic junctions needed to be conquered rapidly and mostly intact. Otherwise, the advance slowed down or came to a halt, partly as a consequence of supply problems. But most of these traffic junctions were in cities, and the German spearheads – Panzer or motorized infantry divisions – were ill suited to conquer cities, especially when defended. The same was true for major river crossings, which were especially rare across broad rivers such as the Dnieper, Dvina or Don. This dilemma was never solved and was a cause of constant command friction, delays, and heavy losses in the spearheading units.

The prolonged battles for Mogilev and Dnipropetrovsk were examples of the problems caused by transportation junctions in cities.[16] Poor infrastructure also applied to the quality of the roads. Most roads in the Soviet Union consisted of dirt that turned into nearly impassable seas of mud after rain or during the melting of winter snows. They were also never intended for the large number of vehicles that passed over them during the German advance. And while many railroad lines were also of lesser quality, the primary issues here were that the Soviets used a different gauge and lighter locomotives. So, if the Germans wanted to use the railway network, they needed to convert it to the German gauge or capture enough Soviet railway material (with the delaying factor of unloading goods at the German-Soviet border). By late 1941 and early 1942, the conversion, often poorly executed under the pressure of operational demands on railways that were never intended to carry the heavy German locomotives, became a constant source of problems. At the same time, the stocks of captured Soviet railway material never reached expectations. Organizational problems further hindered the efficient use of railways. It was not until spring 1942 that many of these problems were solved in most areas under German control. At around the same time, however, a new challenge arose: partisan warfare. Until the Germans left Soviet territory, their lines of communication were frequently threatened and often temporarily broken.

The German army had four means of transportation to overcome the distances and deliver the goods from Germany to the Russo-German-frontline: railways, motor vehicles, aircraft and ships, the last being a very marginal issue not further discussed here. Much has been written about railways in the east and some of their problems have already been examined.[17] Two other issues warrant a mention. First, while railways were effective in bringing forward many goods, they were not flexible enough for the new kind of operation arising from the use of mechanized formations. Second, the constant fluctuations in demand from the frontline overtaxed the agencies in charge of loading and controlling railway traffic. Additionally, the troops were not sensitive to the needs of the railways, often cannibalizing communication equipment, snow fences, supply and maintenance installations and even railway lines. Even with all of these problems – and due in no large part to the lack of motorized transportation – the railways constituted the backbone of the German supply system in the east, thereby shaping the course of German operations more often than recognized.[18]

The railways could only operate to a certain point behind the front, and all traffic from these railheads to the frontline or supply depots could only be carried out by vehicles. While motor vehicles could load more goods, drive faster and further, and needed fewer personnel than horse-drawn transport, the scarcity of vehicles prevented the German army from exclusively using such transportation in the supply system. The general lack of motor vehicles posed several dilemmas to the German army, beginning with production capacities and ending with the balancing of supply forces. A relatively weak automobile industry hampered production. The rearmament programs of the 1930s – including the build-up of a mechanized force and the Luftwaffe – drew both technical expertise and workers away from this industry. The production of trucks was always in competition with tanks or half-tracks and received a lower priority. The trucks that were produced were then needed for a variety of combat-related tasks: to motorize combat and support elements in the mechanized forces, to tow all kind of heavy weapons, and for the supply system. Even if the build-up of mechanized forces was limited, thereby freeing up production for trucks, there never would have been enough trucks to adequately fill the supply system. Another dilemma existed within the supply services. Based on the experiences of the western campaign and in anticipation of the vast distances and the need for the Panzer Groups' operational freedom and flexibility to perform their decisive thrusts, the German army formed special supply columns to be used by the Panzer Groups as moving depots. While this gave the Panzer Groups a higher supply capability, it drew trucks from the regular supply columns and weakened supply possibilities for the remainder of the army, thereby widening the already existing gap between a highly effective but small spearhead and the bulk of the forces. In an attempt to at least minimize these problems, the German army desperately sought any motor vehicle available. This led to an extraction of vehicles from the German domestic sphere, as well as an extensive use of captured vehicles from the short campaigns before Barbarossa, especially those of French origin. While these vehicles added depth to German transportation capabilities, they also created new problems. These, as well as some of the issues discussed above, will be seen in the next source, a report given by the 198th Infantry Division's staff officer for motor vehicles:[19]

I) Formation

The division was formed in November 1939 in the Protectorate as a division of the 7th wave. The vehicles were predominantly drawn from units that already had the Polish campaign behind them. [...] The allocation of no all-terrain vehicles at all – with the exception of a few special vehicles for the Signal Battalion 235 – during the formation and later as well had an especially detrimental impact on the division's previous operations. Therefore the anti-tank units and the leadership only had commercially available vehicles at their disposal. All forwarded requests in this vein remained unsuccessful.

Once again before the Eastern campaign, a request for the allocation of all-terrain passenger cars for at least the infantry and artillery regimental staffs, the artillery battalion staffs, the leaders of the anti-tank units and the staff of the Engineer Battalion 235 in view of the Eastern campaign was forcefully made to the XXXth Army Corps. Subsequently, during the campaign, the division was nonetheless allocated only 1 *Kübelwagen* and 5 Mercedes 170 V vehicles without four-wheel drive. The fittings for the fuel and equipment trucks were not delivered during the division's formation, but had to be procured by the division itself on the open market, which caused severe difficulties, only increased by the division's formation in the Protectorate.

The formation of only one permitted motor vehicle workshop platoon was carried out only by personnel with completely inadequate equipment. It was only during the western campaign that this workshop platoon with its improvised installations became fully operational. The authorized towing vehicle for towing defective motor vehicles was never attached to the workshop company.

Many divisions suffered from gaps in motor transportation right from their initial formation. The lack of heavy trucks, all-terrain vehicles and all kinds of necessary special vehicles such as half-tracks, workshop trucks, radio vehicles, properly equipped motor ambulances, and so on, can be found in nearly all divisions, including the favourably equipped Panzer and Waffen-SS Divisions. Due to the lack of adequate production, gaps had to be filled with requisitioned vehicles from the civilian economy, which had to be converted for special tasks as shown here by fuel and equipment trucks. Also common was a lack of maintenance units. This especially resulted from the contest for technically trained men, which were also needed by both industry and the Luftwaffe. Those sent to the army were mostly sent to the mobile units with their huge vehicle parks (the same being true for special equipment such as recovery vehicles, tools and machines). What was left went to the infantry divisions, and newly formed units often did not receive even enough specialist personnel for their smaller units.

II) Exchange of seized vehicles for German [vehicles]

Equipped with these vehicles, the division participated in the campaign in Denmark and France. In France, the division could replace all losses in ample manner by captured motor vehicles, with the result that the division consisted of around 75% German and 25% captured motor vehicles.

On 2. and 4.3.41, thus 8 days before the transport to the Balkans, the ordered exchange of captured motor vehicles for vehicles manufactured in Germany took place. 22 motorcycles, 40 passenger cars and 134 trucks were exchanged. This exchange had an especially harmful effect on the motor vehicle stock of the division. The division was forced to give up its whole captured motor vehicle stock, which was in very good condition, while the division it traded with – the 253rd Infantry Division, which had to exchange with 3 divisions on the whole, and which was allowed to keep special vehicles and especially urgently needed motor vehicles of German origin – could bring its most worn out vehicles to the exchange. With few exceptions, the exchanged motor vehicles, including tires, were in very bad condition.

While the division had forced up the tonnage by using captured trucks, the vehicles it received in the exchange were without exception on the lower level of their tonnage class. Due to this, the division suffered a tonnage loss of 45 tons. Immediate and repeated demands to the Special Staff Volckheim [...] responsible for the exchange action, resulted in at least 22 trucks being exchanged for vehicles of a higher class of tonnage, although only used vehicles were allocated, without any possibility of choosing others. To remedy the most urgent shortage, 5 additional heavy trucks were attached to the division.

The greatest difficulty lay in the necessary reestablishment of the operational readiness of the exchanged motor vehicles, which could not be executed before the transport on 10.3. and was not set in motion before arriving in the Balkans.

In addition, a restocking of the missing vehicles within the framework of the exchange was rejected. The division had to march to the Balkans missing the following vehicles: 24 motorcycles, 13 sidecar motorcycles, 7 passenger cars, 6 trucks, 1 bus and 9 special vehicles.

The enormous booty of French motor vehicles, as well as the access to the French civil economy for production and requisition, filled the most urgent gaps in the German motor park and allowed for the expansion of the mobile units. While French booty was by far the largest, the German army also massively relied on captured vehicles from other enemies, including those found after the British retreat from Dunkirk. It is certainly debatable whether the German army would have been able to undertake Operation Barbarossa without those stocks of captured vehicles. No fewer than 84 infantry divisions, three motorized infantry divisions and even one Panzer division were primarily equipped with captured vehicles. Additionally, many of the army's motor transportation units were outfitted with captured trucks.

III) Balkan campaign
    [...] The total losses which occurred during the Balkan campaign were not covered by replacements, so that the number of missing vehicles has again increased.

IV) Refreshing by the German Liaison Command Bucharest
    To discuss the question of refreshing and other requirements for the division's equipment, the divisional quartermaster was ordered to the General Army Office and to the General Quartermaster in Berlin. [...] While the allocation of a second motor vehicle workshop platoon and all-terrain vehicles was rejected, 3 medium trucks were obtained from the Liaison Command and allocated to the horse-drawn bakery company 235. Despite numerous requests and personal visits, the division received only one of the already allocated and supplied trucks. [...] During the period of refreshment, the infantry anti-tank companies formed 5cm ATG platoons. On the whole, it was necessary to make 6 5cm ATG and 6 ammunition trailers mobile. For this purpose, the allocation of 12 1.5 ton trucks A-Type or 12 motor vehicles 69 or 12 medium all-terrain passenger cars was requested at the Liaison Command. An allocation of special vehicles did not occur again. Just to make the guns mobile, 3 commercial medium trucks were allocated to the division. The remaining 9 trucks had to be extracted from the handed over 3.7cm ATG platoons. Since those old light trucks were quite inappropriate for towing the heavy guns, there had to be an exchange for medium trucks inside the division, which were missing from other positions.
    In addition to constant telephone communication and continuous reports and requests, repeated personal visits were undertaken relating to the period of refreshment, including those on 5.4., 29.4., 10.5., 30.5., 17.6., and 27.6. by the divisional quartermaster and the Divisional Engineer with the Quartermaster and the motor vehicle administrator of the Liaison Command. [...] Among other things, the Chief of the General Staff of the 11th Army remarked: 'It will be naturally impossible that the division goes into the Eastern war with such a motor vehicle stock.' [...] The Corps and Army could not help materially, since the Army depots were in the process of being built up and closed until the beginning of the Eastern campaign.
    Despite the serious efforts of all superior commands, the Liaison Command responsible for the division's refreshment did not succeed in compensating for the losses of the Balkan campaigns, not to mention the large shortage of vehicles. All in all, the refreshment brought the division an increase in motor vehicles of

8 motorcycles, 9 passenger cars and 11 trucks (including an additional allocation of 3 trucks for the 5cm ATGs and 3 trucks for the bakery company 235) up until the beginning of the Eastern campaign. During the deployment for the Eastern Campaign, the division lacked the following vehicles: 32 motorcycles, 7 passenger cars, 12 trucks, 1 bus, 9 special vehicles, 2 motor ambulances.

While the time-delay effect of the Balkan campaign on Barbarossa is much discussed, it is clear that this operation had a negative effect on logistics. This included significantly more wear on the vehicles than on average, which only increased the gaps in vehicle stocks. Furthermore, the diversion of 15 divisions to the Balkans from the deployment to the east caused much friction and delay for other transports. Units that had participated in the Balkan campaign should have been refreshed in May and June 1941 as a priority but, as the report shows, this was not the case. Even more problematic for the upcoming campaign was the lack of all-terrain vehicles even for combat units such as the ATG platoons.

V) Eastern Campaign
   1) Deployment in the bridgehead Sculeni, losses due to enemy fire.

      In addition to high losses in men and material, the division's first deployment in the Sculeni bridgehead already also brought the division heavy losses in vehicles, in particular by strong artillery bombardment and aerial bombing, which also affected the rear sections in Jassy. Already the division has lost 30 motorcycles, 6 passenger cars, 17 trucks and 1 motor ambulance from 22.6. to 2.7. just through enemy fire. Up to this point, all special requests after losses were directed to the XXXth Army Corps, which did not appear to be promising. Order [of the] XXXth Army Corps motor vehicle officer of 30.6.41 reads as follows: 'The replacement of lost motor vehicles is only to be expected if the total losses have reached more than 10% of the division's motor vehicle authorized strength. It is therefore asked to refrain from individual requests, but rather to limit to [filling] out the required reports of vehicles falling out. The difficult motor vehicle situation at the 198th Infantry Division is moreover known to the corps command. If losses exceed 10% of the authorized strength, a fully filled out Form 6 is requested, indicating the distribution of the losses among individual units and any types of unique vehicles lost. Everything has been done by the corps command to help the division.' At this time, the number of missing motor vehicles already amounted to 157 motor vehicles from an authorized motor vehicle strength of 1,006, i.e. 16%. Despite this severe weakening of the motor vehicle stock, no allocations of any importance took place, even the more so as the allocations from the normal channels of supply did not show any increase corresponding to the losses.

   2) Private acquisition of motor vehicles

      In a meeting of the commanding general of the XXXth Army Corps with the divisional commanders, the latter agreed to accept the private purchase of motor vehicles, in order to compensate for the entirely inadequate replenishment and to make the division with its motor vehicle inventory operationally ready for the war in the East. Forced by the need and the will to maintain the division's operational readiness, private car purchases in Romania were initiated. As a result, by the middle of September 1941, the division was able to provide its motor vehicles stock with 54 motorcycles, 3 sidecar motorcycles, 17 passenger cars and 21 trucks. On order [of] Eleventh Army on 12.9., car sales in Romania had to be discontinued again.

Marching into the Soviet Union with an under-strength, partly worn-out motor vehicle park that in many cases did not fulfil demands such as all-terrain ability or cargo loading capacities, the division's high losses right from the beginning of the invasion were not surprising. Losses reached the aforementioned 16 per cent of the stock only two weeks into the campaign, an ominous foreshadowing of the upcoming months. Such losses reduced both units' mobility and their supply capacities. It is then no surprise that German units tried desperately to fill the increasing gaps in motor transport by any means, including buying vehicles on the Romanian private market. Most of these vehicles were used despite not being fit for cross-country operations. Receiving spare parts was also difficult, so the breakdown and falling out of these vehicles was only a matter of time.

3) The impact of road conditions and the use of repair services

Constantly deployed at the front, the division had to march along horrible 'roads', due to periodic precipitation, during the battles in Bessarabia and Ukraine. In total, about 1,700km were travelled in modest stretches to the local area, which had to be driven mainly in low gears. This resulted in very considerable wear for the entire chassis, but especially in the steering and suspension and, what is more, in the engine itself, which had a significant increase in oil consumption and a decrease in the performance. Over time, the heavy stress on the suspension– quite apart from numerous spring bridges – caused a considerable decrease in the load-bearing capacity of the trucks. As a result of the continually increasing breakdowns, it was necessary to establish numerous vehicle collection points, which inevitably became later operating sites for the 235th workshop company. With the increase in vehicle breakdowns and the resulting number of vehicle collection points, the fact that the 235th workshop company only had one vehicle workshop platoon and thus cannot be deployed with one platoon advancing while the other works is again and again decisively disadvantageous. This resulted in long towing routes to the vehicle collection points, with no tracked vehicles available to surmount this problem. Burdened with such orders, the troops and the workshop company's heavy commercial vehicles were exposed to extreme wear and tear in the prevailing road conditions. Maintenance work was further complicated by the circumstance that, on the one hand, there were no workshops for the maintenance of motor vehicles in the country itself, and, on the other hand, the troops did not have any scheduled repairs. This deficiency had to be remedied to a certain extent with the help of makeshift repair vehicles, which decreased the tonnage available for use.

4) Spare parts supply

The increasing decline in spare parts supply was a decisive factor in the maintenance of motor vehicles. The distances to the army motor vehicle depots were – like all supply routes – so large that the tours there could only be undertaken exceptionally. The stockpiles in the army motor vehicle depots themselves were extremely small in relation to demand, so that the workshop company was compelled to make spare parts itself in a makeshift manner and with great expenditure of time. On the other hand, motor vehicles were lost because the required spare part, which could not be procured by any means, was missing. In this way, motor vehicles whose general condition by no means justified being out of commission nonetheless had to be written off. Replacement engines were obtained only to a small extent, so a lack of suitable tow vehicles resulted in numerous motor vehicles left as total losses. These were cannibalized in the interests of the motor vehicles still in operation.

5) Reorganization of the division

As a result of the high personnel losses, the division was forced to dissolve an infantry regiment except for one battalion on 17.8. The largest motor vehicle gaps could be compensated for by the motor vehicles which were thereby released.

Not even two months into the campaign, the combined effects of an under-strength motor vehicle park consisting of vehicles generally not suited for the conditions in the east, the high demands on those motor vehicles, and structural problems such as the lack of spare part depots and maintenance and towing capacities, eroded German motor transport capabilities. This had severe consequences for units' supply, as well as for their mobility. Only the reduction of unit size could close the most urgent gaps.

6) Reconditioning during the operation in the Dnipropetrovsk bridgehead and captured motor vehicles

During the operations in Dnipropetrovsk bridgehead, which led to stable conditions for the maintenance of motor vehicles, it was possible for the division during the four-week period of the fighting to catch-up with the neglect of the motor vehicle maintenance during the advance. During this time not only had the 235th Workshop Company repaired up to 120 motor vehicles per week, but the troops' provisional maintenance units have also carried out a great deal of repair work in an outstanding manner, so that the number of vehicles in repair fell noticeably and only those repairs which lacked the necessary spare parts for completion remained unfinished. In recognition of the difficult motor vehicle situation, especially of the supply services, First Panzer Army and IIIrd Motorized Corps, already helped the division in the last period of advance and combat with the temporary allocation of corps [supply] columns and the bringing of supplies in close proximity. [...] At the conclusion of the battles in the Dnipropetrovsk bridgehead, which brought high losses for the division, the division succeeded in capturing some motor vehicles. Here, amongst others, 10 tractors were seized, which could be made operational by the workshop company over the course of time. [...] The number of missing vehicles at this time after the inclusion of the motor vehicles supplied from the army motor vehicle depot, private purchases and seized goods amounted to 42 motorcycles, 77 sidecar motorcycles, 6 passenger cars, 49 trucks, 1 bus, 10 special vehicles and 6 motor ambulances. 40% of the total losses resulted from enemy action.

In August, most German advance axes experienced operational stops of varying lengths as a consequence of exhaustion and growing supply problems. This was expected by the military leadership, but it was presumed that the Red Army was beaten at that time. Fighting in most areas, such as the previously mentioned Dnipropetrovsk bridgehead, instead confronted the Germans with a different reality. Instead of pausing and filling up the depots for a second operational phase, German forces were involved in hard, supply-consuming combat. Only minor reserves of supply goods could be accumulated in depots near the front. Maintenance of vehicles also suffered. With the imminent worsening of road conditions due to the upcoming autumn rains, the prospects for future operations were dire. Massive breakdowns could be expected to occur, as the next section indicates:

7) Losses during the march from the Pavlovka-Snamenka area to Makejevskoj
   How much the division's motor vehicles were wasted, however, was reflected in the catastrophic impact of the march from the Pavlovsk–Snamenka area to Makejewoskj (380km). Together with a slight frost, heavy rains had softened the roads and made them so impassable, that all motor vehicle traffic had to be stopped. During this period, the division was compelled by orders of First Panzer Army to proceed with the march with foot and horse drawn troops, without regard for the motorized sections and supply units, so that the troops were increasingly distant from the division's supply basis. Despite the strong wind, the drying out [of the roads] lasted a long time as a result of a constant alternation between frost and rain so that it was not possible to wait for the road conditions to be completely suitable for motor vehicles. As far as possible, the marches were carried out during the night and early morning hours, when the frozen ground still gave motor vehicles a hold. Since motor vehicle traffic was generally tremendously heavy due to the standstills that lasted for days, this condition constituted only a temporary improvement; the motor vehicles had to cut their way through mud and morass partly on and partly next to the roads. The motor vehicle material was no longer able to cope with such a high strain. Thus, 21 motorcycles, 10 sidecar motorcycles, 18 passenger cars, 17 trucks, 4 motor ambulances and 1 bus fell out on the 380km-long route, though these figures did not constitute a final result as the march movement had not yet been completed due to further rain. As a result, the number of missing vehicles has risen to a total of 61 motorcycles, 87 sidecar motorcycles, 24 passenger cars, 66 trucks, 10 motor ambulances, [and] 2 buses. Not included in this figure remain the numerous motor vehicles, which broke down on this route, have been sent to maintenance, and are not yet operational again. In order to collect these fallen out vehicles, two motor vehicle collection points were

set up in Novo-Nikolayevka and Guljaj Pole, where the division's workshop platoon was deployed to work. During the march of the motorized sections on this 380km-long impassable route, the tractors captured in Dnipropetrovsk rendered invaluable services in collecting the broken vehicles. Without them, the losses undoubtedly would have been much greater.

8) Losses of the fuel [supply] column
      For example, the long and poor supply routes had a particularly strong effect on the fuel column's truck inventory. It was assigned to the division in December 1940 with 7 Magrius trucks built in the years 1936/38 and 4 Chevrolet trucks manufactured in 1939. The last-named trucks were traded for 2 Ford, 1 Opel and a MAN truck in the exchange action. By 16.8.41, all the trucks swapped by the 253th Infantry Division and a Magrius truck had already broken down because of engine and differential damage and due to general wear and tear. On 30.8., 3 further Magrius trucks and 2 Ford trucks newly allocated in the meantime were lost. On 20.9., two trucks were loaded [on a train] for repair in the army motor vehicle park in Breslau. The last truck was a total write-off at the beginning of September because of a broken frame and bearing failure. In the case of the column's Magrius trucks, these were commercial trucks formerly used as long distance lorries, which had already driven more than 100,000 kilometres when they were assigned to the column, and in this state they were involved in the campaigns in the West, in the Balkans and in the East. For instance, one of the trucks written off on the basis of general wear and tear, manufactured in 1937, had a kilometre reading of 400,000km.

This short discussion about the fuel columns not only provides a detailed view of the problem of integrating civilian vehicles into the army, but also indicates the wide variety of trucks in use, as well as the condition of many trucks on the eve of Barbarossa. The following section sums up all of the division's problems, which were typical for the Eastern Army.

VI) In this context, the division again reported that beyond that [difficulties of supply], the same conditions apply with regard to the troops' motor vehicle material, with the corresponding consequences for the motorized units' operational readiness and the supply of the entire troops. In order to compensate for the shortages of the division's equipment (only one motor vehicle workshop platoon, a horse drawn bakery company) and the lack of tonnage space in connection with the high combat equipment requirements of the troops from the beginning of the Eastern campaign with the enormously long supply routes, the division was forced from the very beginning to resort to using the total tonnage of the baggage train for supply, whether through central deployment by the division or by distributing its trucks for those lost by the second group [the food supply section of the battalions]. In order to meet the stringent demands of the almost uninterrupted marches and battles, it was to be expected that the troops had to abandon their baggage. It was later only possible for the division to supply the troops with the most essential luggage , that is to say that winter clothing left in Jassy was shipped to them.[20]

VII) The continuous change in the division's subordination[21] may have been particularly disadvantageous in the motor vehicle supply with new allocations, spare parts and tires. In total, the division changed its subordination 25 times during the war. [...]

IX) In summary, the reasons for the current extremely strained motor vehicle situation are as follows:
1) Shortcomings in the formation of the division: a horse drawn bakery company, assignment of only one motor vehicle workshop platoon, allocation [of] predominantly obsolete and exclusively commercial motor vehicle material, no towing-tractors.
2) Loss of tonnage and decline in the motor vehicles' operational capacity due to the exchange of captured vehicles for German ones.
3) Failure of the refreshment period and in filling the vacancies before the Eastern campaign.
4) The enormously long and exceedingly bad advance and supply routes with their tremendous wear.
5) The heavy losses due to enemy action.
6) No allocations of motor vehicles corresponding to losses during the Eastern campaign.
7) Constant plummeting of the spare part supply and the lack of any local workshops.

If motor transportation situation was precarious at the beginning of the war in the east, it grew desperate in the following years. Not even the Panzer divisions, the German army's spearheads, could escape the problem, as the following report of the 8th Panzer Division from 1943 indicates:[22]

The division submits below a report on the present vehicle situation:
I) The majority of the division's vehicles date back to the time of formation in the year 1938. Insignificant reallocations later took place merely after the Polish campaign. Approximately 80% of the present vehicle stock dates back to this time. After the deployment of the division in the French, Yugoslavian, and Russian campaigns, general signs of fatigue now emerged in all of these vehicles as a result of their age, especially as the overloading of maintenance installations and difficulties in procurement of spare parts down to insignificant exceptions doesn't allow for careful and complete overhauls.

Even the make-shift refreshment in spring 1943 in the Nevel-Gorodok area brought as a final result no improvement in the vehicle situation, as no complete overhauls could be carried out during this time. In addition, numerous vehicles that, to be sure, were to be repaired but not completely overhauled in the course of the refreshment broke down during the division's deployment for bandit fighting during this same period of time. New vehicles, however, were not delivered to the division. After uninterrupted large scale combat since the beginning of July 1943, those still operational but very heavily used vehicles are no longer sufficient for their tasks.

II)

A) The Current Vehicle Situation

Establishment Number	Actual Number	Operational	Repair	
			Short Term	Long Term
2407	2790	1314	841	634
Number In %		47%	30%	23%

The number of the operational vehicles is excessively low in comparison to the establishment number because the establishment number also includes the vehicles that have to be sent to the Heimat for long-term repair (27%). A repair of these vehicles at the previous base in Minsk (moved on 20.10) was not practically possible due to the low capacity of the army motor vehicle park.

The number of vehicles in short-term repair (30%) will rather increase than decrease due to the over-taxing of the antiquated vehicle material.

B) Main Damage to the Operational and Short-Term Repair Vehicles
  1) Approximately 50% of these vehicles require a replacement engine because cylinders and pistons are severely turned out and crankshafts and bearings are damaged.
  2) Approximately 25% of the vehicles use up to 10 litres of motor oil per 100km.
  3) Approximately 15% have damage to gear boxes to change speed and differential.
  4) Approximately 20% have breaches in the frame, springs, and cranks.
  5) Approximately 10% have broken drive shafts and half shafts.
     A number of these vehicles (some 30%) that are necessary for the movement of the men, weapons and equipment must be moved by towing, which again has the consequence of an over-taxing of the still operational vehicles. Those vehicles that will be arriving from the Minsk repair station in the coming days (some 30) will only change the above-mentioned numbers minimally.

C) Procurement of Spare Parts
   The well-known difficult replacement part situation has an especially negative impact on the division because the antiquated vehicles have become worn-out and therefore require replacement parts more frequently.

III)

A) For example, the shortage of vehicles has led to one Panzer Grenadier Regiment with a combat strength of 300 men of which 90 are immobile. At this time, 150 men in total from the combat strength are immobile.

B) The lack of any supply vehicles with the transfer of an armored halftrack company and 2 self-propelled light field howitzer batteries (Wespe) has an especially negative impact.
   The most necessary vehicles for this must be provided from the available troop vehicles so that the mobility of this unit was further limited (see III A).

C) Due to the limited equipping with all-terrain vehicles – some 25% of the establishment number – the mobility of the division is further limited.

D) The available tonnage receives a further reduction as a consequence of the majority of the vehicles being able to carry at most only 75% of their nominal cargo load.

IV) In conclusion, one can say that the division can again be fully ready for action after the opportunity for a sufficient complete overhaul—with a correspondingly ample delivery of spare parts – and an allocation of around 25% new vehicles – in correspondence with the number in long-term repair (at this time already for many months). A quick remedy for the raising of operational ability can however only occur with the reallocation of transport room for ____ men, to at least make the current combat strength fully mobile.

One can clearly see in this report the dilemma between troop mobility and supply demands. This was intensified by the transferring of units without any supply vehicles, which then had to be drawn from combat units. The effects of an older vehicle park, which not only led to more breakdowns, but also reduced transport capacity while simultaneously increasing consumption of fuel and lubricants, was also made clear in the document. So the longer the war in the east lasted, the more German units had to rely on horse-drawn supply. The additional requirement of manpower could be only satisfied due to massive influx of *Hilfswilligen* or Hiwis, Soviet soldiers who more or less voluntarily fought for the German side. This issue will be discussed in more detail in chapters 5 and 6.

Supply through the air was used in German offensive operations in 1941/42 only to a small degree. In addition to supplying armoured spearheads that pushed beyond their lines of communications, it was mostly used to transport personnel and equipment of the Luftwaffe itself. But when the tide turned and the Red Army went on the offensive in winter 1941, supplying encircled German strongholds became a major issue. Holding several key strongpoints, especially in the areas of Army Group North and Centre, such as Demiansk, Staraia Russa, Kholm or Suchinitischi, broke the back of Soviet offensive efforts, denying it essential lines of communication to supply the advancing forces. And supplying those encircled positions was only possible by air transport. What worked under severe strain in the winter of 1941/42 became somewhat of a defensive strategy with dire consequences for German troops in upcoming years. 1942 saw the most well-known German airlift, the one for the encircled Sixth Army in Stalingrad. Less well-known is the airlift for Velikye Luki in the central theatre of the Eastern front.[23] A Soviet offensive, attempting a breakthrough in the direction of the Baltic, started a few days after the Soviet counterattack at Stalingrad. The Red Army achieved an encirclement of the strategically important city of Velikye Luki after a few days and tried to push further westward, but was stopped by arriving German reinforcements and its own supply problems, due in large part to the bypassed German-controlled Velikye Luki sitting astride numerous communication and supply lines. The German counter-thrust only reached the western outskirts of the city and freed a small group of the beleaguered garrison, but it failed to retake the city. Considering the size of the Soviet and German forces in combat and the overall situation on the Eastern front, Velikye Luki was a German defensive victory, but a bloody one. The foundation of this victory was the nearly two-month stand of the almost 7,000-man garrison of Velikye Luki, which was only possible due to air supply. An idea of the problems and the size of the airlift can be seen in the final report of the commanding *Luftwaffenkommando Ost* (Air Force Command East, the overall command of air force units operating in the area of Army Group Centre in 1942):[24]

6. Deployment of flying units

During the fighting for Velikiye Luki, the flying units of *Luftwaffenkommando Ost*[25] faced the difficult task of supporting the ground forces in the defence and later in the attack. In addition to this task, the supply of the encircled garrison still took place, which, as a result of the development of the situation, increasingly forced the mass of the combat forces to be used for the supply mission. [...]

E) Air supply
aa) Supply by bomber formations

Since the encircled parts of Velikiye Luki urgently needed supplies, a large part of the bomber formations were used to drop weapons and ammunition, medical supplies and rations. In every possible type of weather, by day and night, supply containers were dropped over the city, [and] later on the citadel and eastern railway station. All the crews who were deployed to drop supply goods achieved unparalleled performances through their missions, despite low-altitude flights often carried out against the heaviest defence. Heavy losses occurred during the attempts to drop supplies to the garrisons of the citadel and the eastern railway station, which were compressed into a narrow space. All possibilities (air drops using the lower cloud cover until the approach run, approaches by low level flight with a steep climb shortly to the air drop altitude before the target, twilight and night drops, targeted air drops of supply containers [food, medicine, infantry ammunition] without parachute) were exhausted. In doing so, it turned out that the dropping of supply containers on small-area targets like the citadel (250m x 120m) represents a task which cannot be solved by horizontal dropping. With the approach of the supply aircraft, the enemy, who had worked all the way up close to the ramparts of the citadel, fired a blocking barrage over the airspace of the citadel with infantry and anti-aircraft weapons of all calibres, which was broken through by the He 111 at air drop altitudes of 80-200m to carry out their missions.

bb) Supply by *Stuka*

In addition to the bomber formations, *Stuka* formations were also deployed for air drops for the first time. This use became necessary due to the strong defence and the small drop targets. During the dive, 'supply bombs,' were dropped, with and without parachutes, into the smallest areas – i. e. into single 'hedgehogs'. All the supply bombs dropped without a parachute hit the target area, but they were partly broken by the hard impact and often could not be found due to the absence of smoke signals. The supply containers dropped with parachutes drifted for the most part and fell into enemy hands.

cc) Supply by cargo-carrying gliders

The use of the tow-planes to Velikiye Luki resulted in excellent successes despite the strong enemy defence and bad weather situation. For the use of gliders it was necessary to land a glider guide in Velikiye Luki, who was able to check the suitability of the landing field and to take all necessary measures for the landing of the cargo-carrying gliders. A daylight mission of cargo-carrying gliders with tow-planes up over the target could only promise little success with the strong defences appearing around Velikiye Luki. In spite of this, 4 missions were successfully carried out during the day.

With missions at dawn and dusk the disadvantages of the night take-off or, to be more precise, night landing had to be accepted, since the advantages of the unseen approach offered a greater guarantee for the successful execution of the orders. Eight Go 242s[26] were dragged to the target in night missions and landed there with the help of paths of positioned flare and flare signals.

In an action that recklessly disregarded [the enemy defence], the garrison of Velikiye Luki was supplied by the landing of 17 cargo-carrying gliders with ATGs with crews, assault groups, machine gun ammunition, flamethrowers, rations, medical equipment and mail. Due to the lack of any news of their fate, it must be concluded that two cargo-carrying gliders landed in enemy territory.

The landing on the County Fair Street in Velikiye Luki, and later on the area of the Eastern railway station demanded great skill and quick decisiveness. Due to the inadequate landing possibilities in such a confined space, a partial destruction of the supply equipment which had already been brought into the target area by crash landings could not be prevented.

In heroic, voluntary efforts, the glider pilots have brought material and moral support to the units fighting on the ground for further stubborn defence.

The long endurance of the garrison of Velikiye Luki under the toughest conditions of combat and weather was made possible only by the air supply of the combat transport and gliders formations, which was carried out with the greatest grit and highest commitment. Without their commitment, the defensive power of the encircled units would have soon come to a standstill as a result of the loss of weapons and a lack of ammunition. [...]

G) Numerical overview of missions, successes, losses

16) Missions and dropped bombs: In the period from 25.11.42-19.1.43, 298 reconnaissance aircraft, 1,393 bombers, 46 nuisance raiders, 403 *Stuka*, 1,554 fighter, 310 bombers and 94 *Stuka* with supply missions, [and] 25 gliders were deployed. A total of 4,163 aircraft. Dropped bombs: 1,450.1 tons.

17) Successes

[...]

291.27 tons supply goods, 12 mortars, 4.36 cbm of fuel dropped by aircraft

23.6 tons supply goods, 4 guns, 17 machine guns, 74 soldiers (gun crews and assault groups), 12 flame-throwers, 3 mortars transported by gliders

[...]

18) Losses

Material: Aircraft: Total losses: 1 Ju 87, 4 Fw 189, 1 Ju 52, 6 DFS 230, 6 Bf 109, 11 Go 242, 17 He 111, 1 FW 190 = 47 aircraft

[...]

Crashes 60-100%: 2 Ju 87, 3 He 111, 2 Bf 109, 1 HS 126 = 8 aircraft

[...]

Crashes below 60%: 3 Ju 87, 19 He 111, 3 Bf 109, 1 DFS 230 = 26 aircraft[27]

Total losses of aircraft from 25.11.42-15.1.43: 81 aircraft

19) Personnel losses:

A) Flying personnel: [...] 17 officers, 133 NCOs and men

The small target areas were the main issue, a problem that had already been under discussion in winter 1941. Soviet fire concentrated over such small target areas made air drops nearly impossible and caused heavy losses. Tests with *Stukas* failed to achieve a positive result and the problem was never solved by the Luftwaffe. One possible solution – if the target area was not too small – was the use of gliders. As mentioned in the report, this solution led to a host of new problems. The training of glider pilots, who were often lost in the operations as few strongpoints were relieved, was demanding. Once again, a lack of resources was compensated for by a man's commitment and courage.

The source also mentioned the constant dilemma of the command: how to divide its aircraft between the two tasks of supporting ground forces and supplying the encircled troops. In the case of the operations in Velikiye Luki, this became more pressing, when from late December on, German relief actions were in need of all available air support, while at the same time supply stocks in the city were depleted. On a strategic level, the lack of adequately trained crews and the demands for multiple air-supply operations led to trainer crews from flight schools flying supply missions at the front, which had an adverse effect both on the quantity of trained pilots and on the quality of their training. This was a decisive factor in the weakening of the Luftwaffe in 1942/43.[28]

Another interesting aspect of the air force report was its overwhelmingly positive tone. While the army recognized the air force's achievements, its final note on the air supply was much more sober and less heroic:[29]

Experience: Despite all efforts of the aircraft crews involved, the air supply of Velikiye Luki was not enough to provide the garrison with the necessary weapons and ammunition, food and medical supplies for the purpose of carrying out the fight. At the time when the dimensions of the strongpoint would have permitted a major deployment of supply aircraft and gliders, this could not be carried out due to bad weather. When the weather permitted the deployment of the Luftwaffe, the strongpoint had been so narrowed by break-ins and breakthroughs that the bulk of the aerial delivery units dropped had drifted to the enemy's side or could not be recovered because of heavy enemy fire. The enemy's strong anti-aircraft and fighter defence forced air drops from high altitudes. When the garrison had been compressed into individual strongpoints, which were no longer connected, it was therefore attempted to drop supply containers without parachutes from *Stuka*s. The contents, however, were for the most part destroyed on impact.

Also interesting – especially when considering the wide variety of goods required – is the final list of supplies flown into Velikye Luki:[30]

Final summary of supplies, weapons, etc., transported to Velikiye Luki by air, between 29.11.42 and 7.1.43
   Ammunition: 164.332 tons
   Rations: 5.248 tons and 7.500 rations of tobacco
   Fuel: 0.33cbm
   MG oil: 0.05cbm
   Anode battery: 290 pieces
   Flashlight battery: 500 pieces
   Flashlights: 650 pieces, plus 50 flashlight bulbs
   Bulbs: 50 pieces
   Radio equipment: 2 B1 and 2 D
   Heavy field cable: 20km
   Electrical tape: 100 rolls
   Vacuum Tubes RV 2 / P 800: 20 pieces
   Field handset: 4 pieces
   Accumulators: 2 units
   Medical material: 3.25 tons, including 1 amputation and 1 surgeon's kit
   Mail
   Iron crosses: 4 packages
   Light mortars: 6
   Heavy mortars: 4
   MG 42 with accessories: 10
   MG 34: 8
   Heavy machine gun 34: 4
   7.5cm Pak: 4 (including crew)
   Telescopic sights for 4.5cm Pak (r): 2
   Spare parts for MG 34 [...]
   Spare parts for MG 26 (t) [...]
   2 packs with cold-resistant grooved ring collars for heavy field howitzer and heavy 10cm guns 18.
   1 battery-locksmith case
   [With cargo-carrying gliders]: 1 engineer assault group (15 men)

As already seen, the supply item delivered in the greatest quantity was ammunition. In order to keep the troops fighting, replacement weapons, rations and fuel were of course also required. Medical supplies were much more an issue of morale than of actual combat need, as were letters from home. Also flown in were special weapons, such as the powerful 7.5cm ATG and engineer assault groups with flamethrowers, especially effective in urban warfare. To maintain communication with the outside and to influence and perhaps even manipulate the garrison, radio sets and everything needed to operate them, such as accumulators and tubes, were also brought into the city. Seemingly minor items such as flashlights had to be flown in, as they were essential for patrols on long winter nights so the Germans could maintain control over the frontline. So too were cold-resistant spare parts for guns and tools for gun maintenance. We have only a few indications of how much of the previously mentioned goods actually reached the encircled garrison.

While air supply was helpful in some special situations, it often proved a waste of resources. It required a sizeable infrastructure and high-quality personnel to work, and the losses in men and material were high, especially considering the relatively small amount of supplies delivered (and actually received). Even worse was the fact that the successful operations in winter 1941/42 awakened unrealistic expectation about the possibilities of supplying encircled forces of any size for long periods. This resulted in a sanguine attitude towards encirclements at the highest German command levels that was as essential for developments on the Eastern front in 1944 as Hitler's ill-fated orders on fortresses and holding positions.

Medical services were essential in keeping the German *Ostheer* fighting.[31] Determined Soviet resistance, as well as the sheer size of the Red Army, caused German losses to rise to levels far higher than in previous campaigns. This placed a heavy burden on medical units right from the beginning, as the following source of the 14th Panzer Division, fighting in Panzer Group 1 on the German southern wing, illustrates:[32]

During the campaign in Russia, altogether 3,153 soldiers were treated by the medical service of the 14th Panzer Division in the time period from 22.6.until 31.8.1941. Of these, 2,019 were wounded and 1,134 were sick.

Specifically, the cases were distributed among the medic companies or the clearing station:

Main Dressing Station	Period of Deployment	Total	Wounded	Sick
Medic 1/4				
Wlodzimierz	24.6 - 27.6.41	35	32	3
Lutsk	29.6 - 1.7.41	240	192	48
Zhytomir [...]	10.7.41	25	25	
Kotscherowo	18.7 - 20.7.41	130	100	30
Tolstaja	31.7.41	17	12	5
Schpola	31.7 - 4.8.41	145	51	94
Kirowgrad	5.8 - 8.8.41	85	42	43
Beljnyj-Bossad	6.8 - 7.8.41	17	12	5
Nowe-Tschigirikowka	15.8 - 18.8.41	80	34	46
Ssolonenjkoje	19.8 - 31.8.41	512	293	219
Dnepropetrovsk	26.8 - 27.8.41	37	37	

Main Dressing Station	Period of Deployment	Total	Wounded	Sick
In the operation trucks and during the march			49	49
Medic Company 2/4				
Korzec	6.7 – 9.7.41	400	265	135
Makarow	16.7 – 20.7.41	275	264	11
Boguslav	28.7 – 1.8.41	245	133	112
Preton-Iaschlyk	3.8 – 5.8.41	52	32	20
Alexandrija	7.8 – 15.8.41	345	88	257
Losowatka	17.8 – 20.8.41	87	60	27
Ssurskoje	23.8 – 30.8.41	354	275	79
During the march			23	23
Total:		3153	2019	113

Four surgeons of the companies, who with the operation assistants in almost uninterrupted work during their particular deployment, bore the brunt in caring for the wounded, are especially deserving of recognition.

The ambulance platoons 1/4, 2/4 and 3/4 covered altogether 109,000km during the transport of the wounded from the front line to the main dressing stations or to the main dressing stations in the medical installations lying in the rear areas, sometimes under enemy fire and thereby transporting 2,928 wounded and sick.

In the reporting period, the two medic companies carried out 38 blood transfusions. The donors were members of the companies.

During the campaign against Russia, the medic units have 6 fallen and 24 wounded in their own ranks.

The numbers cited above include only men treated by the medical units – neither dead nor missing soldiers were included. But wounded men alone counted for 30 per cent of the divisional personnel for the first two months of the invasion of the Soviet Union. Many of the wounded men, as well as most of the sick, returned sooner or later to their units.

While sick soldiers were already a problem during the summer, the German army had to adjust to a completely new situation when the campaign against the Soviet Union dragged on into winter. Not only were winter clothes such as quilted jackets, gloves and earmuffs arriving slowly and in completely insufficient numbers, but the troops were physically exhausted by the nearly permanent advance since 22 June 1941. All of this is reflected in the following source, sent by the 123rd Infantry Division to its superior army corps in November 1941:[33]

The division's state of health has continually deteriorated lately. This fact is not so much revealed through a massive occurrence of severe illnesses, although serious colds have increasingly arisen in this form. What is noticeable in comparison is the severe deterioration of the troops' general state of strength. In this way, the resistance of the individual man is considerably reduced. This makes itself noticeable above all in an abnormally severe susceptibility, which, as already stated, manifests itself not so much in serious life-threatening illnesses, but rather much more in the relatively high percentage, especially in the infantry regiments, that has arisen of minor illnesses of the respiratory organs, rheumatic illnesses, as well as pictures of general exhaustion.

The current deployment does not allow for these illnesses to be treated properly, thus an unacceptable percentage of the troops will fall out. On the other hand, productivity is considerably reduced as a result. This state of exhaustion frequently leads individual men to an excessive apathy that is accompanied with a reduction of the defensive will against sickness, which under current circumstances must lead to a further worsening of the general state of health.

With this comes the danger that it will be accompanied by a severely increasing lice infestation. [...]

In this way, a sharply growing number of skin diseases have lately occurred. To be sure, these constitute no serious threat. In contrast, an outbreak of typhus would be very alarming. The severe lice infestation would facilitate a fast spreading of the disease, and at the same time, the generally poor state of strength of the troops must lead to a very unfavourable influence on the course of the disease.

A further worsening of these conditions thus can only be avoided when the troops are given the opportunity for some time in a quiet position to take the necessary measures for the restoration of reasonable health conditions.

Parallel with an improvement in the state of strength, the radical treatment of lesser illnesses as well as a true de-lousing on a grand scale would substantially improve the combat strength.

This source is especially striking since it points to a deteriorating health situation that was predicted to become severe in a few weeks, at a time when the Army Chief of Staff Franz Halder and the Army Groups and Armies' Chiefs of Staff met in Orsha to discuss the further course of war. They agreed there – with few reservations – to undertake a last push on Moscow in the hope of ending the war in the east. But it was clear that an operation with troops as described in the report of the 123rd Infantry Division was doomed from the beginning. Worse, it would have severe consequences when the German offensive was continued beyond its culmination point.

Rest and time for personal hygiene was urgently needed, but the demands of the rapid advance and the lack of manpower frequently did not allow for such things. As a consequence, troops were full of lice, and the German military leadership feared the diseases spread by lice, such as typhus fever. The lack of hygiene also promoted dysentery. While these hygiene issues were especially concerning for frontline troops, they were also an issue for those in the rear.

A major problem for the Wehrmacht in handling disease was the interaction of soldiers with the Soviet civilian population. The remaining civilian population was often prone to illnesses due to a lack of food, as well as the presence of numerous children and elderly people. While a complete separation of the two groups was simply not possible, the German army had to divert some of its overstrained medical resources in hopes of at least controlling the civilian population and containing the outbreaks of serious diseases before they could spread to the military units – of course an issue primarily caused by harsh German occupation policy. Termed the 'regulation of the [population's] health', this issue became more and more pressing for units in the east, especially those engaged in positional warfare who remained in specific sectors for longer periods of time. The following source is such an example from the 87th Infantry Division, holding a section of the front sector in the Velizh area in Army Group Centre's northern sector. The order was issued by the IVb, the divisional doctor:[34]

> The regulation of the health of the population that is contaminated by typhus, typhoid fever, [and] dysentery is of essential importance for the protection of the troops against epidemics.
>
> The combating of infectious diseases [and] lice within the troops and civil population, the stopping of the civil population's wandering and a complete separation of housing are hereby urgent.
>
> For the implementation I order:
>
> 1) In every station district a station district medical officer is appointed (appendix). He is the adviser of the station district or station commander for all questions and measures of the regulation of health. The instructions given by him on behalf of the station district commander are to be implemented promptly by the town commanders.
>
> 2) An epidemic troop is to be established with every station district medical officer (for composition and detachment see appendix), which is to be used for the continuous control of his area and the execution of his measures.
>
> 3) By headquarters' order, the reporting of every case and suspicion of infectious diseases is made a duty for a) the troops, b) Russian doctors on hand, c) mayors and the population.
>
> 4) The station commanders arrange that one accessible sauna and one delousing chamber next to it are available for the civil population of their areas and are used frequently. Pay attention to the construction of proper, sufficient civilian latrines and their use.
>
>   The town commander regulates provisions for ill civilians by decree to the mayor.

The German army's medical services and medical staff were generally effective in preventing dangerous diseases from becoming epidemics. But the increase in pressure on German troops, especially when the combat situation become more and more unfavourable from the summer of 1943 on, had a very negative effect on the health situation of German soldiers, especially those in the front line. Military necessity frequently clashed with health considerations, and the former generally won out. The following report by 306th Infantry Division, then fighting in the Nikopol sector, gives an insight in this dilemma:[35]

After consultation with the divisional doctor, I report on the state of health of the fighting troops:

German engineer company marching in the Ukraine, summer 1941. The endless plains of the Soviet Union forced German troops to undertake long marches that exhausted the infantry. (BAMA RH 26-76/21)

German engineers crossing the Dnieper by force, summer 1941. Broad Soviet rivers proved difficult obstacles to overcome for German troops. (BAMA RH 26-76/21)

German trench near Naumovka, Velizh area, 1943. Beginning in early 1942, large sections of the front reverted to positional warfare – a strategy that needed to be relearned by the German army. (BAMA RH 26-205/94)

Troops of the 371st Infantry Division in a bottleneck at a river crossing during the breakout from the Kamianets-Podilskyi encirclement, March 1944. Note the various uniforms as well as the many horse-drawn vehicles. (Private archive of Marco Sigg)

Units of the 371st Infantry Division during their retreat in southwestern Ukraine in February 1944. Harsh weather conditions hampered troop movements and had negative effects on the troops' health. (Private archive of Marco Sigg)

German infantry supported by an assault gun advancing in open order in the Ukraine, summer 1941. Combined arms were an essential part of German tactical success. (BAMA RH 26-76/21).

Ferrying of an assault gun over the Kasplia River (Vitebsk area), spring 1942. (BAMA RH 26-205/94)

An assault gun passing a horse-drawn column, Ukraine 1941. One of the German army's fundamental problems was the lack of adequate means of supply for the rapidly advancing Panzer troops. (BAMA RH 26-76/21)

Part of the staff of the 385th Infantry Division in April 1942, Ukraine. The divisional commander *Generalmajor* Karl Eibl, the twenty-first soldier of the Wehrmacht (and second of the army after Erwin Rommel), decorated with with Swords to the Oak Leaves, died six months later during the Soviet winter offensive after being accidentally wounded by Allied Italian troops during a frontline reconnaissance. (Private archive of Marco Sigg)

Generalleutnant Hermann Niehoff (centre), best known for his command of besieged Breslau in 1945, during his staff's celebration for receiving the Knight's Cross, late June 1944. He earned the award for his command of the 371st Infantry Division during the breakout of First Panzer Army from the Kamianets-Podilskyi encirclement. (Private archive of Marco Sigg)

Improvised sled production by a German supply unit, autumn 1942. The German troops started preparing for the second winter in the Soviet Union much earlier than in 1941 – a lesson learned after the high casualties and breakdown of the supply system. (BAMA RH 26-205/93)

Construction of a log causeway, central Russia, 1942. Warfare in the generally undeveloped forest and swamp regions of central and north Russia forced the German army to build its own infrastructure. However, the lack of men, machines, and material only allowed for makeshift solutions. (BAMA RH 26-205/94)

Soldiers try to pull a truck that has slid off the road, Ukraine 1944. The road conditions, especially after rains or in the thaw period, hampered German movement and supply. (Private archive of Marco Sigg)

Garden of a German supply unit. Due to difficulties in the logistical system, self-supply became essential for German troops. (BAMA RH 26-205/93)

Soviet civilians building positions near Velizh, 1943. The longer the war endured, the more the German army had to rely on Soviet manpower for auxiliary tasks. (BAMA RH 26-205/94)

A German NCO prepares tactical training on a sand table, 1942. The level of detail demonstrates the degree to which the German army sought to train men and leaders even under the difficult conditions of the Eastern front. (BAMA RH 26-205/94)

Destruction of an abandoned truck on the German retreat in the Ukraine, March 1944. Long retreats under difficult conditions not only caused the German troops to suffer materially, but also affected their combat morale. (Private archive of Marco Sigg)

Recreation home of the 205th Infantry Division in Baslovo, 1942. A peaceful area that allowed German soldiers to recuperate from the horrors of the front line. (BAMA RH 26-205/93)

Sleeping room in the recreation home of the 205th Infantry Division in Baslovo, 1942. Even if very Spartan from a modern perspective, it was luxurious compared to conditions on the Eastern front. (BAMA RH 26-205/93)

The 'attraction' of the 205th Infantry Division's recreation home: two German Red Cross Sisters. German women were rarely seen in the German-occupied Soviet Union. (BAMA RH 26-205/93)

Cemetery of the 205th Infantry Division in Novosokolniki area, 1942. Burying comrades in proper circumstances – when possible – was an important hygienic measure and proved essential for combat motivation. (BAMA RH 26-205/93)

Makeshift graves of German soldiers killed in action against Soviet partisans, spring 1942. (BAMA RH 26-205/94)

Note: We gratefully thank Dr Marco Sigg for offering us pictures from his private archive.

a)   all cases of non-transmissible diseases will remain with the troops.
b)   Given that the troops have had no bath – or washing facility for 2½ months, they are completely ridden with lice.
c)   60% are afflicted with scabies, 20% have lower leg abscesses or extensive cellular tissue inflammations.
d)   Under normal circumstances, 25% of the fighting troops must undergo military hospital treatment for 3–4 weeks.
e)   The combat power suffers from complete physical exhaustion. It has been detected several times, that individual soldiers were no longer responsive or their drive for self-preservation was completely extinct.

Under these circumstances, the increasing breakdown of the German army's morale from late 1943 on is not so surprising.

Even working under the over-optimistic presumption of a short campaign, German supply means were barely adequate. When the *Blitzkrieg* approach failed and the war in the east turned into a long-lasting one of attrition, the German supply system could not cope with the demands placed on it.

Two issues connected to the logistics of the German armies in the east have still to be discussed. First, in hopes of lowering the demands on the supply system, the German military leadership planned for the troops to live off the land. This would significantly reduce the amount of rations and thereby relieve the means of supply. Second, the supply system strongly relied on safe lines of communication, which were all the more important in consideration of all of the deficiencies previously discussed. Both issues are closely connected to German occupation policy, the focus of the following chapter.

Chapter 5

The Occupied Rear: Pacification, Exploitation and Mobilization

Since Operation Barbarossa's *Blitzkrieg* was designed to crush the Soviet Union within a brief period of time, the German army put very little thought into designing an occupation regime. Once all Soviet resistance had been smashed by the German army within the three-month period calculated by the high command, both the army and Hitler expected that administrative power would be immediately turned over to civilian authorities. Focused on achieving such a quick and decisive victory and expecting support from SS formations in eliminating resistance in the rear, the army dispatched a mere nine security divisions – three to each army group – to pacify its rear area. In the summer and autumn of 1941, these units had already proved to be unable to fulfil their mission, and the failure to destroy the Soviet Union in one blitz campaign forced the army to create an ad hoc occupation policy in early 1942 that continued to evolve throughout the course of the war.[1]

Army practice shifted between callous neglect, violent coercion and calculated conciliation from 1941 to 1944. Despite it never achieving a unified policy that guided its actions across the expanse of the occupied territories, several guiding themes emerged as early as summer 1941 in the army's approach that continued throughout the course of the occupation. First, it sought a quiet and pacified rear area in which all traces of resistance and opposition were destroyed. This was necessary for its second objective: the economic exploitation of the region. Working in conjunction with Economic Staff East and other civilian agencies, the army assumed an extremely important role in the devouring of the Soviet Union's resources, particularly military equipment, raw materials and, most importantly, food.[2] The latter proved decisive in determining the army's relationship with Soviet civilians. In order to shield the German population from any further cuts in rations and to save what promised to be a strained supply system from delivering large amounts of food to the front, the army was expressly ordered to live off the land. In other words, the fields of the Soviet Union were to provide the army's sustenance during the campaign. In order to ensure that the Soviet Union provided the necessary materials to not only feed the Eastern army, but also to fuel the global war against Great Britain and an increasingly belligerent United States, the German army prepared for a quick, yet exceedingly violent campaign, which was framed by what historians refer to as the 'criminal orders'. These directives ranged from regulations governing the relationship between the army and the SS-*Einsatzgruppen*, utilized to eliminate all manifestations of resistance, particularly from male Jews, to the abrogation of military justice when it came to dealings between soldiers and civilians. The army also issued the commissar order, which demanded the execution of all Soviet political officers captured in battle.[3] Finally, the most important order in determining occupation practices was the 'Guidelines for the Conduct of the Troops in Russia'.[4] The order began by stating that:

1) Bolshevism is the mortal enemy of the national socialist German *Volk*. Germany's struggle is aimed at this subversive *Weltanschauung* and its carriers.
2) This struggle demands ruthless and energetic action against Bolshevik agitators, guerrillas, Jews and the complete elimination of all active or passive resistance.
3) Extreme reserve and the sharpest care is in order towards all members of the Red Army – including prisoners – as one should expect treacherous combat practices. Especially the Red Army's Asiatic soldiers are devious, unpredictable, underhanded, and callous.

After discussing the various racial and ethnic groups found in the Soviet Union, it then switched focus and highlighted the economic foundations of the campaign:

8) Economic goods of all types and seized military goods, especially food and fodder, fuel, and articles of clothing are to be saved and secured. All squandering and waste harms the troops. Plundering will be punished with the heaviest penalties according to military law.

Though the army's period of occupation was deemed to be brief, it was nonetheless based on violence and exploitation.

Within two weeks of the initial invasion, the 7th Infantry Division's commander released an order that highlighted the importance of the Soviet Union's raw materials for the Reich.[5] On 5 July 1941, he established the division's food requisitioning policies to his subordinate commanders:

The General Quartermaster of the Army's General Staff emphatically points out that, in consideration of the entire food situation of the Reich, the time of unlimited falling back on food supply stocks are over.

The homeland must be relieved wherever it is possible. To protect the stocks in the homeland, as well as to relieve the supply system on the technical grounds of transportation, it is *the highest requirement* that the troops live extensively '*off the land*'. That this is extra work for the troops must be accepted.

In regards to supply from the land, every soldier needs to keep in mind that *stocks of captured goods* are Wehrmacht stocks that *can only be distributed according to the prevailing ration rate*. Any wasting and every additional consuming of captured food stocks falls back once again on the supply situation of the homeland.

Captured good depots that cannot be completely exploited by the troops are to be reported to the Divisional [staff section] Ib/IVa and to be guarded until they can be taken over by the division.

The *troops* must in any case supply themselves with: *oats and potatoes*.

The *division* is in any case ready to provide: *bread and meat*.

Self-butchering by the troops is undesirable at this time because the meat provided by the division is then either taken additionally or it remains lying there and spoils. Due to our supply situation, each spoilage of foodstuffs is a sin against the entire [centralized] German food economy. Self-butchering is only necessary when the division can only distribute 1 day's rations due to the excessive heat.

Vegetables, spreads, sugar, spices and drinks should be obtained by the troops themselves when possible. The division provides these foodstuffs only on a *temporary basis*. Just because they are on the troops' menu does not mean the troops must expect to receive them. [...]

Evening food [rations] will be distributed from 7.7. only every two days. One evening meal must be acquired by the troops according to the rations set by Field Manual 86/1. Towards this goal, self-butchering can take place to the necessary extent.

We want to always keep in mind:

England wants to starve Germany.

Russia has the means that Germany needs.

As the division commander made clear, German occupation goals were seen as vital not just for the war in the east, but also for the larger struggle against the British Empire. While the army has been rightfully criticized by historians for ignoring the larger strategic issues of the war in favour of emphasizing operations, clearly some officers understood the importance of the Barbarossa campaign for a favourable outcome to the global struggle. This directive also contains the essence of the German struggle to effectively exploit Soviet agriculture during the war; while the order attempted to set limits on the troops' foraging, it simultaneously encouraged them to take the initiative in finding their own nourishment.

As a result of an over-strained supply system, a focus on the army locating its own food in an area dependent on subsistence agriculture, the German belief that the fertile land of the east should provide for them and not the 'inferior' Slavs, and a delegation of authority to the lowest levels when it came to living off the land, such policies inevitably resulted in confrontations between German soldiers and Soviet civilians. Unable or unwilling to distinguish between 'legitimate' and 'wild' requisitioning, the troops frequently plundered Soviet peasants and their farms. The town commandant of Kholm reported in late summer that:

Despite the sharpest orders and despite supervision, the number of cases of German soldiers extorting cattle and foodstuffs from the population (sometimes through physical abuse) has increased. It is primarily a matter of villages lying outside of Kholm in which commandos appear and 'organize.'[6] Here, farmers often have their last piece of cattle taken away [and] in a few cases, money and valuables are stolen. Those parties affected then come to commandant's office and complain.

So, for example, on 11.8.41, a unit passing through drove away an inhabitant's last cow, punched him in the face, and allegedly took away a contribution of 3000 rubles.

A 75-year-old woman from Brzkoie (some 5km south of Kholm) came to the commandant and stated that on 17.8., a cavalry unit appeared, wanted to drive away her only cow, and when she begged on her knees for the cow to be left, a soldier hit her. The woman had marks from being hit on her face. Then the soldiers rode away and took with them a sheep and several chickens without payment or receipt.

A woman came to me with a voucher, which confirmed that an *Obergefreiter* (without his field post number) had taken a cow for 3 *Reichsmark*.

Since these are probably troops from outside of Kholm and from other divisions, the commandant asks for redress.[7]

Such behaviour played an important role in turning those sections of the population that initially welcomed the Germans into resisters. This was not an insignificant issue. In order to Sovietize the western fringes of the Soviet Union in the 1930s and early 1940s, Ukraine, Poland, and the Baltic States had been terrorized by Soviet power. Mass arrests, deportations, shootings and famine resulted in the imposition of Soviet control, but at the cost of any support from the local populations. Numerous German soldiers testified to being greeted by these various ethnic groups as liberators freeing them from the Bolshevik yoke, and it is clear that anti-Soviet attitudes could have been capitalized on by the Germans if any real attempts had been made.[8] Nazi racial policy and the army's myopic focus on operations to the exclusion of all other considerations ensured, however, that in 1941 no such effort would be forthcoming and German practices in the occupied east transformed such potential support into outright resistance. One German soldier fighting in the Leningrad region noted that:

Last evening, Russian peasants dragged a dead cow here and made a loud clamour over their loss. With right! Some German soldier had killed the animal because he had a craving for liver. He took that with him and left the rest lying there. That arouses dissatisfaction with us and the careless black butcher[9] received an appropriate punishment. Now he had created another family of future partisans.[10]

Partisan activity remained a constant worry for the German army during the entirety of the campaign. This was partly based on ideological concerns: as the 'Guidelines for the Conduct of the Troops in Russia' made clear, the army expected irregular resistance as it believed that the 'Judeo-Bolshevik' leadership of the Soviet Union actively encouraged such underhanded methods of fighting. It was also based on the Germans' understanding of the campaign they were going to fight. As panzer spearheads drove deep into the rear of the Red Army, their supply lines grew correspondingly long and difficult to secure. In hopes of smashing the partisan movement before it could become a major irritant, the army resorted to coercion and violence. The army's traditional response to guerrilla warfare was based on military necessity and it manifested itself in what were known as collective measures: the arrest of an entire village, taking of hostages, burning down a community or the execution of suspected partisans. An order issued by Sixteenth Army in October 1941 elucidated this policy.[11]

a) Civilians convicted of sabotage or espionage are to be shot by an order of a responsible commander. When suspicion isn't adequate for this, the commander can order a collective measure against the town or village in question. This is to be determined by the degree of destruction and the extent of suspicion. In case of repeated sabotage, for example on the means of communication, it is recommended to take hostages and to task their relatives with the guarding of the telephone lines.

b) Only when these measures by the troops unexpectedly fail to lead to success, can suspicious male civilians and conscripts be transported to the civilian camp in the prisoner of war transit camps, on order of the corps. [...] Authorization to send convicted civilians to these camps can only be given in extreme emergencies. Such civilians are deported with accompanying guards on the railroad.

The army followed this traditional Prusso-German practice during the Second World War, though its actions on the Eastern front were clearly radicalized by Nazi ideology.[12]

Even though partisan activity failed to materialize into a true threat to German operations until 1942, scattered Red Army troops who managed to escape the large-scale encirclements proved to be an irritant to the Germans.[13] The following document provides an example of how a German collective measure was ordered and carried out by an artillery regiment during its advance:

The end of the 426th marching group on the road from Dorochova to Oserki took rifle fire on 21 July 1941 around 1900 hours from terrain overgrown with bushes and shrubs by the village of Puchova. A medic stepped out of the column and was shot at a distance of 5 meters by a civilian. The medic company then returned fire from its side. On my order, the bush and shrub covered terrain and the cornfields in the direction of the village were combed-through by members of the signal section under *Leutnant* Ullrich and by medics. I gave *Leutnant* Ullrich the order to proceed ruthlessly and to make use of summary justice.

Since some time passed before the beginning of this action and because the combing through took a long time, the commando found no one else in the area around the village, with the exception of two young women, who were lingering in the sunken terrain in a suspicious way. *Leutnant* Ullrich surrounded the village and ordered it to be searched. The village inhabitants finally admitted that the Bolsheviks had stayed in the village and claimed that all of the Bolsheviks in the meantime had left the village in the direction of the east. The village inhabitants had obviously supported the Bolsheviks or themselves participated in the sniper attack. Through a translator *Leutnant* Ullrich made the facts known [eds. the 'facts' in this case were merely the *Leutnant's* suspicions as noted above] to the assembled population of the village and explained to them the now following reprisal action. He had the draft-age men of the village – altogether 7 men – shot by a rifle salvo from his men in the face of the remaining population and burned the entire village. *Leutnant* Ullrich's behaviour from the submitted report is approved by me. It corresponds to the meaning of orders given by me.[14]

The mass shooting carried out by the artillerymen highlights both the army's brutal approach to anti-partisan measures, as well as the latitude given to officers in formulating a response.[15] It also illustrates the army's approach to occupation during the months of the advance. Civilians were seen as irritants and only those deemed threatening received any attention at all from the army. Focused on achieving victory on the battlefield, the German army simply ignored the bulk of the civilian population, only interacting with it when the Germans requisitioned food, needed intelligence, or viewed it with suspicion and fear.

As the German advance slowed in late summer and early autumn, the war behind the front took on a new ferociousness. During the last weeks of August and into the beginning of September, German anti-Jewish policy degenerated into one of pure mass murder.[16] The earlier emphasis on male Jews of military age now evolved into a policy that encompassed all Jews, no matter the age or sex. Large-scale shootings, such as the one at Babi Yar in which over 33,000 Jews were murdered by SS units and Ukrainian auxiliaries, also demonstrated the army's involvement in the Holocaust.[17] Recent scholarship has conclusively demonstrated that army units, from the army level down to the regimental level, were involved in the murder of Jews and did so on their own initiative.[18] This was encouraged by army propaganda, which markedly increased in stridency as the army prepared for what it hoped would be the final weeks and days of the campaign in the east. Alongside *GerneralFeldmarschall* Walter von Reichenau's infamous order and the similar ones issued by *Generaloberst* Herman Hoth and Erich von Manstein, the 123rd Infantry Division issued an order of on 2 october first promulgated by *Feldmarschall* Wilhelm Keitel in late September.

> The struggle against Bolshevism demands a ruthless and energetic crack down, especially against Jews, the main carriers of Bolshevism.
>
> Therefore all cooperation between the Wehrmacht and the Jewish population, which is either openly or secretly anti-German, and is used for various preferential auxiliary services for the Wehrmacht, is prohibited.
>
> Passes, which confirm the use of Jews for the Wehrmacht's purposes, are not to be issued in any case by the military agencies.
>
> The exception is merely the use of Jews in specially constructed labour columns that can only be used under German supervision.[19]

Such orders were an attempt to both motivate the troops for one final effort, and to make clear the stakes of the campaign: Bolshevism and, by extension, Jews constituted a mortal threat to Germany that needed to be eradicated.

The rear-area war against partisans and the development of the Holocaust on the Eastern front soon merged. The following two documents, generated by the 221st Security Division, illustrate the evolution of army policy towards Soviet Jews and how it was entwined with the army's responses to the irregular resistance. The first dates from July 1941.[20]

> On 17.7., a sentry and a motorcycle messenger were shot at in Bialystok by unknown perpetrators.
>
> As a reprisal, Military Administration Headquarters 549 set a comprehensive raid in Bialystok on a day determined independently in agreement with Regional Defence Regiment 45 and the police units in Bialystok that is to be carried out with all severity.

Suspicious people are to be arrested. At the slightest resistance, weapons are to be immediately used. Hostages (especially Jews) are to be taken into custody, whose shooting by the slightest disturbance is to be ordered.

In July, Jews were taken as hostages in response to partisan activity and were the first to be threatened with execution. By September, German policy had already become radicalized, as the following war diary entry from the 221st Security Division demonstrates.[21]

The section Rübekeil reached the final goal of the Bobruisk-Mogilev road in the cleansing action ordered by the Commander [Army Group Rear Command] Centre. During the time period 10-12.9., altogether 2 officers and 160 men were taken prisoner. 1 Communist and 22 Jews were shot due to support for the partisans.

As the report notes, while the army brought in 162 prisoners during the operation, those executed for supporting the partisans were overwhelmingly Jews. Here, the army's prosecution of the war against insurgents had bled over into the regime's ideological goals. The fact that both the army and the state not only viewed Jews as the backbone of any resistance in the rear area, but also as the mainstays of the Communist Party and its infrastructure, meant that they disproportionately received the brunt of German anti-partisan brutality during 1941.

The army's targeted violence and callousness towards the civilians was only exacerbated during the 1941/42 winter crisis. As the army faced an existential struggle to survive the Red Army's ferocious counter-attack, freezing temperatures, and a supply system that had almost entirely ground to a halt, Soviet citizens in the occupied areas were now viewed in an entirely utilitarian manner. The following record of a meeting at the headquarters of Eighteenth Army's Chief Quartermaster in December 1941 clearly indicates the army's total disregard of civilians not seen as useful for its survival.

Prisoners of War. 800,000 tons of bread cereals in a year
  Distinction: working prisoners and prisoners in rear camps
  The number of working prisoners reduced to the absolutely necessary mass. These will be better fed. This comes at the expense of the Heimat.
  Question to examine, how few prisoners can I get by with?
  All those unable to work are to be deported and not fed.
  Make sure that the prisoners really receive the portion they are entitled to.
  Treatment of the prisoners should be correct. Currying favour, cigarette exchange is forbidden.
  Establish small workshops to improve the clothing, etc. The confiscation of clothes from the civilian population for prisoners.
  Civilian population: Feeding is a crime. The wandering of the civilian population is to be stopped with all means. Once again on the order of the Commander-in-Chief, the sharpest separation of the population from the soldiers is pointed out.
  At this time, transport of refugees cannot be undertaken. The army cannot help. The civilian population is to be abandoned to its fate.

The fact that Eighteenth Army was carrying out the siege of Leningrad at the same time is surely not coincidental; in both cases, the Germans viewed civilians exclusively within the concept of military necessity and in both cases their fate mattered little in the context of the army's attempt to achieve final victory on the battlefield.[22] This document, however, also points the way to the further evolution of the army's occupation policy, as civilians and prisoners of war who could be exploited by the Germans for labour and production were to be mobilized into the German war effort. Such developments, however, would have to wait for the conclusion of the winter crisis.

During this time, when the very survival of the Eastern Army seemed in question, the army became much more radical in its approach to occupation policy. On the one hand, its scorched earth practices designed to stem the oncoming Soviet tide simply exposed civilians to the unforgiving elements. An order issued by XXXIXth Motorized Corps on 7 December 1941 ordered that 'the city of Tichvin is to be destroyed as thoroughly as possible before the final pulling-out' by German troops.[23] Its subordinate unit, the 8th Panzer Division, noted in its war diary that 'destruction commandos' needed to be established to carry out this order, to ensure that:

> every house, every bridge, and every building that could be used as shelter is to be destroyed, without consideration for the inhabitants. Food and fodder that cannot be taken with the troops is likewise to be destroyed.[24]

By eliminating both shelter and food during the dead of winter, such policies obviously doomed countless Soviet civilians to death in late 1941 and early 1942. At the same time, fears of partisan attacks in the rear areas mushroomed during this period of crisis and the army responded by instructing its troops to maintain vigilance and inculcating in them ideological beliefs first mentioned in the pre-invasion orders, such as the 'Guidelines for the Conduct of the Troops in Russia'. The following directive, issued by the 126th Infantry Division, highlights these points and also betrays the division commander's anger at what he considered the unprofessional and lazy behaviour of the men under his control.

> The fundamental guidelines for combating partisans are contained in the directive 'The Commander-in-Chief of the Army, Gen. St. d.H./Ausb.Abt. (Ia) Nr. 1900/41 v. 25.10.41', distributed on 10.11. to the battalion level. In addition to it, special points for partisan combat have once again been emphasized by the army. They are published below in excerpts and are to be followed.
>
> 1) Snow and ice, as well as murky, foggy weather with a prolonged darkness setting in very early, favours not only the possible appearance of enemy paratroopers, but also the operations of partisans and enemy raiding parties that usually close in on villages, highways, and railroads noiselessly on snowshoes, and can reach far behind the front.
>
> All the greater must everyone's vigilance and discipline be, even for those troops billeted far behind the front. Here, an incomprehensible naïveté is often especially found.

2) Every responsible commander and soldier must continually be clear that we are standing in enemy land and are dealing with an opponent whose character traits are treachery and insidiousness. Again and again, the Russian finds voluntary or forced support through the population. The trusting nature of the German soldier is all too often exploited to his harm. Caution and suspicion towards the Russian population is therefore necessary.

This includes not only the disarming and supervision of the inhabitants' behaviour. Especially important is the constant checking of the numbers of the male as well as female population regarding comings and goings (agents, spies!)

All troops must learn to report unusual occurrences and suspected cases concerning agent activity, partisans and so on immediately to the counter-intelligence agent at their superior command or directly to the Division's section Ic [Intelligence].

3) All troops, and in this context this applies especially to those not deployed directly at the front, must take the necessary security measures against hit and run attacks. These require constant inspection and, where applicable, the modification through the responsible troop commander. Especially in cold and snow storms, the sentry must be particularly strictly supervised. Through frequent relief, the attention of the sentries should not be merely maintained, but rather increased.

[...]

5) Monitoring of the cross-country traffic also belongs to the guard and security service against partisans. This extends to:
   a) Limiting traffic to a purely local 'traffic'
   b) Prevention of all traffic over wide areas
   c) Examination of baggage and the sleds
   d) Checking of passes.

These four points are to be continually checked through spot testing. Only through these means can one achieve the effective confrontation of the enemy's means of intelligence transmissions – the fundamental prerequisite for all partisan and agent activity!

6) During a long stay in a village, the readiness and discipline of the troops is to be checked through frequent practice alarms. There should be no villages with troops in them that cannot immediately respond to surprise occurrences with prepared countermeasures.

The largest reproach is attached to the commander and the troops who have neglected blood-saving measures out of laziness.[25]

By emphasizing the fight against 'an opponent whose character traits are treachery and insidiousness,' and demanding the men take appropriate measures against such an enemy, the order suggests that the commander believed his men had been too lenient in their dealing with civilian population. Such a reading complicates a narrative that exclusively focuses on German brutality in the east. Nonetheless, it is also clear that civilians felt the sting of German occupation during the winter crisis, as the army implemented whatever policies it deemed necessary to survive the resurgent Red Army during the depths of winter.

The fate of Soviet soldiers taken captive by the German army provides perhaps the best example of how German policies in the occupied east evolved during the first two years of war. During the fighting of 1941, German operations culminated in large-scale encirclement battles in which over three million Red Army men were taken prisoner. German treatment of this massive number of men was simply criminal. Ideological beliefs – including the fear that Russian POWs were carriers of Bolshevism, as well as their alleged racial inferiority – intersected with pragmatic concerns – the disinclination to divert food intended for the army to prisoners and other logistic issues – to create the greatest mass mortality that the army was directly responsible for. More than two million men perished as a result of mass shootings, exposure to the elements, disease and, most importantly, starvation.[26] As the report reproduced above issued by the Eighteenth Army's Chief Quartermaster in December 1941 illustrated, prisoners of war on the Eastern front were a commodity – only working prisoners were to receive the necessary rations to survive. This in and of itself was a revolutionary change in German policy towards Soviet POWs caused by the winter crisis and the realization that the war would stretch into 1942. Such a transformation of policy was reflected in a document issued to the 207th Security Division. As part of its mission in pacifying Estonia and a sliver of Russia-proper in the Lake Peipus region, the division dealt with prisoners of war. A rubric received by the division in December 1941 highlighted the daily deaths faced by POWs, the increasing use of such men for German labour projects, and the importance of race in determining treatment of prisoners: among those groups of prisoners released, ethnic Russians were conspicuously missing.

Monthly Report
  A) Stock at the end of month following the model of appendix i
  B) Arrivals in last month
    a) pp.
    b) in Army [Group] rear area
    c) pp.
  C) Left in last month
    a) died, shot
    b) escaped
    c) given to the SD
    d) given over to responsibility of Luftwaffe
    e) given up to the *OKW*'s POW organization
    f) released
    g) total
  D) Labour Action on the first of the month
    a) supply for the troops
    b) road and bridge construction, street maintenance (without Organization Todt)
    c) building and position construction (without Organization Todt)
    d) Organization Todt
    e) operations, construction, and maintenance of the railroad
    f) business, industry, and trade
    g) agriculture

      h) Luftwaffe (so long as not discharged from the supervision of the OKH)
      i)   other work
      k) total (further distinctions are not to be made)
  E) Releases in the past month
      a) Lithuanian
      b) Latvian
      c) Estonian
      d) Ukrainian
      e) Romanian
      f) Finnish
      g) Ethnic German
      h) White Ruthenian
      i) Caucasian and security service, as well as translators
      k) Turkic
          h, i, and k only for auxiliary guard service, police
      l)   total[27]

This shift towards a policy that now recognized the productive value of prisoners of war reflected broader trends that permeated the army's approach to occupation policy. The realization that the war would now last at least one more year and that positional warfare reminiscent of the First World War had become the norm for the northern and central fronts meant that elements of the field army's command moderated their policies in hopes of winning support from the Soviet population under its control, ranging from *Generalfeldmarschall* von Reichenau's famous memorandum of early January 1942 to First Panzer Army's more conciliatory policies in the Caucasus.[28] An order first issued by the OKH on 10 May 1942 that was distributed by Third Panzer Army to its subordinate units three weeks later highlighted the shift in German intentions.[29]

> The goal of the struggle that the German soldier leads in the East is the destruction of Bolshevik power. The attitude of the troops towards the peaceful population, as long as they see German soldiers as the emissaries of a new just order, will not be affected in this way. As nowhere else in the occupied European territories, the German has the opportunity in Russia to have his claim to leadership voluntarily recognized by the population. Essential for this is the nature of his behaviour. He should be perceived as master in the east. Mastery should never degenerate into contempt towards the defenceless vanquished. The Russian is obedient and willing when he is treated strictly but fairly. The trusting basis of the population is to be used for a quick pacification of the conquered territory.
>
> It is wrong and detrimental to our own interests to see the native population as without rights and honour on account of their outward proletarian appearance, because, as experience shows, this was only camouflage against Bolshevik terror. *The German soldier protects the property of the labouring and peaceful population, he respects the sense of honour of Russian women and girls, he supports the reconstructive work in the rear areas. He must know that capricious acts create opposition, sirs up embitterment and therefore threatens the security of our troops.*
>
> Unavoidable forced measures that must be taken for the continuation of the war and which extensively assail the rights of the inhabitants are to be made

understandable to the population if possible. The requisitioning of cattle and other goods, whose seizure would have a disgruntling effect, should be tasked to the village elders (*Starosten*) if possible. Through his behaviour, the German soldier is to prove to the civilian population that he is a member of a culturally advanced people, whose dominion will have the effect of releasing the population from the Bolshevik yoke.

On the other side, the mastery of the occupied territories and the exploitation of the countryside demands hardness. All weakness and softness would be out of place. Where civilians revolt against the military authorities' orders, where they act violently towards or threaten a member of the Wehrmacht, or plan or carry out an act of violence of any type is to be immediately and ruthlessly cracked down on per the previously distributed directives on order of the responsible officer.

These perspectives are of importance for are all measures of the troops. He who avenges cruelties of the Red Army on the defenceless and innocent civilian population helps the enemy cause. The soldier must be the best propagandist for the Greater German Reich though his strict but just treatment of the population.

Such an order indicated two important points. First, the very fact that the army felt the need to issue such a directive indicates that its men had behaved violently towards the Soviet civilian population during the advance and subsequent winter crisis. Second, the army clearly understood that its objective of winning the war militarily would be impaired by a chaotic and rebellious rear area and it hoped to placate the occupied population in order to avoid such problems. These types of ideas and policies trickled down the army hierarchy to the division level across the breadth and depth of the front.[30] For example, the 7th Infantry Division deployed in the centre of the front, ordered that:

the troops are again to be instructed that their demeanour towards the population needs to be correct. Every instance of violent attacks gets around, undermines the trust in the German armed forces and gives Soviet-Russian propaganda welcome fuel and impetus.[31]

Other divisions implemented more tangible policies designed to assist Soviet civilians survive the occupation. Encircled in the Demiansk Pocket by superior Red Army forces and dependent on air drops for its own supplies, the 123rd Infantry Division nonetheless initiated a communal food program for the population in its midst in May 1942.

In order to improve by a small measure the hopeless food situation for some areas of the Russian civilian evacuees until the onset of other assistance, the following provisions should be immediately started:

1) The sector commander will responsibly determine in consultation with the respective military doctor those localities in which the food situation is so bad that aid measures need to be introduced.

2) In those localities as determined in accordance with number 1, communal feeding is to be established throughout the sector. In general, the communal food should consist of a warm soup each day, and should be disbursed to

the civilian population not local to the area, under the supervision of the German security organs and with the assistance of the responsible Russian mayor. Appropriate measures must be taken so that the entire evacuated population is actually treated equally and, for example, no double portions.

3) For the evacuees' food, the sectors are to allocate food in the fixed ration rates for the Russian population that works in the service of the German Wehrmacht as long as the stocks allow. The numbers being fed is to be reported at the same time in accordance to number 6.

4) In return for this food, the population is to be used for work for the Wehrmacht (also quarters and defensive position construction), as well as for agricultural help. The communal feeding is to be exploited for propaganda for us when possible.

5) Any costs (outside those in accordance to number 3) will not be paid for by the Reich.

6) The section commanders must be clear that this additional food comes at the cost of burdening the entire transportation system. Therefore, especially strict standards are to be applied. The localities identified in accordance with number 1 are to be immediately reported to the Division Ib [quartermaster] about the necessary developing communal feeding with the details of the number of evacuees that need to be fed and with the section of economic troops tasked with feeding them.

7) I request that the section groups, deployed for as an intensive cultivation of the fields as possible, are above all to ensure that the minimal available seeds should not used at the last minute, but rather to take measures to ensure the protection of the sprouting seeds in order to benefit fully from the securing of food.

This document also indicates the division's attention to the region's agricultural resources; clearly, the German army's occupation duties encompassed far more than merely securing its lines of communication and supply. It also suggests that the division commander recognized the shift in the balance of power in the east. The army that invaded the Soviet Union in June 1941 had suffered grievous and irreplaceable casualties in terms of men and equipment and victory could now only be achieved if the occupied population remained quiescent or could perhaps be encouraged to fight on behalf of the Reich.

Simultaneous to the army's implementation of more conciliatory policies were attempts by the Reich to more systematically exploit the manpower resources of the occupied territories. In spring 1942, the Nazi state instituted a new programme designed to deliver Soviet citizens to work in Germany's fields, mines, and factories. Led by Fritz Sauckel, *Gauleiter* of Thuringia, the Reich Labour Action's tentacles spread widely through the occupied east, working in concert with institutions such as the Economic Staff East, the SS, and the army. An order issued by the 8th Panzer Division's quartermaster in May 1942 made clear the army's role in the process.[32]

The very great need for workers in the *Heimat* demands the transfer of around 2,000,000 people from Russian territory.

The organs authorized with the recruitment of Russian workers by the General Plenipotentiary for the Labour Action, *Gauleiter* Sauckel, are to be supported by the units in every respect.

The army was thus inextricably involved in what eventually became a massive program of kidnapping and population displacement.[33] While millions of workers from the occupied east were eventually sent to Germany, the army also utilized hundreds of thousands of Russian men and women for its own purposes, from building and maintaining roads, to constructing defensive positions and improving lines of communication. A November 1942 order from Fourth Army emphasized the importance of civilian labour to the army itself.[34]

Due to the prevailing scarcity of prisoners of war, an increased use of civilian labourers as single workers and in labour columns will take place in the future.

These labourers must be treated differently than prisoners of war. Before requesting such labour forces, each military user of this labour must carefully consider the requirements of the civilian work force, such as securing food and shelter.

The deployment of civilian workers in labour columns especially requires precautionary measures in the following sense, as the danger exists that members of the labour columns could be unwilling to work or could flee from working through illicit means. Such people are easy loot for the gangs.

The issue of food, however, remained the most pressing for both occupiers and occupied. Unfortunately for German forces at the ground level and the starving civilians surrounding them, the German High Command squashed attempts, such as those of the 123rd Infantry Division, to feed the occupied territories' population. In August 1942, the OKH delineated the field army's responsibilities for civilians.

With the increasing difficulties in supplying the Russian civilian population with food directly before the harvest, the proposals from command authorities have become more frequent to place food from troop stocks at the disposal of the civilian population in the army and rear areas. As understandable as these proposals are from the troops' standpoint and as desirable as this would be for the fulfilment of the requirements in the interest of population's labour power and its willingness to work, their carrying out are just as untenable.

The serious situation of the *Heimat*'s entire food situation itself makes it necessary for the population in the occupied territories to be left a minimum of food and in particular the circle of those who eat from German rations needs to be limited to the most necessary extent. Furthermore limited transportation capabilities, which can only partially satisfy all its users and due to the heavy troop demands for supplies of arms and ammunition and other goods of all types, only a relatively minimal space is allowed for food supplies on the trains, which in addition to the on-going supply, is barely sufficient to create the necessary stocks for the mud period and winter. All assistance from army stocks can therefore only have a negative effect on the troops' own supply.

Supply for the civilian population is exclusively the task for the economic authorities.

The distribution of food from the troops' stocks must be categorically prohibited and can only be limited to temporary assistance in individual cases subject to the application of strict standards, if a timely reimbursement of food is to be maintained by the economic authorities.

The OKH clearly recognized the benefits of feeding civilians in order to successfully carry out its other programmes, specifically those involving labour. Once again, however, severe supply difficulties intersected with the army's utilitarian interpretation of military necessity and Nazi ideology, resulting in the end of policies that could have at least alleviated some of the worst effects of German occupation. This hard line taken by the High Command was mirrored by the actions and policies of many front-line units. Even the 123rd Infantry Division found itself straddling the line between conciliatory initiatives and simple violence. In an order it issued in October 1942, the German army's struggle to reconcile its competing visions of an occupation order based on a mutually beneficial relationship with the peasantry and one based on violence was clearly articulated.[35]

The relationship of the troops to the population is decisive for the combating of agent- and partisan activity in Demiansk combat area. In general, the population has proven itself willing and hard working. Several parts are even prepared to provide armed support for the troops. There are within our area, however, still citizens who find it the best when the population has experienced a strict, but sympathetic treatment. It is essential that the population is convinced by our just behaviour and strictness, even in the future, and simultaneously feels itself protected from enemy agents by the consistency of our actions. Every weakness on our part will also be seen by the Russian population as a military weakness. This further undermines their obedience and trust in the troops. This would ease the work for agents and partisans.

The authority to carry out punitive measures against the population lays solely in the hands of the town commanders, the commander of the guard detachment, and the division. Sentences are to be imposed as non-judicial punishments (for example, imprisonment, if necessary with increased labour, including after the normal working hours, money and payment in kind). Corporal punishment is only to be used against men. It should be limited to exceptional cases. Punishments are to be recorded and filed.

German occupation policy continued to transform in 1943, marked by the catastrophic defeat suffered by Sixth Army at Stalingrad and the subsequent hasty retreat by elements of Army Group A to escape a similar fate in the Caucasus region. The army now fully committed to total war and this motivated its ever-evolving occupation policy. Two documents generated by the 126th Infantry Division, which was operating in Army Group North, highlight this transition at the divisional level. The notes from a meeting between members of the division and a group of Russian elders who administered villages in the region illustrate the army's approach to occupation.[36]

1) Necessity of the total effort in the struggle against Bolshevism:
   a) total mobilization in Germany and Europe
   b) total effort of the Russian population
          goal: quick end to the war
   c) reference to the methods of the Soviet regime.
2) Evacuation for the protection of the population (especially children) from the rigours of war
   a) entire settlements (village-wise)
   b) no deportation to Germany, but rather temporary assignment to a new homeland
   c) vacation, postal service for those left behind for a labour action
   d) volunteers (advantages: food, clothing)
   e) for the care of children, mothers or other suitable females
3) Closing Remarks (Vlasov)
4) Counter-intelligence – Espionage Danger

Three interesting points emerge from this document. First, the army was now explicitly demanding that the Soviet population, in concert with that of other European populations under German control, be mobilized in service of the German war effort. Second, forced evacuations had now become part and parcel of the daily activities of German units in the east, as civilians, their livestock and belongings were deported to the German rear in order for the Germans to exploit them for the war and simultaneously to deny their efforts to the advancing Red Army. Third, the mention of Andrei Vlasov, the Russian general who was captured in 1942 and then decided to collaborate with the Germans by heading the anti-Communist Russian Liberation Army, highlighted tangible efforts on the part of the army to yoke Soviet society to the service of the German war effort.[37]

The second document issued by the 126th Infantry Division in April 1943 was an attempt to convince its men about the necessity of Soviet manpower for the war effort and what this meant for the treatment of Soviet nationals.[38] The commander argued that

In order to ensure a successful execution of the labour service duty, a mental adjustment of the entire German occupation power towards the Russian people is necessary. Headquarters and agencies must know that those Russians conscripted for labour duty and volunteers cannot be treated as a mass of humanity who should be led to the slaughter, but rather as labour strength that the front, as well as the rear area services, urgently need and without the Russian people, the Russian farmer will never be able to survive. Under all circumstances, therefore, care must be taken so that those conscripted for labour duty and volunteers are treated and regarded as comrade-in-arms and that naturally, discipline must be maintained. It falls to us German officers and soldiers the task of making these people reliable allies of Germany, who are decisively interested in the outcome of this war and who are steeled against Bolshevik propaganda. While there are guidelines for the treatment of *Hilfswillige*, German agencies must be conscious that these *Hilfswillige* also have relatives and peasants and that likewise these relatives and peasants must be treated as humans from the side of the German occupation power, or then the action could lead to a danger for ourselves. From the German perspective, one must reckon that the enemy sees the *Hilfswillige* movement as great danger to himself and will try hard to sharpen our behaviour towards the Russian people. Disappointments from the ranks of the *Hilfswillige* are surely to be expected, but the unit commanders and German agencies should not be discouraged by them, and superiors should be especially not tempted to let the other *Hilfswillige* suffer. The responsible agencies and superiors must stress fairness, organizational strength, understanding and care. There is naturally always a place for strictness and discipline. Arrogance and brusqueness must, however, cease; likewise snide remarks in German. Russians should, if possible, eliminate their mistakes and also reprimand them themselves, punishments for specific actions should be announced ahead of time. One must always keep in mind that the Russian is a person, who will by and large willingly work when he is treated fairly, but who also possesses a marked sensitivity.

This remarkable directive amounts to the division commander attempting to recast his soldiers' attitudes towards the Soviet population. Of course, the transformation of mentalities proved far more challenging than simply issuing orders reversing policy, and these types of decrees were impossible to enforce, especially as the increasing reliance on Nazi propaganda in 1943 and 1944 contradicted this approach (see chapter 7). Also of note in this document is the focus on *Hilfswillige*. By 1943, Soviet volunteers – either out of conviction or in hopes of receiving food and escaping the worst of German occupation policies – had become increasingly important to the army. As the following report by the 7th Infantry Division makes clear, natives now constituted significant components of German units.[39]

The infantry division has 1,448 *Hilfswillige* slots according to the combat strength table. Of these, 475 positions before 10.4.43 and 835 after 10.4.43 have been filled by *Hilfswillige*. The necessity of the employment of *Hilfswillige* is fully recognized.

The following experiences have occurred up until this time:
1) Behaviour of the *Hilfswillige*.
   The *Hilfswillige* recruited by the troops themselves (from prisoners of war and civilians) have in general shown themselves to be industrious and reliable. In contrast, the majority of the *Hilfswillige* allotted from the transit camp require supervision.
   Contrary to expectations, there was no resistance and no attempts to escape during the Buffalo Movement [see chapter 1]. The division, however, has only 475 well-chosen and watched *Hilfswillige*.
   The danger of espionage exists. Traffic between the *Hilfswillige* and local civilians cannot be stopped. The *Hilfswillige*, especially those with the supply troops, gradually get to know the entire divisional area. Indeed, how extensive the enemy's knowledge about our intentions that can be traced back to the collaboration of the *Hilfswillige* cannot be stated.
2) Division of the *Hilfswillige*
   Hilfswillige are not suitable in positions of trust. They are also not suitable in cooking and handicraft positions. In addition, they are not to

be trusted with the maintenance of German uniforms and equipment and have previously not been trained to our handicraft standard.

As drivers, co-drivers, and mechanics, they have proven themselves for Russian vehicles, not, however, for German vehicles.

When there is an existing knowledge of horses, they are suitable for riding horses and taking care of them. A good bit of understanding and attention is nonetheless missing for the care of German horses.

3) Area of Employment by the Individual Weapon Sections

Deployment with the combat troops comes into question only for a very limited number of especially chosen *Hilfswillige*.

In the baggage train of the combat troops, especially the infantry, they are likewise to be used only to a limited extent because the baggage train has to carry out numerous individual and night trips to the front positions.

On a larger scale, they can be joined into closed moving ammunition squadrons and supply troops. It must be considered, however, that an increased number of German personnel for guard duty and surveillance must be employed with the higher numbers of *Hilfswillige*.

Against this, the war in the east has brought each soldier so much additional work in road, shelter and fortification construction, that the *Hilfswillige* concentrated into *Hilfswillige* construction companies, not only ease this burden, but have become an urgent necessity.

4) Freeing Up of Combat Soldiers

The theoretical number of soldiers freed up by the employment of *Hilfswillige* cannot be reached because

a) the troops' baggage now primarily consists of soldiers who possess neither the mental nor physical preconditions to be a combat soldier.

b) the supply troops heavily consist of older age groups and last sons and so on.

c) even the baggage and supply troops must possess an element of defensive strength to defend themselves.

The following guidelines for the employment of *Hilfswillige* result from this:

1) The troops are to be supplied *Hilfswillige* not numerically, but rather according to urgently needed jobs and from well-disposed peoples.

2) *Hilfswillige* are not acceptable as cooks, hand-workers or drivers of German vehicles.

3) Some 800 *Hilfswillige* for permanent posts are suitable for an infantry division, primarily in driver and co-driver positions.

4) Each Grenadier Regiment and Engineer Battalion urgently desires a *Hilfswillige* construction company of about 120 *Hilfswillige* in addition to the 800 *Hilfswillige* in permanent posts.

The contradictions and prejudices that formed the basis of German occupation policy clearly emerge in this document. On the one hand, the army's need for Soviet manpower was quite evident and the 7th Infantry Division ordered that its men treat the volunteers as allies in the fight. On the other hand, it was evident that Germans did not entirely trust the natives in their ranks based on both experience and ideology, and the casual racism that underlay beliefs such as the Soviets being incapable of taking care of German horses or driving German vehicles meant the *Hilfswillige* were not exploited as fully as possible. Nonetheless, the integration of Soviet men into the ranks of the German army heralded a new stage in the army's approach to the war in the east.

In fact, during the Stalingrad campaign, the 24th Panzer Division even utilized Soviets for combat roles, as the following report notes:[40]

> The Division is trying to increase combat strength through all kinds of means. Numerous *Hilfswillige* are hired as craftsmen, drivers, cooks and ammunition carriers. Individuals have proven themselves as machine gunners, even entire rifle groups from Russians were formed. In this way around 700 soldiers have been freed for the front.

The shift to total war was made adamantly clear by Ninth Army (code-named Group Weiss during the planning period for Operation Citadel) in May 1943. The army command's order indicates the Germans' attempt to systematically exploit the Soviet Union's resources – food, natural resources, and manpower – in a way that far surpassed all previous measures.[41]

Special Order for the Registration and Collection of Prisoners of War, Labour Power and Plunder Seized Goods, as well as for the Military Administration

I) In General
  1) Total war demands the total employment of all labour power and the complete registration and collection of all materials important for the war. Every prisoner of war and civilian capable of labour equals a worker, every captured weapon a savings of raw material and labour output. The supply of workers to the Heimat is therefore of decisive importance. The value of prisoners of war and the maintenance of their labour power and the necessity of a complete registration and collection of seized materials are to be looked at from this point of view and made clear to all soldiers.
  2) The registration and collection of all prisoners of war, workers, and plunder seized materials will be centrally led. For this registration and collection, as well as captured goods, staffs will be deployed and equipped with sweeping powers of command, passes, external identification, and executive bodies (army sectors special army patrols). They are empowered to enforce their orders in situ.
      The captured goods and registration and collection staffs are to be supported by the troops in every respect with the postponement of their own special interests. [...]

II) Registration of Prisoners of War
  1) The prisoners of war are to be immediately shipped rearward by the troops to the divisions' prisoner of war collection points. [...]
      An overstraining of these prisoners of war must never happen. [...]

2) The selection of *Hilfswillige* for the troops occurs in the prisoner of war transit camps of Group Weiss. The divisions will be allocated *Hilfswillige*-candidates in correspondence with their vacant spots and the number of the delivered prisoners of war.

3) The treatment of POWs is to be given the necessary attention by all superiors. Sufficient food and shelter according to local circumstances is to be provided. It must be accepted by infusing into every soldier that it depends on the preserving of the labour strength of each one of the prisoners to its fullest extent. Wounded and sick prisoners are to be medically treated.

   The POWs are allowed to keep pieces of clothing and equipment (above all mess tins, drinking mugs, spoons, etc.). It is to be drummed into the heads of the POWs that they will receive no replacements for the clothes and equipment that they give away in exchange for tobacco, etc. [...]

III) Registration of Workers

With the occupation of villages and towns, all draft-age men, separated from prisoners of war, are to be collected and left to be led back in cooperation with the POW installations.

The female population capable of work is initially to be locally registered and deployed for work there.

The recruitment for the Reich Labour Action in the Reich will be carried out as soon as possible by the deployed worker registration and collection troops.

IV) Registration of Seized Goods

1) The troops can only keep seized goods required for the replenishment of their own needs, with the exception of the following guns:

   7.62cm Howitzer-canon,
   20.3cm Mortar

   The seized goods not needed for replenishment are to be obligatorily given up in the interests of other troops under the responsibility of the commander.

   Every senseless cannibalization of vehicles and weapons etc. is to cease. The troops are to be immediately instructed about this. The carrying out of this order is to be supervised.

2) The troops are already to begin with the recording and collection of captured goods if possible. [...] Especially important is the recovery of optical equipment and weapons. In addition, individual pieces from weapons, equipment and vehicles that are no longer completely useable are urgently required as replacement spare parts and for repair maintenance. Captured field kitchens are first and foremost foreseen for POW installations.

3) Captured food and fuel stocks are to be immediately reported to Group Weiss so that they can be systematically used in order to relieve the supply situation. [...]

V) Military Administration

1) In the recently occupied territories, the administration is to be established again by the Army Corps Headquarters according to the previously issued orders as soon as the situation allows for it. Orders for the transfer of rear areas to Group Weiss are to be enacted in a timely manner.

2) The following measures are to be immediately taken with the occupation of villages and towns:

   a) Registration and concentration of all draft age men (compare with III.). An immediate and thorough search for hidden Red Army men, soldiers, weapons, and ammunition, as well as enemy agents left behind, in cooperation with the Field Gendarmerie and the Secret Field Police. Over and above that, enemy radio sets, passenger pigeons, and messenger dogs are to be searched for, as the enemy has recently used dogs again for the transmission of intelligence. A careful thorough search of the planned quarters for built-in explosive charges. Above all caution by the lighting of the oven, as experience shows that explosives are not only behind doors and under carpets, but are also built into chimneys.

   b) Under the threat of the death penalty, the population is to be called upon, through posters on walls, to give up weapons and ammunition, as well as to report hidden Red Army men and people in the villages not from there. Posters will be sent to the divisions.

   c) Immediate arrest of the village elders employed by the Reds and other leading personalities and search for suspicious elements with the aid of informants [*Vertrauensleuten*].

   Enemy agents are to be immediately handed over to the Secret Field Police branch, for the quickest transfer to the *Abwehr* [German military intelligence]. As long as they can be convicted by the unit, suspicious elements are to be sentenced after the decision of an officer with the disciplinary authority of a regimental commander.

   d) As local agents, *Hilfswillige* who have already proved themselves should be deployed at first, so far as possible. They should wear civilian clothes to camouflage themselves for this purpose. A further task for these *Hilfswillige* must also be to find trustworthy people within the resident civilian population. With the selection of trustworthy people from the civilian population left behind, the greatest caution is required, especially towards such people who have already stood in German service and now voluntarily offer their services again.

3) The replacement of the village elder positions requires an especially thorough vetting of the persons selected for that position. The discrete questioning of as large as possible circle of people is the best way to avoid mistakes. The newly appointed mayor is immediately to record all inhabitants found in the town in a list of inhabitants. They are further instructed to report immediately to the nearest Wehrmacht office Red Army men and people not native to the area.

4) For the treatment of the population, the raising of labourers and so on, the previously given orders are valid. Encroachments are to be prevented under all circumstances. It depends on to again win over for German interests the population aggravated by the events of the winter.

5) Illegal collection of the population's private property or extortion of foodstuffs is plundering. Plundering is to be cracked down on with all severity. The troops are to be instructed again...

Several themes emerge in this document. First, the importance of prisoners of war for labour and for filling the ranks of the *Hilfswillige* was emphasized and with this came a demand for proper treatment of them. This suggests that similar earlier orders were not being carried out by German soldiers, as well as the fact that the army recognized the values of these men for the war effort. Second, the integration of civilian workers – both male and female – was to continue apace. Third, Germany's industrial weakness relative to its enemies led the army to implement a massive scavenging and recycling program. Finally, treatment of the surrounding population consisted of strict security practices leavened by attempts to win over hearts and minds. In many ways, the essence of German occupation goals in the Soviet Union – shorn of the ruthless anti-Semitism and anti-Bolshevism that provided the occupation with so much of its destructive energy early in the war – is captured by this order.

Six weeks later, the 7th Infantry Division – operating under the designation 407th Infantry Division during the lead-up to Operation Citadel – released its own version of Ninth Army's order to its men. Similar issues are covered in this order, as the necessity of civilians for the Reich labour action, as well as the importance of Soviet POWs and scavenged material for the war effort, was discussed. The primary difference is that the division order attempted to convince the men of the necessity German policies in the East. Equal parts cajoling and evidence based, the order placed the occupation policy of 1943 into the larger context of the entire war in hopes of persuading the individual German soldier to carry out the policies deemed necessary for victory.[42]

At this time, the need for labour in the *Heimat* and in the eastern territory is in no way covered. The consumption of raw materials is in the process of continually rising, the situation on the raw material market is critical. Both areas are of a decisive nature for the war.

Up until now, the attitude of the troops to these things in no way corresponds to their true importance. A fundamental change must be created here through continual instruction of all soldiers and officials. In particular, it is again found that our previous attitude towards Russian prisoners of war and the civilian population was incorrect and its effects have brought tremendous setbacks in the *Heimat* as well as in the eastern territory.

All threatening of the population is to be avoided in the future. The population is to be clarified about [anti-partisan] special measures through reasonable explanation, propaganda-prepared interventions of the Russian mayor, and all other available means. The appearance of brutal rape is to be avoided. All measures in the future will be uniformly guided from above to avoid individual duty stations working against one another and thereby conditionally influencing the civilian population from various points of view.

1) Labour Action

During the beginning of the Russian labour action in *Heimat* industries, there were terrible experiences that were induced by the lack of rations, clothing, and general care. The efficiency of German workers was thereby only about 30% achieved. After the elimination of these grievances, the efficiency of the Soviet workers increased to the present level of 70-130%. The illness numbers sunk to 2% against the cases of illness for German labour at 3%. In contrast, the number of illnesses in the eastern territories increased from 5.1% to 25.7% in the year 1942 as a result of a poor diet. The curve is still sloping upwards.

Care in all areas is significantly easier and better in the Reich than in the East. There are measures underway to eliminate the previously existing evil after taste with being sent for the labour action in the Reich. The East insignia that all eastern workers in the Reich had to wear previously has been abolished. The people can go out on specified days and visit public entertainment sites. The Soviet worker proves his gratitude for this care through increased labour performance.

The occupation of the eastern area demands a tremendous quantity of labour. Every time territory is gained, this number increases. Due to the existing lack of labourers, the volume of work can only be raised through an increase in the efficiency of work force labouring in the east. Through the improvement of diet and proper treatment, success has already been achieved.

Forced measures in the pursuit of labour are to be avoided. Propaganda alone must lead to the goal. The demands on labourers are absolutely to be paid. In future operations, a worker-registration and collection organization will be deployed early on. It is to be supported by the troops, in which the registration and collection of specialists is especially important.

With complete recognition of the troops' concerns in the operational area, the troops are again and again to be instructed about the labour action's decisive importance for the war. Every soldier sets an example for the population through his conduct and therefore decides in miniature the success of the labour collection action.

2) Prisoners of War

The flawed treatment of the prisoners of war in the winter 41/42 is heavily to blame for today's existing labour shortage. On top of that, these things became known in the Red Army and this led to a dramatic fall in prisoners of war and deserters. Every Russian feared captivity and fought therefore to the end. The result was an increase in our own casualties.

Before the first improvement of the prisoners of war's lots, the number of deserters had shrunk to 2-3%. After the better treatment became known, six months later it was already 17%. The proportion continues to increase. The fundamental order Nr. 13 (7. I.D. Ic Nr. 1177/43 geh., from 7.5.43) particularly emphasized a preferential treatment of deserters. This issue continues to have importance attached to it, and it will into the future as well. We must see in every deserter a future soldier for the Vlasov Army, who will help us fight, or at least be a worker who produces our weapons and ammunition.

If this thereby promotes the undermining of Russian military strength and at the same time delivers missing workers to our economy, the troops will have saved much blood in this way.

The campaign 'Russians desert to Russians' is underway. It is to be continued with all means. Its effect was weak at first, an increase is to be recorded. Its true effects will be displayed during future operations. The collaboration of the troops is to be constant and by all means necessary.

Prisoners of war and deserters are not stay with the troops in any case. According to the respective orders, they are to be sent to the division. Their quick passing on to collection camps is prepared.

In respect to the care and relief of our own industry, they are to be left their cooking plates, mugs, spoons, clothes, boots, etc. The confiscation of these things by the troops requires articles to be newly made in the *Heimat* and shipped on the long transport routes. They burden the means of transportation that is already continually strained through supply for the combat troops and troops going on leave.

The troops need to be made urgently aware of these things.

3) Captured Goods

The front cries out for weapons and equipment. Both are dependent on the availability of enough workers and sufficient raw materials (including scrap material). Presently, large amounts of weapons and equipment flow into newly established units so that sometimes our needs cannot be immediately and completely covered everywhere. We are therefore quite dependent on captured goods for this year. If the combat troops take what they need, then it doesn't count against the replenishment of its authorized strength. All accumulated goods of all types should not be left behind to deteriorate but instead they need to be reported through the channel to the divisional staff officer for weapons and equipment. The assistance of all soldiers, especially unit commanders, is absolutely necessary in consideration of its decisive importance. Russian 7.62 cm field guns and cannon and 20/30 howitzers[43] will be supplied to other fronts for deployment. Rubber-tired wheels from artillery pieces and vehicles are in no case to be taken away. [...] Not only are complete weapons important, but so is each individual piece for the repair of already available weapons.

Even the simplest soldier must know that nothing is worthless. Unnecessary destruction is to be absolutely avoided. Previous collection actions have brought undreamed of success.

In addition to this, it must again be pointed out that the soldiers' dealings with the weapons, equipment, and clothing entrusted to him leave much to be desired. There is not one Russian village in which there aren't dozens of civilians running around with pieces of German clothing (socks, sweaters, boots, underwear). The assumption that torn clothing is no longer usable is incorrect. 2 pairs of completely torn socks are as good as a new pair.

The continual repeated instruction of the troops as well as the responsible rank's supervisory authority must start here and be put swiftly right.

This order is to be destroyed after perusal by the regimental and independent battalion commanders. It is to be only passed on orally to battalion commanders by the regimental commanders.

The flip side of mobilizing the population and its resources for war was ensuring that the population did not impede the German war effort. By late 1943/ early 1944, the Soviet partisan movement had evolved into more than an irritant. It threatened the lines of communication in the rear areas, and it also became an increasing worry for the troops at the front. In response to this, Hitler and the OKW issued an order in December 1942 that demanded the army use any and all means to defeat the insurgency. By early 1943, the order had worked its way down the army's hierarchy to the divisional level.[44]

Reports submitted to the Führer [show] that individual members of the Wehrmacht who have been deployed in the fight against gangs have been later called to account due to their behaviour in combat.

Concerning this, the Führer has ordered:

1) In combat against gangs, the enemy employs fanatical, communist-schooled fighters, who shrink from no outrage. More than ever, this is about to be or not to be. This struggle no longer has anything do with soldierly chivalry or with the agreements in the Geneva Convention.

If this struggle against the gangs both in the East and in the Balkans is not conducted with the most brutal of means, the available forces will no longer suffice to master this plague in the foreseeable future.

The troops are therefore authorized and obligated to apply in this combat any means without limitation even against women and children if it will only lead to success.

Considerations, no matter the sort, are a crime against the German *Volk* and the soldiers at the front who have to bear the results of the gang attacks and who can have absolutely no understanding for any mercy towards the gangs or their followers.

These principles must also rule the application of 'Combat Directive for Anti-Partisan Warfare in the East.'

No German deployed in anti-partisan warfare will be called to account either for non-judicial punishment or with a court martial *due to his conduct in the struggle against the gangs and their followers.*

The commanders of the troops deployed in anti-partisan warfare are therefore responsible that:

all officers in subordinate units are promptly instructed about this order in the most emphatic way;

their legal advisors immediately receive notice of this order;
no judgments shall be confirmed that contradict this order.

In many ways, this order only sanctioned what was already occurring on the ground all across the front. Such practices, however, were not the only ways in which the army responded to the growing insurgency. The following January 1943 report by the 207th Security Division provides a snapshot of the problems faced by this unit and how it responded to them.[45]

General Situation:
I) Estonia: Cases of sabotage against telephone lines have recently increased. In some cases, it could be simple thievery, as sabotage cannot be irreproachably proven.

Flares have again been observed in connection with enemy aircraft incursions.

Scattered enemy air incursion planes have also dropped bombs without, however, causing any appreciable damage.

A larger fire broke out in a horse stall in the horse rehabilitation home in Värska [...] in which considerable damage was done to the horses. Presumably sabotage, an investigation is underway. Otherwise, the situation is unchanged.

II) Russian Area
a) Field Commandant area Gdov: At the end of the reporting period in Field Commandant (V) 611 Gdov, further scattered appearances of small troops of plundering gangs, 12–20km northeast, east and southeast of Polna.

Increased incursions of enemy aircraft, flares are also seen at the same time. Bombing from the planes was also noted; however, they fell in open terrain and caused no damage.

The train station in Gdov (a wooden shed) burned down. Cause: presumably a defect in the chimney.

b) Local Commandant – Pleskau [Pskov] area
On the eastern border of the local commandant area and in the area of the adjacent neighbouring divisions, large joint actions were commenced against the strong gangs that had cropped up. Gangs were repeatedly met. The bandits suffered considerable casualties in dead and wounded during combat. In this way, the gangs dispersed and withdrew to the north and northeast. At the end of the report period, no gangs were noticeable in the area.

Incursions of enemy aircraft and bombings have increased. Pleskau [Pskov] was bombed multiple times. Negligible damage to the south airfield and the train station. Numerous large fires have been noted in Pleskau [Pskov], including one in which a large garage burned down. Causes of the individual fires have not yet been determined. Presumably sabotage, investigations are underway.

In Detail:

I)   Estonia:

Paratrooper taken prisoner:	2
Paratrooper shot:	1
Gang helper, already reported, shot after conclusion of interrogation:	4
Sabotage or thievery of telephone wires:	8
Parachutes with loaded bags observed:	2 [...]
Balloons armed with explosives:	2 [...]
Bombings:	2 [...]
Fires:	1 (in Värska where 26 horses burned to death, 12 were severely injured and 19 were lightly injured)
	In addition, a fire in the oil shale plant Kiviolo. Cause: gross negligence of the worker proven

II)   Russian Area:

Firefights:	16 (of which four were [partisan] attacks)
Gang members shot in battle:	25
Gang members taken prisoner:	7
Gang members, already reported, shot after the conclusion of their interrogation:	21
	(includes 6 members of the earlier reported 17 member terror organization Gdov; 7 of these were given to the SD and 4 were released)
Civilians shot due to crimes:	4

Own losses: Dead: 3 (Estonians), Wounded: 7 (1 German, 2 Estonians, and 4 EKA [local combat section]

Captured Goods: 4 sub-machine guns, 1 light machine gun, 1 rifle (German), 6 rifles, 15 hand grenades, 900 rounds rifle ammunition, 15 pairs of skis and explosives

Rail detonations:	1
Thwarted rail detonations:	3
Bombing raids:	17 (of which 12 on Pleskau [Pskov])
In which dead:	1
Wounded:	4 (2 German soldiers)
Fires:	7 (during a fire in a large garage, 12 trucks were burned up with 2 trailers and communication equipment)

As the document indicates, German rear-area formations spent much of their time securing economic installations and resources, in addition to their more proactive patrols and raids on real and suspected partisan camps. While many of the army's anti-partisan operations during the war proved to be nothing more than murderous actions that targeted civilians and created 'dead zones' in which nothing remained that could support an insurgency, the 207th Security Division clearly engaged an actual enemy in northwest Russia. Equally clearly, the division neither waged a brutal war of extermination against partisans and their supporters, nor did it attribute every accident to a ubiquitous insurgency. Its treatment of captured partisans, however, spoke to the general attitude towards Soviet civilians that permeated the army.

While the fight against insurgents constituted the primary task for rear-area units, frontline units were also frequently forced to carry out missions against partisan units in their rear in order to secure their lines of communication. The following order issued by the 126th Infantry Division in December 1943 highlighted the seriousness with which the army approached partisan war. The German way of war emerges in this document, with its emphasis on decisive leadership, the importance of speed and mobility, and the necessity of destroying the enemy's means of survival.[46]

Advice for the Partisan Hunt
1) Only the active partisan hunt leads to success. Decisive and energetic NCOs are to be divided as leaders of the hunt patrols. They receive their orders from the division or the town commandant.
2) The hunt patrol follows the same tactics as the bandit. It never goes on streets and never through villages; rather it goes aside from these through forest and swamp. Every movement has to take place silently. It can only work with signals and whispered speech. The patrols also never go on the same path as the day before. They scout out bandit paths and trails and [then observe by] listen[ing] in on them.
3) All remote lying huts, hide outs and earthen bunkers that could offer the bands shelter are to be destroyed by the patrols. Everything that could support life must be taken from the bandits.
4) Attire and equipment for the patrols must be adjusted to their mission. Everything that is unnecessary is to be left behind. Weapons and equipment are to be worn so that they don't rattle (see item 2). With increasing depth of snow, the patrols must be able to move on skis.

5) The bandit always has the carelessness of the German soldier to thank for his success. When he can avoid it, he doesn't fight. When he receives surprising fire, he almost always scampers off; the same thing when he realizes that the opponent that he meets is prepared for defence. All patrols must have their weapons ready to fire at all times. When advancing near bandits, fire cover is especially important.

6) When the patrol ambushes a bandit troop, it must know that almost always the bandit leader marches in the front; in the second position is generally the Politruk. What marches behind the bandit [leaders] is generally not important.

The bandit loves flanking manoeuvres; he often only apparently retreats. Therefore security for the flanks!

A further piece of German occupation policy in 1943 – one that was closely connected with its anti-partisan and labour mobilization policies, as well as its scorched earth retreats – was its increasing use of forced evacuations of Soviet communities. In all three cases, the Germans wanted to both deny the Soviets' – the Red Army or partisans – manpower and use that same manpower for its own purposes. By this point in the war, the evacuation of civilians had become part of German combat divisions' everyday activities. As this order issued by the 7th Infantry Division in preparation for its participation in the 'Buffalo Movement' – the scorched earth retreat out of the Rzhev salient – indicates frontline divisions were intimately involved with this aspect of German occupation practice.[47]

1) It is planned to evacuate:
   a) workers between 13 and 50 years old preferably without dependents.
   b) local auxiliary police and all those people in service and interests of the Wehrmacht and their dependents
   c) the population on both sides of the new position, namely 15km east of it and 5km west of it

2) All evacuees are to be left cattle and foodstuffs so long as they can carry it on the marches. In particular, all available horses, sleds and wheeled vehicles are to be left to the civilians for the transport of foodstuffs and the necessary household goods.

3) Male inhabitants, who appeared to be suitable as *Hilfswillige*, can be kept with the troops. After a probationary period, they can transfer into the *Hilfswillige* units, as long as they have already declared for it.

4) All food stocks, so long as they cannot be definitely allocated among the troops, are to be used to provide the population being evacuated with food for the march. The sections of the population remaining in their villages are only to be left the absolute minimum.

   The evacuated population is to be left livestock (milk cows and small livestock) to secure their supply during the march and in their new area, while the section of the population left behind is allowed only a few milk cows for the supply of milk for children and the sick.

5) It is to be guaranteed that the evacuated section of the population is able to keep all its livestock and property that it carries with it and that nothing

is taken away so that it is possible for them to participate in the spring cultivation and partially secure its own supplies for the coming year in their allocated area. The slaughtering of pigs and small livestock should be permitted for those being led to the rear, if necessary.

6) In those areas where the food stocks ordered for supply are not fully used, they can be transferred to the troops.

The available cattle in the divisional areas – as long as it is not needed for the supply of the evacuating civilian population or to cover the most vital needs of the section of the population remaining behind – is to be made immediately available for butchering and use through the administratively responsible unit.

The independent collection of beef cattle by individual units remains prohibited and is to be prevented through the sharpest measures. Discipline suffers through uncontrollable slaughtering and requisitioning and a fair distribution is therefore made impossible.

While forced evacuations could result in chaotic upheavals for the civilians involved, as numerous deportations hastily took place with insufficient food or transport, others, such as this one, were well-planned and demonstrated the army's desire to utilize them for the German war effort. The document also highlights the German emphasis on ensuring that the area's economic goods would be kept from the advancing Red Army.

German occupation policy in the Soviet Union was thus in constant evolution between 1941 and 1944. At times, ideologically-inspired ruthlessness motivated the Germans to murder and starve millions of Soviet civilians under their control. This was contrasted by periods in which the army carried out more conciliatory policies designed to help civilians survive the rigours of occupation and hopefully contribute to the German war effort. Two constants, however, ran throughout the period of occupation. First, the mobilization of the Soviet Union's material and manpower resources was the predominant concern of the army's occupation policy. Second, violence remained the army's primary means of dealing with the civilian population. Even during periods when the army attempted to win over the hearts and minds of the civilian population, the threat of violence remained present and the increasing partisan movement only exacerbated this tendency. The final document in this section demonstrates how engrained and matter of fact the application of mortal violence had become to the *Ostheer*.[48]

Civilians who clearly flee the approach of German soldiers are to be immediately shot. At a closer distance, they should first be called out to. If the appeal is obeyed, they are to be arrested and delivered to the [Staff] Section Ic.

Likewise all civilians are to be shot that attempt to oppose or escape any such measures, including evacuations.

This order is to be made known through the village elders in all towns and villages that have not been evacuated.

Chapter 6

Sustaining the German Army in the East – Replacements and Training

This chapter will look at three issues: how German troops were trained for their service in the east, what kind of replacements were sent to the Eastern front, and finally what measures the army undertook in addition to sending reinforcements in order to cover the high losses suffered during the war in the Soviet Union.

The German army was spilt into two main organizations: the Field Army for operations and the Replacement Army for recruitment and training. This relatively clear line between the institutions increasingly blurred as the war dragged on, especially due to developments on the Eastern front. The call for more men led to the forming of Reserve Divisions and Field Training Divisions, which were first created in mid-1942 and used for rear security, occupation tasks, anti-partisan warfare and coastal guard duty in the west, thereby freeing up forces for combat tasks in the east. On the other hand, decreasing time devoted to training, as well as a lack of weapons and equipment in the Replacement Army, denied a proper training to the recruits. Furthermore, the high losses of low-level leaders could not be replaced adequately. All of this forced frontline units to take over increasing numbers of training tasks.

The length of this basic training differed during the course of the war, not only according to crisis situations, but also between the different branches of the army. Twelve to sixteen weeks were usual for riflemen, with eight weeks the absolute minimum, while panzer crew members trained for sixteen to twenty-one weeks. Due to a permanent flow of information, as well as continual exchanges of officers, NCOs and men, the Replacement Army was kept well informed about the training necessities (although, as we will see, the question of achieving such necessities is altogether different). The information was channelled and summarized in guidelines for basic training every three to six months. The following source is the first such guideline from October 1941.[1] The introduction of the guidelines stresses a training that prepares for the conditions in the east by acclimating the soldiers to a spartan life and giving them a sense of the war (including the enemy's typical behaviour) to overcome the first shock of the battlefield. At the same time, a feeling of superiority needed to be inculcated into the soldiers. This was an essential, yet often underestimated, aspect of German combat power and motivation. German soldiers would often fight in nearly hopeless situations, their confidence based on their belief in their own superiority as soldiers, as well as on willpower. Both attitudes were part of the education of the soldier (in comparison to the rather technical training on weapons and tactics).

1) The experiences of this war, especially of the campaign in the East, are to be used extensively for the training and education of the Replacement Army. It is essential that the Field Army's experiences are brought to life in the training of the Replacement Army. The training must carry the whiff of war and be conducted so that after the conclusion of basic training, the recruit can be appointed to the field troops as a full-fledged fighter based on attitude, hardness, agility and military skill. Therefore, the imparting of these war experiences must initially take into account the recruit's meagre powers of imagination and, with progressive training, allow him to grow into the life and spirit of a good field soldier and into modern combat. It is essential therefore that the self-confidence of the recruit is raised and that the conviction is roused that the German soldier can cope with *any* adversary and any difficult and dangerous situation through determined action, well-considered use of his weapon and his own courage.

2) The utilisation of war experiences can occur in following ways:

   a) Drawing on war experienced officers and NCOs. These include: lectures by combatants, preferably with sketches or at the board, with the use of slides on small combat sections and individual deeds, the use of front reports and *Wochenschauen* [weekly propaganda movies] of the propaganda companies in a similar way, and stories at comradely gatherings, to give the recruits a vivid and clear picture of war's reality.

   b) Transfer those insights gained from under section a) into similar combat exercises, that correspond as near as possible to reality. Hereby the assigned enemy has to conduct themselves as the Russians or English fight. A short compilation on the Russians' combat practices, as far as they concern small tactics, is produced in Appendix 1. The combat practices of the British are similar especially in their toughness und tenacity, their good camouflage, observation of the combat area and their devious conduct of war.

   c) In all branches the recruits must be educated to *hardness*. This hardness must find its expression in the will and the ability to bear hardships, such as long marches, simple quarters, meagre rations and inhospitable climate, and in the determination and self-confidence that are also necessary to carry forward an attack against a stronger opponent until the enemy's destruction and to hold one's ground in the defence against an opponent superior in number and weapons. [...]

   d) Prepare the recruits of all branches on the combat practices of the opponent, especially on the possibility of raids at any time, day or night, and at every opportunity. This training must be handled, so that after the basic training the soldier cannot be confounded by anything and is not surprised by even a very unusual situation.

In addition to these general guidelines, the issues most important for each specific type of formation were also transmitted within each unit. Those for the infantry and motorized infantry are compiled below:

The following areas of training are to be carried out with special emphasis:

1) *Observation* of the combat area, recognition and addressing of targets, becoming familiar with the terrain, and estimation of distances.
2) *Orientation* in terrain day and night without maps, with simple sketches, compass, by sun and stars.
3) Reconnaissance patrol and stealth exercises [...]
4) In the attack, use of one's own heavy weapons and artillery fire or artificial fog to advance. During a break-in, firing on the move and assaulting with the will to destroy the enemy who does not surrender in close combat. Increased close combat training with all available means and weapons. [...]
5) Combat in woods and for and in villages is to be increasingly practiced.
6) Night training and training in fog to acclimatise the recruit to these types of combat are especially necessary. While doing so, seeing, hearing, movement and orientation at twilight and during the night, reconnaissance patrol missions, attacks, raids and defence against them, security and sentry service.
7) Defence: Construction of the position according to [Infantry Training] Manual 130/11 with a considered adaptation to the terrain, skilful camouflage and use of spade. Increased use of changing positions for light machine guns and all heavy infantry weapons. Educate [the men] that there could be big holes by neighbour[ing units] in the defence of broad front sections, which have to be mastered by fire, sealing off and counter attacks. The enemy who has broken into our positions also has to be destroyed by heavy weapons in close combat. The positions of heavy weapons, especially anti-aircraft guns, are to be selected as 360 degree defence. [...]
8) Defence against tanks. No tank fright can arise among the infantry. He must know that he is protected in the tank foxhole and that he is in the position to destroy tanks with his equipment. [...]
9) Fire effectiveness with all weapons is to increase. The primary emphasis should be placed on combat firing exercises[2] against well camouflaged targets. Also firing at twilight or in the night is to be especially practiced. Every recruit must master his weapon to perfection even under the most difficult situations. The training with the M.G. 34 is to be promoted with stronger emphasis. Care and maintenance of weapons are an important area of training. Good riflemen are to be trained with the telescopic sight and the semi-automatic rifles.
10) The defence against aircraft with infantry weapons is of special importance. Air attacks are not to be passively endured. [...]
11) Marches are not only carried out on roads, but also on lanes and cross country with available equipment. In principle, all marches are to combine a tactical idea with constant combat exercises. Night marches are to be practiced often.
12) Physical exercises are to be adapted to the training area, for example, cross country running for habituation to continuous activity, hand grenade throwing in regards to close combat and so on.

German basic training aimed for soldiers who mastered their weapons, could work together with other weapons and types of units, had an eye for the terrain, and could act independently, the last being a general principle of the German army since the pre-First World War era. Issues especially stressed as a consequence of the campaign in the east included defensive positions, unit defence against tanks and aircraft, and night fighting. Such issues had rarely arisen in the short campaigns of 1939 and 1940, as German forces were primarily on the offensive, encountered few enemy attacks and profited from air superiority, if not air supremacy. In the east, many units already had to go over to the defensive temporarily in the first months, as demonstrated in chapter 1. The sheer size of the theatre, as well as the fluidity of the combat situation, did not allow for a continuous front line, and so many advancing German units were attacked by Soviet tanks or aircraft. The Red Army was also more accustomed to night fighting. Additional issues that became important were described in chapter 3.

Men trained in the Replacement Army were formed into march battalions, numbering up to 1,000 men, to be sent to the front. The German army was organized territorially, which meant that German divisions were connected to a clearly defined area from which to draw recruits. The replacement units functioned as an intermediate level between the field unit and the recruitment area. So, for example, the 73rd Infantry Division originated from Military District XIII (Nuremberg), which consisted primarily of Franconia. Its Infantry Regiment 170 received replacements from Infantry Replacement Battalion 170, its Artillery Regiment from Artillery Replacement Battalion 173, and its Engineer Battalion from Engineer Replacement Battalion 17. This connection was vitally important for the combat power of the German army. Field units were bound to a territory, allowing them to draw from the traditions and symbols of that region. It also enhanced the units' cohesion, as soldiers from the same region shared comparable values and identities.[3] This explains the relatively high effort the army directed towards maintaining this system. Furthermore, the ties between the field and replacement units allowed for an exchange of personnel, which increased the realistic nature of combat training, as well as giving war-weary men an opportunity to take a break from the front. Finally, and perhaps most importantly, the men trained in the replacement units were already acquainted with the men with and under whom they would fight in future. So, integration into the field unit started with basic training, an important factor for the unit's cohesion.

There was a second type of replacement unit, the so-called convalescent companies. These consisted of men so severely wounded or ill that they had to be sent back to Germany for recuperation and recovery. They were collected and retrained (or used as trainers, depending on their rank) at the replacement unit and then sent forward. These men, combat experienced and already well integrated into their units, were of high value for the divisions. Only officers and a few specialists were sent individually or in small groups to the front.

This system worked well during the short campaigns of 1939 to 1941, when periods of quick, intensive operations alternated with longer periods of rest and refitting. Few replacements had to be integrated during an operation or campaign, and if this was carried out in a defective manner, it had only a minor impact. The moulding and training of new low-level leaders, as well as specialist training, was carried out between campaigns and not within the framework of combat divisions, but instead in the Replacement Army. This idea prevailed in the German military apparatus in summer 1941, since the German military leadership expected another short campaign. As it became clear in autumn 1941 that at least a second campaign would be necessary in 1942 to finally destroy the Red Army, the first adjustments were planned. But at this stage, the massive losses in men and leaders, combined with the permanent logistical crisis – which did not allow the movement of replacements in significant numbers – led to a near collapse of the German replacement system. In response, the German military expanded the Replacement Army. In 1941, for every soldier in the Replacement Army, three were in the Field Army; by 1942, this ratio approached two soldiers in the Field Army for one in the Replacement Army. Therefore the Replacement Army was expanded by 50 per cent in size.[4] This quantitative expansion and the demands for replacements from the front troops had consequences for the quality of the replacements, which increasingly became a source of complaints by field units, as the following sources from 1942 show. The first is from Engineer Battalion 173, subordinated to 73rd Infantry Division, fighting in the Novorossiysk area:[5]

There were some suitable men in the replacements. A large part, however, is almost unfit for front service due to physical ailments (hardness of hearing etc.) or susceptibility to diseases (age group 1907). The replacements' level of training is not sufficient in terms of engineer tasks and military basic training.

In addition to the lack of both adequate basic and specialist training, the first signs of the evanescent German manpower pool appeared, with the need to send men to the front with physical handicaps.

More detailed in describing the training deficiencies of freshly arrived replacements is the following report by 8th Panzer Division, fighting under Army Group North's command:[6]

The training of the replacements shows considerable gaps in all branches. The shortcomings that have arisen are not only traced back to carelessness and the individual's lack of discipline, but reveal a cursory and hasty training.

In detail:

1) Weapons training

The soldiers are not yet fully familiar with their weapons. By far the largest part of the replacements is, for example, not able to disassemble the lock of the rifle with certainty, to fix the magazine butt plate, or to carry out the exercises of loading and securing properly according to regulations. 40% of the recruits are not trained on light machine guns. Of the remaining 60%, only a few are adept at handling the machine gun, such as changing the barrel and lock, [and] the detection and elimination of jamming.

Of the replacements distributed to the heavy mortars, only a very few people had previous knowledge.

The greater part of the replacements is neither informed on the use of the stick grenade 24, nor is it trained in throwing it.

On the other hand, the ATG and light infantry gun riflemen had training on the gun.

2) Training in firing

In training in firing, considerable deficiencies occur, particularly in the most elementary things, such as loading and securing, taking up the slack of the trigger, and all types of combat firing positions. Furthermore, the firing technique and the calmness during targeting must be significantly improved. This applies to the same extent for shooting with the rifle, as well as with the light machine gun.

3) Utilization of terrain

Here, the replacements lack the quick confident eye for the favourable position. In the use of entrenching tools, as well as in the camouflage of their own entrenching work, great deficiencies are evident, especially with regard to the experience gained in the deployment in the East. The use of the prismatic compass is only mastered by a few, map knowledge generally does not exist.

4) Group training must be characterized as insufficient. Collaboration and the ability to move in a closed unit are nowhere to be seen. It must be begun with the simplest forms of deployment and development exercises.

5) The mental and physical condition of the replacements is average. The replacements consists of 2/3 *Reichsdeutschen* and 1/3 *Volksdeutschen* (resettlers from Bessarabia, Romania, Poland). A part of these *Volksdeutschen* has strong language difficulties. Among them are some illiterates. 2/3 of the replacements are from the birth years 1922-1924 and 1/3 of the men are over 27 years old. Above all, the older cohort is particularly vulnerable and weak and will only gradually adapt to the suddenly changed circumstances. The good will to cooperate and the willingness to serve are universally present. All recruits show keen interest in the training.

To sum up: Regarding the actual state of training of the replacements, the division considers a thorough three-week training necessary, followed by an additional two-week training in the front before any deployment for attack.

There were hugely important gaps in the training, such as an insufficient understanding of weapons, especially with the light machine gun that formed the backbone of the German infantry's firefight tactics. Crews for heavy infantry weapons were also unevenly trained and were generally not ready for combat. But even with the soldier's individual weapon, many training deficiencies existed, including targeting, combat use and maintenance. These flaws severely undermined the individual feeling of superiority, as the German soldier in the field missed his target or experienced a jammed weapon in the firefight due to lack of cleaning and oiling his rifle or machine gun. Complaints about the inability to use terrain and the building of positions are also interesting, as these were clearly stressed in the training guidelines from autumn 1941, as seen above. Finally, the physical and intellectual quality of the replacements, in this case the forwarding of Germans from different regions outside of Germany (often pejoratively called 'booty Germans'), who often spoke broken German and therefore had problems in following training exercises, was also noted in the report. On the flip side, the Panzer troops profited from being favoured when it came to replacements.

They often received younger men, here represented by 2/3rds of the replacements between the ages of eighteen and twenty years old.

A third report from 186th Grenadier Regiment – the regiment mentioned in chapter 2 in conjunction with Werner Ziegler while fighting in Novorossiysk – shows a sinking combat morale of the replacements not fully overcome by their formation while in the Replacement Army. More strikingly, it precisely explains the consequences of the adding replacements of dubious quality:[7]

The replacements were not suitable as a result of their low combat experience. Especially striking is the general phenomenon that the replacement men lacked combat will and enthusiasm, drive and hardness. While they overestimated the effect of enemy defensive fire during the attack, in which the example of their leader did not motivate them to advance faster, they are not nearly active enough in defence. Instead of engaging every opponent, they keep quiet out of fear of betraying their position to the enemy through their fire. The burden of fighting lays mainly with the old soldiers, whose conduct is admirable. In contrast to the old fighters, the replacements strive to leave the frontline with just about any minor wound or sickness. The best part of the unit's regulars, who could have had an educational effect on the replacements, has become casualties. The remainder of the old men, which as before is still dutiful, is incapable of having an educational effect on the replacement due to the constant employment in such a state of mind. This is a phenomenon that is attributed to fatigue and the overstraining of nerves. With appropriate rest and relaxation, this phenomenon can be rectified. In this period of rest it could be possible for the company commander, through many lectures, conversations, and lessons, to enhance the inner firmness of the replacements, their enthusiasm and combat joy. The necessity to educate the replacements to hardness, to carry out intensive training under special consideration of mountain warfare and Russian combat conditions, must thereby not be disregarded.

The lack of both quantitatively and qualitatively adequate replacements therefore led to a burnout of units, as well as the loss of an experienced and high-quality core.

It became increasingly difficult to replace those men who formed a formation's backbone and additionally fulfilled the important roles of integrating replacements. This issue, which first arose in 1942, was more of a problem for the infantry divisions, who were rather low on the list of replacement priorities. The majority of the best and most motivated men went as volunteers earlier into military service. These men frequently chose the Luftwaffe, Waffen-SS or U-Boat service, and those going to the army generally went to the Panzer troops. While many of those men would have made good NCOs or even officers, the consequences of an unbalanced distribution were units packed with many over-qualified soldiers, who could not be promoted due to the lack of positions, while other units suffered from a lack of men able to become even NCOs. This was certainly the case with the regular infantry divisions. Further strain came from the tendency of each service branch to form its own ground forces. The surplus personnel of the Luftwaffe that was transferred into the ill-fated *Luftwaffen-Feld-Divisionen* (Air Force Field

Divisions) – essentially infantry divisions with excellent soldiers, but poorly trained for ground combat and led by officers and generals unfamiliar with this type of fighting – was only the first such step. The expansion of the Waffen-SS, which accelerated in 1943, also drained personnel from the army, both in quantity and in quality. In combination with a strategy of forming permanent new units instead of feeding the existing ones, this led directly to the already mentioned infantry crisis, breaking the backbone of the German field army. The final blow for the traditional units and the system beyond came with the massive losses in summer 1944 and the command changes after the 20 July plot. This included the formation of the so-called *Volksgrenadier* Divisions under the newly appointed Chief of Replacement Army, *Reichsführer-SS* Himmler. The German army afterwards was only a shadow of its former itself, and comparisons with other armies after this period of time only have minor relevance in discussing combat power.[8]

Another issue of replacements emerged in the winter 1941/42 when the German army had to adapt to the changing nature of war, namely those of low-level leaders and specialists, as mentioned in the source below:[9]

> The time that is available for the division after its relocation to a suitable area for refreshing will be tightly measured and must be completely utilized.
>
> The most important preparatory work is the development of instructors, NCOs and specialists. Due to the high losses in the division especially in this regard, the accelerated commencement of this training is especially urgent.
>
> Therefore all troop sections are to organize immediately *courses for the training of NCOs, instructors and specialists*. All *instructors* for this purpose should only be divided among completely suitable officers and NCOs, who have conspicuously proven themselves and preferably have some success in this field. The lack of suitable teaching personnel makes it necessary to consolidate the training courses in the panzer regiment, the artillery regiment, and the rifle regiments as well as the rifle brigade. This brings with it the advantage of the standardization of training.
>
> As long as the teachers belong to the front-line sections of the division, their withdrawal is to be immediately requested at the division. [...]
>
> For the selection of the *course participants*, proving themselves before the enemy is above all decisive. [...]
>
> A duration of some 4 weeks is initially foreseen for the training courses. [...]
>
> By 12.1.42, the Rifle Brigade 8, Panzer Regiment 10, Artillery Regiment 80, Tank Engineer Battalion 59, Anti-tank Battalion 43, Tank Signal Battalion 84, Light Anti-aircraft Battalion 92 have to report to the division: a) the place where courses are held, b) the date of commencement, (c) the [personnel] strength of the courses.
>
> By 16.1.42, the training plans have to be submitted to the division.

To rapidly provide the necessary low-level leaders as well as specialists, the German military leadership reacted in its typical manner, namely by decentralizing the process. Instead of building up courses at home in the Replacement Army, which was already overstrained by the demands for more recruits and its own expansion, frontline units should choose men that had proven themselves in the last month under front conditions and train them right behind the front. This saved travel time, which could easily take several weeks for the men to travel back and forth, as well as administrative work. It also had the advantage of instituting a warlike training that fulfilled the demands of the frontline units. While these initial courses in winter 1942 were improvised, they were quickly institutionalized in most divisions, often in the so-called divisional combat school. The task of the combat school was described as follows:[10]

1) The combat school's objective is the development of independently acting, clear thinking, versatile, decisive and energetic NCOs, whose character paired with passion and technical as well as small tactical skills to convince and electrify subordinates and is example to them.
2) In addition to the use of their own weapons, all NCOs are to learn to cooperate with the heavy weapons that fight with them. Here, especially NCOs of the heavy weapons are to train in the flexible control of fire and in the rapid forming of fire concentrations. The NCOs of the Grenadier companies are to learn above all the immediate exploitation of fire.
3) Candidates for platoon- and group leaders are to drill in the technical handling of weapons and equipment, in close-combat and destroying tanks and in the giving of commands, as well as be instructed in the training of subordinates.
4) To that effect, those trained in the combat school include a) especially proven *Unteroffiziere* to platoon leaders, b) young, inexperienced *Unterroffiziere* and older good *Gefreite*, in special cases also Grenadiers, to group leaders, c) young, inexperienced *Unteroffiziere* and *Gefreite* of the machine gun, infantry gun and ATG companies to commanders of their weapons and group leaders.

At a divisional level, only the lowest level of leadership – the NCO – was trained. But as one can see from the tasks they were responsible for, NCOs had very different roles in the German army than in most other armies of the time, especially in tactical leadership. Officers, primarily company and battalion commanders, were trained in courses at Army or Army Group level, also a newly introduced innovation begun in winter 1942.

These two developments – the need for additional training for newly arriving recruits and the decentralized training of low-level leaders – as well as the need for training with newly introduced weapons, made training capabilities in the field units necessary. The divisional combat school was one such step, while others were taken in the field replacement battalion. It was the field replacement battalion that finally became the training facility for divisions in the east, as the following source shows:[11]

1) Purpose of field replacement battalions:
 The field replacement battalion is the 'field training battalion' and at the same time the personnel reserve of the Eastern army's divisions.
 With the field replacement battalion, the divisions should be given the opportunity by evaluating combat experiences to:

A) train arriving replacements to become full-fledged Eastern fighters,
B) train group and platoon leaders for their demands,
C) Further training for the front fighters – especially through attack training – and to train specialists of all kinds.

As losses are the heaviest with the infantry and the engineers, the main task of the field replacement battalion is to train infantry and engineer replacements and sub-leaders.

To A): Newly arriving replacements, such as march companies, convalescent companies, etc., are to be trained in each division for several weeks in the field replacement battalion, as long as the combat situation allows for it, before deploying in the front. The same applies to the training of NCOs, who are supplied from the Replacement Army and are not yet suitable as a group or platoon leader as a result of their previous use. It is also not possible for the Replacement Army to fully train the replacements on automatic weapons (especially the machine gun) due to the lack of such weapons. The missing training is to be supplemented in the field replacement battalion.

To B): The formation of platoon and group leaders (sub-leader training) is of decisive importance in the present state of numerous divisions and in the continuing duration of the war. In consequence, divisional combat schools have been established in infantry divisions, light infantry divisions, and mountain divisions. The divisional combat schools are to be incorporated into the field replacement battalion. They count as a company. The commander of the divisional combat school (B-position)[12] can be used as commander of the field replacement battalion depending on suitability.

To C): Due to the duration of the positional warfare, it is also necessary to develop the older front fighters for other types of combat. In this case 'attack training' is of particular importance. If there are personnel reserves (leader reserve[13]) in the field replacement battalion, the same applies to them. The introduction of new weapons [and] the need for specialists of all kinds requires the implementation of special courses in the field replacement battalion. Furthermore, the field replacement battalion can be utilized to train the alarm units. All kinds of combat experiences can be evaluated by further trials in the field replacement battalion.

The structure of the field replacement battalion must therefore be adapted to the respective situation.

2) Training subjects:
In the case of an overabundance of subjects, the emphasis should be placed on:
Reconnaissance patrols and assault group activity
Co-operation of all infantry weapons
Close-combat training,
Anti-tank close combat,
Sniper training,
Night fighting.

At the same time, the field replacement battalion is the winter combat school of the division.

3) Structure

The field replacement battalion is to consist of the battalion staff and 2 to 5 companies. Only the command, instruction and supply personnel are fixed in the unit, while the personnel to be trained are subject to considerable changes, depending on the deployment and situation of the division. Thus, for example, the following structure may be appropriate for a division to which a march battalion had been recently added:

Staff

2 training companies for infantry training,

1 training company for heavy infantry weapons training,

1 company [at the] disposal [of the commander] (engineer training, signal training, other specialists),

1 sub-leader company (divisional fighting school)

On the other hand, it is possible that in another division, to which no march battalion or replacements were added, the field replacement battalion consists only of

1 sub-leader company (divisional combat school),

1 company [at the] disposal [of the commander] (training of specialists of all kinds),

1 company for close combat and assault group training (men removed from the front for advanced training).

4) In particular, the following is pointed out:

The training of the sub-leaders must continue independently of all combat operations.

The most appropriate officers and NCOs are to be appointed as instructors, especially to set up and get used to each other in the first training period.

Anti-gas training belongs to the basic training of every soldier and is therefore also to be pursued in the field replacement battalion.

The field replacement battalion can only fully fulfill its task of being the field training battalion of the division when the leadership does not deploy the battalion prematurely in critical situations for combat, but pursues the training as planned independent of the situation.

In addition to further training for replacements and NCOs, the Field Replacement Battalion was also not only the unit where new weapons and tactics could be tested, but also a place for the further training of men whose long stretch in the trenches had decreased their effectiveness in offensive actions. The training for newly arrived replacements in the field replacement battalion allowed for their step by step integration into frontline units, as well as for the men to adapt to conditions in the Soviet Union. When the combat situation allowed for such a period, units that carried out these programmes clearly suffered fewer losses of new men when they were again engaged in combat. But even when armed with such knowledge, German units were often forced to deploy the field replacement battalion in crisis situations or to release the replacements prematurely to the front. The demand to train NCOs independently of combat action was often impossible due to the lack of men. Interestingly, the training issues stressed did not appreciably differ from the 1941 guidelines.

In addition to filling units with individual replacements, complete units were also sent to the east. Up to mid-1943, these were mostly full divisions. A first wave of divisions was sent to the Soviet Union in the 1941/42 winter crisis to fill gaps across the front. A second wave arrived in the east in spring and early summer 1942 for the German summer offensive. This wave included many allied units. A third and final wave was sent eastward from late November 1942 on to stem the Soviet offensive in the south. After these three waves, only a few new divisions were sent eastward, mostly rebuilt units such as numerous divisions destroyed in Stalingrad. Allied threats in the Mediterranean and on the Channel coast in 1943 drew most newly formed divisions to those regions. The introduction of new troops, however, caused many problems, in some cases due to the composition of the units, while others were due to the special conditions in the east, as the following autumn 1942 report by Sixth Army illustrates:[14]

1) The mistakes ascertained in the report of the Second Army about the formation of divisions with three hundred numbers also occurred in the divisions of the same type subordinated to the Sixth Army. In the case of future new formations, it is then necessary to avoid:

   composition of almost only short-service, men classified as indispensable, numerous fathers with many children and last sons,

   formation by cadre personnel mostly inexperienced in the East, including officers,

   too brief and deficient infantry combat training.

   It proved to be disadvantageous to order the few useful instructors to Döberitz and Jüterbog. Dispatching of a school's instruction troop to the divisions would have been better.

   Equipment with too little motorized transport capacity (only 1 small truck column), with horse-drawn bakery companies, with only one workshop platoon, with heavy military carriages instead of light commercial ones, with too many types (about 100) French motor vehicles and with horses that are too heavy, and thus unsuitable for the East;

   Equipping [the unit] with horses and motor vehicles too late, so that it was no longer possible for the operating personnel to practice before employment.

2) In spite of these deficiencies, the 300-numbered divisions subordinated to the Sixth Army have proven themselves effective not only in attack, but also generally in defence.

3) In order to remedy the identified shortcomings during the winter:

   A) Ruthless eradication of all unsuitable leaders and an increased replacement rate of men with Eastern experiences in contrast to other divisions,

   B) Sustained further education during periods of relative quiet in individual and unit training up to the level of the reinforced battalion. For this, several weeks of relief for each unit. Use and training of individual battalions as instruction battalions at the company commander school of the army,

   C) Remedy of the deficiencies found in the supply units by modifying the table of organization, the table of basic allowances and corresponding supply.

The divisions identified as numbering over three hundred, which primarily arrived in spring and summer 1942 to support the German summer offensive, suffered heavily from all kinds of shortages, be it men or material. While a lack of instructors with experience in the east only exacerbated the problem, the leadership of experienced divisional and, in some units, regimental commanders allowed these units to perform adequately after an initial learning curve.[15] They also profited from being transferred to the east prior to a German offensive, giving them time to settle and adapt to the conditions. Units sent eastward in the winter crisis were often hastily thrown piecemeal into battle and frequently suffered irreparable damage or were completely destroyed.

But even sending smaller units that should have been integrated into existing divisions proved very problematic, as the following report by the 5th Panzer Divisions indicates:[16]

The I./894 is subordinated to the Panzer Grenadier Regiment 13 since 22.11.1943. The experiences made with this unit appear so serious that it is considered appropriate to make higher levels aware of them.

Grenadier Regiment 894 was formed in June 1943 for security tasks on the Atlantic coast from soldiers non-suitable for the East, men who were previously rated as indispensable, in the mass soldiers classified as fit for reduced field service (*Garnisonsverwendungsfähig* – *Feld*) , and deployed in the positions on the coast at the end of July 1943. On 20 October 1943, the 1st Battalion was removed from the regiment, and newly formed after the exchange of non-suitable soldiers. From the day of formation to the day of loading to the east, the battalion had 10 days available, which for the most part still had to be used for work for establishing [the unit].

The battalion was equipped in a way that has not been seen in the East either with our own or with other units. Armament: purely MG 42, namely for each company 12 light and 2 heavy machine guns. In addition, in each company two medium mortars. Combat strength of the companies average 130 men. The equipment for the winter, from the complete winter clothing, to sleds, rescue toboggans, skis up to and including coal for heating was described as perfect.

A training of the battalion with the assigned weapons has almost not taken place at all. During the time of the use on the coast, only training on the immobile defensive weapons was carried out. Only in the reserve company was some terrain training carried out. After the formation of the battalion, a special training on the heavy machine gun and mortar was begun, which however had to be interrupted after five days as a result of transport to the east. Use, handling and maintenance of all weapons, priming and use of hand grenades, and the use of the spade invariably are almost unknown to the battalion. The principles on the use of weapons and the building of positions are also unknown to most officers and NCOs.

During the formation of the battalion, it never trained as a unit at all. Therefore, none of the leaders were trained in smooth cooperation. Because of their short affiliation with the troops, most of them hardly knew each other.

The personnel situation was as follows:

NCOs and men at march out:	800
Thereof with experiences in the East: 8%	60
Thereof with otherwise war experiences (France)	90
Without any war experience 81%	650
Officer situation at march out:	11
of which with experience in the East (mainly partisan war)	5
of which otherwise war-experienced (campaign in France)	3
of which without war experience:	3

A 46-year-old *Hautpmann* was appointed as the leader of the battalion, who until now had been company commander of a bicycle company, and so far had occasionally led a battalion as deputy. He had experience in bandit warfare, but all that is fundamental in the entrenchment and defence of a position is completely new to him. A *Leutnant* was assigned to him as adjutant, who learned about and took over the affairs of the adjutant for the first time at the end of October 1943. His wartime experiences were limited to the war against France. He had not been in the East yet. The same information applies to the special mission staff officer. Of the company leaders two had experiences in the East. However, the experience of the one limited itself to the staff activity. The third company leader was 2 months [in the Soviet Union], and the fourth not yet in the East.

Immediately prior to the start of the railroad transport, the battalion was given replacements from the class of 1925, which accounted for 16% of the total strength. These young men were all grouped together in a company. As a result of imperfect training and inexperience among the leaders and NCOs, these young replacements suffered considerable casualties within a few days, so that now only 9% are still available.

The total losses of the battalion were also comparatively high as measured by combat activity. Within 9 days, there were 180 casualties. These losses are mainly attributed to the lack of combat experience, likewise the comparatively high losses of armament, devices and equipment already in the first 24 hours.

Such a wear-and-tear of people and material would not have occurred in a veteran unit. There, men as well as weapons and equipment come into expert hands. What is lacking in training will be made good in a sound form, be it during the deployment, and weapons are issued only to those people who could operate them.

It seems more appropriate to refrain from such new formations, and to correspondingly replenish the old, combat-proven companies. Only then can such losses be avoided. We cannot afford any superfluous losses in the currently strained replacement situation.

It should also be borne in mind that there is a tradition in the old front regiments and thus the feeling of pride in one's own troop. These are the things which, even in difficult situations, enable the troops to achieve a particularly high fighting performance.

Obviously, these conditions are completely absent in the case of such a loosely composed units as in these new formations. As a result, the fighting spirit of such a force is far less. For this reason too, such a preferred equipping [of the unit] appears to be completely out of place.

Panzer Grenadier Regiment 13 also reports that from 22.–24.11.1943, another battalion was attached to it. Here the conditions were the same as in the case of the I./894. After a deployment of 48 hours, the battalion commander reported that he had only around 250 out of 800 men still in hand! This, too, was not a result of the fighting situation, but merely the effect of the inexperience of the troops and their leaders. The troop itself is the least to blame. It is not responsible for its inexperience, and it must also be acknowledged that the good will is undoubtedly present. This good will, however, can neither replace the lack of training nor the complete inexperience of command and troops.

Once again, the source indicates that manpower deficiencies were not as damaging to the unit as was the lack of men – and especially commanders – familiar with conditions and combat in the east. In this particular case, material questions were not an issue. This source thereby reflects a larger problem that occasioned many complaints in the second half of the war, namely the uneven distribution of new equipment. Many newly formed units received new weapons and equipment while older units had difficulties in acquiring either replacements for lost or destroyed material or newly introduced weapons. This process further weakened older units. An issue not even talked about is the amalgamation of a unit trained as an infantry formation into a tank unit, despite the fact that many of these men had never before seen the inside of a tank. This was certainly a contributing factor to the decline of German Panzer units' combat power in the second half of the war, and is a topic which deserves more research.

Even after the forwarding of replacements and transfers of full units to the east, German manpower in the Soviet Union always operated in a shortage – and it was a shortage that only worsened as the war continued. In an attempt to overcome this scarcity, the German army started to draw manpower from new sources. The most obvious means, yet often overlooked, was to shift men within the army apparatus. A well-known example of this was the tasking of *Generalleutnant*, later *General der Infanterie*, Walter von Unruh, with combing through all agencies and rear units for men to be sent to the front. Beginning in late 1942, his competencies were expanded to federal departments and Nazi party institutions. His success in creating large numbers of soldiers was moderate, but it nonetheless led to conflicts with Armaments Minister Albert Speer, because each drew from the same pool. More important was the shifting within the field army's frontline troops, as the following order from the OKH on the enhancement of the combat power in autumn 1942 shows:[17]

Prior to spring 1943, one cannot expect any significant replacements arriving. We must resign ourselves to this fact, and do everything we can to maintain and increase our combat strength.

Therefore the following measures must be carried out as soon as possible:
1) Complete disbanding of individual units and formations, disbanding and reduction of baggage trains;
2) Replacement of the German soldier by Russian *Hilfswillige* (prisoners of war) in such places which do not need to be occupied by combat soldiers.

In many units this has already been carried out to a large extent, although further measures are still necessary.

3) Deployment of all hereby released German soldiers into the infantry and formation of special branch combat units.

In detail:

A) Disbanding and reduction

1) The disbanding of units and formations (III. battalions [...]) must be a complete one and may not be temporary. It is precisely the 'cadre personnel' and the baggage trains that yield gains in men.

2) Reduction of batteries to 3 guns. The fourth guns have to be parked division-wise with the least amount of German supervision and Russian support personnel. Cannoneers and drivers who are freed in this way cannot be used for filling open positions in the artillery.

3) Reduction of the baggage trains. Even where this has already been ordered and carried out, it is again necessary to examine with the strictest criteria, which parts a) can be completely disbanded, b) can be stored throughout the winter, thus freeing soldiers for combat use. I expect that commanders of all degrees will take drastic measures here.

4) As soon as the winter position is reached, approximately 50% of all horses and a large part of the motor vehicles are to be stored in the hinterland. For the care of these horses and motor vehicles, only Russian *Hilfswillige* and only the absolutely necessary supervisory personnel, which at the same time carries out the training of the *Hilfswillige* (for example as a driver of the horse, a driver, technical staff, etc.) are to be assigned to them.

[...]

5) The reduction and modification of existing tables of organization are in preparation. Correspondingly, we must now proceed. According to these, the following disappeared: about 10% in each battalion and regimental staff, 8 men per battery, all not absolutely necessary motorcycle drivers, messengers, command post clerks and drivers in each engineer battalion, the heavy machine gun group in the cavalry companies of each reconnaissance battalion, some 10% per signal battalion. In the case of supply troops, it is intended to merge all the horse drawn columns and small truck columns into large horse-drawn columns and large motor vehicle columns to save command and crew personnel.

While the order aimed at creating new frontline soldiers, primarily infantry and engineers, it also reveals an often forgotten issue. Losses in combat and rear area troops were not at the same level. In his pioneering study on the 253rd Infantry Division, Christoph Rass has indicated the level in which losses diverged between the rear and front. While many infantry units were virtually destroyed more than once, loss rates in rear area units were rather low, except for extraordinary circumstances (that admittedly became more common beginning in 1944). The difficulty in regulating the recruitment and flow of replacements often led to imbalances between rear services and frontline troops. Orders such as the one mentioned above tried to realize that balance. But there were also limits to the exchange of personnel from the rear area to the front. The last-surviving sons and fathers of several children could not be endangered for morale reasons, while men physically unfit for frontline duty were more ballast than asset. The same was true with older men, but the age limit was continuously raised as the pool of younger men gradually depleted. In addition to the imbalance between rear and frontline troops, the sustaining of cadre units was also a vital issue. While – as mentioned in the order – this led to a real gain in combat power, the issue was more complex than that. Neither rebuilding units from scratch nor integrating completely new units was an easy task, as was demonstrated by the experience of the 5th Panzer Division. The massive dissolution of battalion-level units in 1942 in the traditional divisions and the formation of many new units, such as independent infantry battalions or the already mentioned Luftwaffe Field Divisions, marked the first step in the erosion of the German infantry that would eventually evolve into the infantry crisis. As a result, the German army lost much of its tactical superiority, which had been an essential component of its ability to successfully fight against numerically superior foes.

As part of its internal shifting of troops, Sixth Army also amended some points to the order, thereby sharpening it:[18]

1) In the staff of the Sixth Army (including the army engineer leader and the army signal leader): return of all officers, NCOs, and men commanded to the staff of the 6th Army; reduction of the remaining actual strength by 10-15%; in addition: replacement of additional soldiers by Russian *Hilfswillige*. [...]

2) In the corps and divisional staffs: return of all officers, NCOs, and men commanded to these staffs; reduction of the remaining actual strength by 10%; in addition: replacement of additional soldiers by Russian *Hilfswillige*. [...]

3) Formation of alarm units: all units of the divisions, which are not directly deployed at the front (parts of the signal battalion, supply units, etc.), of all higher staffs (from divisional staff to and including army headquarters), all corps troops and all army troops not immediately fighting at the front.

4) Disbanding of a rifle company in the infantry battalions and of the 3rd battalion in the infantry regiments, for the saving of baggage trains, etc., in cases where the combat strengths are not in a sustainable relationship with the baggage trains' strength.

5) Reduction of soldiers and units not directly engaged in combat in the divisions and likewise in the army troops:
   Reduction of battalion and regimental staffs by about 10%
   Reduction of batteries to 3 guns (removal of the 4th cannon for overhaul and as a material reserve)
   Disbanding of individual batteries. Formation of 6-gun batteries [...]

6) Handover of 2 NCOs and 10 men from each bridging column to the engineer battalions. [...]

8) c) Registration of soldiers not suitable for infantry service, as well as of the last surviving sons from the divisions' units and all soldiers from the army troops in divisional replacement battalions and army troop replacement battalions (directly subordinated to the Sixth Army).

> Training of these replacement battalions for infantry defensive warfare in winter. Deployment is intended only in crisis situations, disbanding and return of the soldiers to their original units in the spring or after receiving sufficient replacements is intended. Use of the army troops replacement battalions only by order of the army command. Beginning of training in the replacement battalions from 5.11.42.

In addition to the measures ordered by the OKH, Sixth Army ordered the disbanding of further units on the lower levels, the reduction of staffs, including higher levels, and decreed that the corps and army levels free soldiers too. Sixth Army at this time was – as seen in chapters 1 and 4 – in an extremely difficult situation in and around Stalingrad and in need of every fighting man for the front.

A further means to gain frontline soldiers was to replace German soldiers in various positions by so-called *Hilfswillige* (literally: one willing to help), Russian men generally drafted into the Wehrmacht for auxiliary services, though in a few cases, they were also used in combat. To be clear: the *Hilfswillige* formed just one group of Soviet collaborators, but they were the most numerically important for the German army in the east, with their numbers estimated between 800,000 and one million. Divisional files reveal that many divisions employed between 700 and 1,500 *Hilfswillige* in their ranks in 1942 and 1943. While the initial use of Soviet prisoners of war – the primary source for *Hilfswillige* – was improvised, the German military in its typical manner developed a set of regulations concerning *Hilfswillige* in 1942 and 1943, including rations, payment, uniforms, insignia and so on. The training for these men aimed mainly at moulding them into convinced anti-communists and thereby reliable auxiliaries. This was directly formulated in the following manual:[19]

Guidelines for the training of the *Hilfswillige*
1) The objective of the training and education of the *Hilfswillige* is to educate them to be reliable fellow combatants against Bolshevism.
2) In order to carry out that training and education, the *Hilfswillige* are to be appropriately concentrated in camps and suitable supervisory personnel and trainers (including interpreters) have to be made available. The following organization of the *Hiwi* replacement company has proven itself here in the camps: for every division one or more *Hiwi* replacement companies. Disposal of training personnel by the division in question. The training personnel train the *Hilfswillige* for their own division and assist with the allocation of the *Hilfswillige* inside the division.
3) [...]
4) Sustainment of the commitment to service and willingness to fight against Bolshevism are important. In addition to a variety and variation in training, this will be achieved by the example and personality of the German superiors and their active care. Strict but fair treatment through an exact knowledge of the Russian mentality, the eradication of Bolshevik influence through systematic military-ideological leadership to educate the *Hilfswilligen* to a reliable fellow combatant for the troops. The belief in the absolute superiority of the German leadership and the German soldier over the Red Army and its members is to be stimulated and sustained.

5) [...]
6) At every roll call, one has to pay attention to bearing and uniform.

Complementing this focus on developing an anti-communist attitude, the training – or rather education – aimed at a strict discipline. Of course this was needed, but the stressing of discipline here was also part of the German perception that Russian 'subhumans' had to be educated to discipline, as they inherently lacked this due to their 'nature'. As with German replacements, *Hilfswillige* were trained in the division to which they were attached. With this decentralized organization, the German army again desired to achieve a rapid deployment, but it also wanted to give divisions control over the process of selection. The divisions thus had a keen interest in choosing those men since they would have to fight with them later. This made the selection of instructors especially important. These individuals had a difficult task, as they needed to educate Russians to become 'reliable fellow combatants', while at the same time convincing them of the 'absolute superiority' of the German military. This became more difficult after the defeat at Stalingrad, but nearly impossible from summer 1943 on, when German victories became very rare events. Even during the years of German defeat, many *Hilfswillige* and other Soviet auxiliaries stayed with their German units, though this was not so much out of conviction, but rather a consequence of the Stalinist policy that deemed these men as traitors and threatened them with severe punishment.

The main purpose of *Hilfswillige* was to free German soldiers for combat duty. How this was intended for various positions can be seen again in the orders of the OKH on the enhancement of combat power in autumn 1942:[20]

B) Replacement of the German soldier
Hilfswillige (prisoners of war) are to be employed in place of German soldiers:
In all units up to and including company and battery as a driver, co-driver, horse and mule-driver, craftsman, technical personnel (locksmith, weapon personnel, etc.) and as working personnel in construction and supply units.
In addition: as ammunition bearers in machine gun companies, infantry-gun companies and anti-tank companies.
In battalion and regimental staffs as cable carriers at telephone sections.
In batteries as gunner 5 and 6.
In engineer battalions as engineers not directly involved in the combat. Example:
Formation of a company from only German soldiers for combat deployment.
Formation of 2 further companies with German cadre, filled with *Hilfswillige*, for bridge building, road and quarters construction, mining and demining, obstacle construction.
In signal battalions in mixed telephone-construction groups.
For building units of all kinds. Only German supervisory staff (ratio 1:10) can be used here.
For supply troops of all kinds. In these, generally, only supervisory staff and the absolutely necessary specialists such as mechanics, bakers, butchers, etc. are to be left.

The purpose of these measures is to free German soldiers. It is not possible that *Hilfswillige* are hired additionally, just to do mindless work, and the baggage train is thus increased without gaining a German soldier. A sharp supervision is also necessary here!

Therefore, *Hilfswillige* were to fill all types of auxiliary service positions. While the requirements for most of these positions were low – and therefore could be brought in line with the Nazi ideological belief of Russians as primitive subhumans – the use of *Hilfswillige* in craftsman or mechanic positions blurred that line. Even when considering all of the boundaries drawn by the German military between German soldiers and *Hilfswillige*, one cannot escape the impression that in this question, military necessity overtook Nazi ideology. This became especially clear in the cases where Russian *Hilfswillige* fought side by side with German soldiers, prompting XIth Army Corps Chief of Staff, *Oberst* Helmuth Groscurth, to write: 'It is disturbing that we are forced to strengthen our fighting troops with Russian prisoners of war, who are already being turned into gunners. It's an odd state of affairs that the "beasts" we have been fighting against are now living with us in closest harmony.'[21] However, even the most fanatical Nazi ideologue had to recognize from mid-1942 on that German troops in the east could not have fought without the help of hundreds of thousands of Soviet men and women serving in the German army and in other agencies, such as, for example, the *Reichsbahn*. Otherwise, the Germans would have had to mobilize the Reich's manpower resources at a much higher level, an issue that was feared by Hitler and many other high-ranking German officials due to traumatic experience of the collapse of 1918. Because of this period of limited German mobilization from mid-1942 to summer 1944, Bernhard Kroener has written that it was 'not quite total war'.[22]

Once German soldiers were freed, units needed to proceed in the following manner:[23]

C) Use of freed German soldiers
    The following is to be done:
    1) infantry (not the last-surviving sons or the physically unsuitable), whose present position will be filled in the future by *Hilfswilligen*, are a) if their training permits, to be immediately integrated in rifle companies, b) to be consolidated in training companies by the division and after sufficient training to be transferred to rifle companies. The divisions may, at their own discretion, also use members of other branches.
    2) Soldiers of all other branches and supply troops, as well as the last-surviving sons and the physically non-suitable for infantry service, are to be registered by each division and are to be trained for winter and positional warfare. They are then available as reserves, which must suffice until spring, for the winter position.

The initial gain of these measures was rather small, as few soldiers could be directly placed into rifle units. Furthermore, these measures destroyed valuable cadres and necessitated the introduction or rebuilding from scratch of new companies and battalions, a demanding task that cost much blood. The units mentioned under point 2 often enough could not fulfil their task due to the lack of adequate training, equipment and especially leadership. They marked the bottom of a poor man's army, often suffering extraordinary losses with minor military effect. The widespread forming of such alarm units in late 1942 was a clear sign of an army that had lost its balance.

German losses in the east were enormous – and continual. In 1942, for example, German monthly casualties exceeded 70,000 in nine months. In this year, the German replacement system could forward more troops than the *Ostheer* lost in only eight months. But when it did so, it never surpassed an additional 30,000 men. On the other side, January 1942 alone saw losses of over 214,000 men, while the *Ostheer* received only 43,800 replacements; the heavy fighting in August 1942 cost the *Ostheer* over 250,000 losses, while not even 90,000 replacements arrived in the east.[24] These massive losses forced the German army to lower training and recruiting standards. While part of that could be compensated for by field training, the quality of replacements decreased. The actual strength of the German *Ostheer* never again reached its peak strength of 22 June 1941 (3.3 million men). While primarily allied units helped to rebuild the strength of the *Ostheer* for the 1942 summer offensive, their destruction in 1942/43 forced the Germans to send more men in spring 1943. Before Operation Citadel, the German army in the east could field nearly 3.15 million men, but from then on – with pressure from the Western Allies rapidly increasing – German strength fell sharply.[25] Combined with a decrease in training quality, this led directly into the defeats of late 1943 and 1944.

Chapter 7

The German Army's Understanding of the War in the East: Ideology and Motivations

In January 1943, the German southern wing in the Soviet Union teetered on the edge of catastrophe. In addition to the Sixth Army slowly dying in the rubble of Stalingrad, elements of Army Group A that had been struggling to seize the oil fields of the Caucasus region had not only been checked, but now faced their own encirclement. For one German non-commissioned officer deployed in the Caucasus, the crisis that faced the German army led to a brutal interpretation of the conflict. In a letter to his wife, he wrote:

> Does war actually have its own laws? I read now 'Not everyone that saith unto me "Lord, Lord," enters into Heaven, but rather those who do the will of my Father in Heaven.' Just now, an elder came to me, someone took his pig. Now he wants to have at least something from it. In any case, he lost his pig. Of course it is for our kitchen, but this is hard for those who affected by it. Should I now give my people less to live on to spare the civilian population? Or am I obligated to care for the men so that they live as well as possible? In general, one says that war has its own law. Thus, the case is settled... You see, the war brings not only a re-evaluation, but a revolution in the moral sphere. [It] has its own law?[1]

For this NCO, the war in the east had developed into one that existed outside the normal parameters or understandings of conventional conflicts. Such an understanding, however, did not necessarily indicate a fervent belief in Nazi ideological tenets; rather it was based on preserving his men in a theatre of war which demanded a brutally utilitarian approach to the civilians in his midst. While his thoughts, doubts, and reflections on the war do not represent every German soldier's approach to the war against the Soviet Union, his conviction that this conflict was indeed different from the army's other campaigns would certainly have been shared by the majority of his comrades who served on the Eastern front.

With the exception of the Japanese war in China, the German–Soviet theatre of war witnessed the longest continuous fighting of the war between armies. It also surpassed all of the war's other conflicts in terms of totality and scale. The army's initial belief that victory would be achieved quickly was soon punctured by the challenges of the eastern theatre, which had failed to materialize in any of the Germans' previous campaigns: terrain and climate difficulties that served to magnify each other; increasingly long and tenuous supply lines as covered in chapter 6; and, most importantly, as chapter 1 showed, an opponent that was prepared to fight just as savagely and desperately as the Germans to achieve victory. This chapter will investigate how the German army and men such as the NCO deployed in the Caucasus understood their task in the east, how they viewed the Red Army, and in what ways the army strove to keep its men in the field. This necessitates an examination of the army's behaviour in the Soviet Union and what drove it to act in such a way.

Immediately after the conclusion of the war, military commentators tried to solve one of the conflict's great puzzles: how did an out-gunned and out-manned German army manage to hold out for so long against such great odds? The early answers to this question dismissed the importance of ideas in motivating German soldiers; rather, notions of primary group solidarity – fighting for one's closest comrades – predominated.[2] This focus on professionalism also diverted attention from the army's participation in the war of annihilation. Instead, German crimes in the Soviet Union were blamed on the SS and other Nazi organizations, while the army was generally portrayed as an apolitical entity that had merely carried out its professional duty by fighting a 'clean' war in the east. This view was crafted by numerous former high-ranking German officers who published memoirs of their service, as well as historians sympathetic to their post-war fate.[3] The growing tensions of the Cold War only reinforced this narrative as the United States looked to integrate a rearmed West Germany into the western bloc. It was only from the late 1960s that historians began to uncover the army's complicity in Hitler's war of annihilation; by the 1980s it was clear that the army had participated on a massive scale in the Vernichtungskrieg.[4] The primary question asked by historians during the twenty-first century has concerned the 'why' instead of the 'what'. Why did the army as an institution and the soldiers themselves stay in the fight until Germany was completely and utterly defeated, and why did both groups commit war crimes?

Historians have identified several different possible answers to these questions. According to one perspective, ideology served to cement German soldiers to the cause, providing them with the necessary mental and spiritual foundation to sustain the war effort some two years after it was clear the Third Reich would be defeated. This same ideology also served to legitimize ruthless behaviour against enemy combatants and civilians, who were seen as not only racially inferior to the German Herrenmenschen, but who also threatened to destroy Western civilization with their Jewish-Bolshevik ideals.[5] Another approach focuses on the professionalism of the German army and the soldier in carrying out their duty. This view holds that German soldiers of all ranks internalized the military ethos that demanded the fulfilment of their mission of defending the Reich from its enemies.[6] Such a perspective is closely tied with emphases on the patriotism of soldiers determined to fight for their country and family.[7] Finally, the idea of military necessity has also been advanced as an explanation for the army's conduct on the Eastern front. In its attempt to emerge victorious on the battlefield, the army resorted to whatever practices and policies it viewed as necessary at a given time. By subscribing to this idea, the army alternated between periods of conciliatory and violent, coercive behaviour towards the Soviet civilian population.[8] Any examination of why and how the army – and by extension its soldiers – conducted itself needs to be put into the context of these four approaches and their interconnections.

The German officer had traditionally been responsible for the care of his men and this included their morale and mental state.[9] Based on its experiences of the First World War, however, the army realized that such efforts needed to be intensified within the context of modern, industrialized war. As the war shifted to a total one during the course of 1916, the army leadership recognized that the total mobilization of the nation's resources for the war effort included the minds of its soldiers.[10] The rationale behind this new emphasis on a soldier's psyche was spelled out by the commander of the 8th Panzer Division during the course of the truly total war waged during the Second World War.[11]

> [...]
> The meaning of Military-Ideological Care
> As the experiences of the First World War taught, next to the outer totalization of the war within the military and economic respects and in the area of labour mobilization, a so-called inner totalization must also take place to confront war weariness from the start as well as its scattered appearances and the ebbing of the spirit of resistance through instruction, clarification and easing of tension.
>
> This occurs through the mobilization and the arousal or stimulation of all mental-spiritual powers in each man, with the goal to remove any doubts and to support and strengthen his will to resist. Such help is all the more necessary the longer the war lasts and the more that the Russian space and war situation burden the mind and soul of every soldier.
>
> The threatening degeneration of the soldiers into primitive, Russian-like brutes should be worked against through constant clarification of the situation, discussions about the point and goal of this war, explanations about the state leadership's measures, and action against enemy propaganda, etc. through the spoken word.

As discussed in the chapter on training, preparing the soldiers for the stresses and strains of combat was clearly a priority for the German army as it realized that the quality of the German soldier would have to make good the numerical inferiority of the army.

Following the army's defeat in the First World War, the Reichswehr continued this process, though the emergence of the Nazi regime in 1933 and the close links forged between Hitler and the defence minister, Werner von Blomberg, led to an increase in specifically National Socialist indoctrination. Such a programme was due in part to the army's leadership attempt to ensure its relatively privileged position within the Third Reich as one of the two (alongside the Nazi Party) pillars of the National Socialist state and in part to Blomberg's admiration of Hitler. He initiated a series of policies designed to draw the army closer to the regime, including the adoption of the Aryan paragraph, the oath to Hitler following President Hindenburg's death, and, most notoriously, the army's active participation in the elimination of the SA leadership during the Night of Long Knives. As German historian Wilhelm Deist has noted, 'all this meant that the "adaptation" and "opening" of the Wehrmacht amounted to a process of almost complete ideological assimilation into the National Socialist regime.'[12] This development was certainly not welcomed by the army's entire leadership, however, and individuals such as *Generaloberst* Werner von Fritsch and *Generaloberst* Ludwig Beck strove to maintain the army's traditional outlook and powers. It was only in 1938 – the year of the Blomberg–Fritsch Crisis – that the regime finally gained the upper hand in its struggle with the army leadership.

The fault lines between the two institutions were laid bare during the invasion and occupation of Poland. Campaigns of murder and forced deportation carried out by the SS aroused army opposition in the autumn and winter of 1939. Hitler quickly solved this problem by granting amnesty to anyone who committed crimes during the campaign, but it had demonstrated to the Nazi leadership that the army was not yet sufficiently prepared to wage the war desired by the regime. It therefore renewed efforts to transform the army's mindset. These efforts especially expanded following the defeat of France in autumn 1940, as the army prepared for the war with the Soviet Union. Coinciding with the establishment of new infantry divisions for Operation Barbarossa, the OKH issued an order in October 1940 that directed officers on how to properly instruct their soldiers for the upcoming campaign.[13]

Ideological Education

In war, a far greater part of the male population fit for military service stands under weapons than in peacetime. For numerous soldiers, this means a considerable lengthening of their time in the service. The Wehrmacht accepts and takes on this task to a greater extent [than other organizations and] therefore expands to educate the soldiers ideologically [*weltanschaulich*] and national-politically, in addition to weapons' training. No doubts can exist that the training of the soldier to be a determined warrior who enthusiastically attacks cannot be separated from a vital national socialist education.

All superiors therefore are to pay special attention to this. In so doing it is not so important to deal with as many themes as possible. What is decisive is that a unified conception exists in the army about National Socialist foundations and that they become the intrinsic values of all soldiers.

The troop commander is alone responsible for the spirit and the attitude of his soldiers. Therefore ideological education of the troops is also his task. This task is of far-reaching importance for the army's schools and courses. The 'Guidelines for the Ideological Instruction' (enclosure) serves as an indication. [...]

Guidelines for Ideological Instruction

The soldier also requires [guidance] in ideological and national socialist areas. Ideological instruction is especially successful when it occurs through a troop commander who knows his men.

The means for ideological instruction and spiritual care are:

Lectures about National Socialist basic principles, reading matter, film, radio, free-time activities. At the same time, the personally spoken word of a spiritually stirring and fresh officer to his troops is always the best means for the soldiers' ideological education.

I) Lectures by the troop commander or lecturer to the troops about national socialist fundamentals.

Theme 1: The German *Volk*

Main point: Clean race, health and capable women. Many children. Soldier replacements (military strength). How many recruits has Germany, for example, in 20 years? Fleeing from the land – a danger for the nation's racial foundations [*Volkstum*].

Documents: The Führer's book, '*Mein Kampf*'; 'People in Danger' from Otto Helmut; 'People and Race,' an illustrated monthly; 'Racial Studies of the German people' Prof. Dr. Hans Günther; 'Population Development in the Third Reich,' by Burgdörffer

Theme 2: The German Empire

Main point: The Structure of the State. Party and Wehrmacht as the pillars of the state. Führer state. Responsibility up. 'State' as living form of the people. From the military strength of healthy people will become the Wehrmacht of the strong state. Prerequisite: utilization of societal manpower.

Documents: The Führer's book, '*Mein Kampf*'; the defence law

Theme 3: German Living Space

Main Point: Goal of the war: securing the German living-(economic)-space, not subjugating the neighbouring peoples. 'Autarky' – Import – Independence for goods necessary for existence. The smaller in protection by the larger peoples.

Theme 4: The National Socialism as Foundation

Main point: a) for a healthy and unified people (see theme 1).

German socialism and front camaraderie (as result of National Socialist instruction!)

b) for a strong empire (see theme 2). Strong leadership. Labour and full utilization of societal manpower. 'Work ennobles.' 'Military service is honourable service.' (Domestic politics!)

c) for the securing of living space. (Foreign policy!)

As this order indicates, the traditional spiritual care that officers were responsible for now took on more National Socialist overtones, thus further politicizing the army and its officer corps. The various lectures highlighted the army's attempt to show the close bond between itself and the Nazi regime, as well as attempt to explain to its soldiers – through the use of Nazi rhetoric regarding race, living space, and *Volksgemeinschaft* – the necessity of the present war.

The OKH's order of October 1940 was complemented by the much more radical criminal orders (see chapter 5) issued in the lead-up to Operation Barbarossa in spring and summer 1940. These orders framed the war as an ideological one from the start and both officers and enlisted men used Nazi racial rhetoric as a means of understanding the extremely violent conflict unleashed by the German invasion. The following order, issued by the 7th Infantry Division less than two weeks after the beginning of the attack, displayed how the army placed members of the Red Army into the racial categories devised by the Reich government.[14]

The enemy has defended himself in the past fighting extraordinarily tenaciously, sometimes – even in desperate situations – to the bitter end. Due to this *dogged style of combat*, our own casualties are also increasing. The Russian, as a dull half-Asian, believes the principle drummed into him by his commissars that he will be shot during any capture. This is the main reason that he doesn't surrender.

Leaflets have been dropped in an increasing manner with the slogan: 'Come to us, you will be treated decently, everything else is a lie.' These leaflets have shown good effect in many places and therefore save blood on our side. In order not to contradict this propaganda, it is necessary to treat Red *Soldiers* who surrender and have possibly seen the leaflet as *prisoners of war*.

Necessary *executions* are as a rule therefore to be carried out so that civilians or other prisoners are unaware of them.

The order also betrays what was becoming an increasingly common practice on both sides of the front: the cold-blooded execution of surrendering troops. While the division attempted to convince the men of halting such a practice in hopes that Soviet soldiers would willingly lay down their arms, its use of terminology such as 'a dull half-Asian' only further perpetuated the notion of the Red Army man as the 'other', and this made such executions that much easier.

The view of Red Army soldiers as fundamentally different from German soldiers – either biologically or spiritually – clearly emerged from an entry in the 121st Infantry Division's Signal Unit's war diary from the summer of 1941.[15]

What animal-like and completely inhuman impressions the first prisoners made on us – completely depraved figures! Or human beings, whose joyless existence that they had to lead, can really be read in their eyes. So appeared the inhabitants of the paradise of workers and peasants! Instinctively we are seized by horror when we imagine how, in the reverse case, these guys would go about in our *Heimat* with our relatives. Once again, how true the words of the Führer would have been when he said that the victory of Bolshevism would mean the destruction of culture and Europe.

Here, in the 10-15 kilometre deep forests, is their very own combat area. For our infantry, however, this deployment means an enormous adjustment, in that the Reds have different tactics in forest fighting that had been usual before with the English, French and Poles.

The Asiatic impact makes itself noticeable. Treachery and duplicity, combined with a superb knowledge of the terrain, are the primary advantages of the Red Army's soldiers.

The officer fights together with his soldiers. Yet, it's the surveillance system of the commissars that forces him [to fight]. Undoubtedly the weaponry is qualitatively and quantitatively good, for despite the shouts of peace for international fraternization and human rights, Russia has rearmed for years in order to prepare for world revolution.

The greatest threat, however, is the innate nature-instinct of the inhabitants of the Russian steppe. The abilities to orient in unfamiliar terrain, to read the trails and tracks, and to adapt to nature, are for us Central Europeans in our large cities, long ago withered away and lost.

Ideological beliefs – both Nazi and those that existed in German society before January 1933 – permeate this document. While 'the Asiatic impact' manifested itself in 'animal-like and completely inhuman impressions,' it also proved to be an advantage for the Red Army, as its allegedly primitive soldiers were more adept at fighting the 'devious' war that raged in cornfields and forests. The Bolshevik system had not only produced the necessary weaponry for the Red Army, but its 'surveillance system' – or its use of commissar and politruks – was what kept the army in the field.

Another German source discussed similar themes in trying to explain the Soviets' tenacious defence:[16]

Copy: Compilation of Observations on the Red Army (from A.E. Frauenfeld[17])
  The resistance of the enemy was exceptionally tough and courageous everywhere. Especially noteworthy was that the enemy's Luftwaffe was as good as completely unnoticed...
  The battle was [*skillfully*] led by Russian infantry, with handguns, machine guns and anti-tank guns, anti-aircraft guns and mortars.
  The astounding bravery, with which the small and smallest groups defended themselves and the scattered remnants and individuals fought until destruction, stands in a stark contrast to prisoner of war statements that unanimously and truthfully report that food is really insufficient for them, that they have had nothing to eat for days.
  The explanation is to be looked for in that:
  The members and above all the functionaries of the Bolshevik Party fight well. They doubtlessly constitute an elite, who see in their duty an example for the others. There are numerous examples for this.
  Another group fights well due to other motives. There are Kyrgyzs, Tatars and all the members of war-like but primitive peoples. For them, there are – similarly as with the niggers in France – only two possibilities in war: either they kill the enemy or he kills them. Surrounded and caught in a hopeless situation, they defend themselves out of desperation.

By the end of summer 1941 at the latest, the German army and its soldiers recognized that the war in the Soviet Union was waged against an opponent far different from any previous campaign. According to the Germans' cynical view, the 'primitive peoples' that filled the Red Army's ranks were motivated by the example and coercion of Communist Party members and commissars to carry out their duties.

This discussion of the Bolshevik state was picked up on by another soldier, whose sometimes perceptive analysis of the Soviet Union nevertheless betrayed both traditional and Nazi prejudices.[18]

In a centuries-long school of suffering, especially in the last three decades of Bolshevik rule, the Russian people has become a victim of nihilism. That was also often the judgment of war correspondents, who described that life for the Bolshevik people had nothing to offer. It was joyless and not overly worth living. One was summoned to the living hell and the empire of shadows. Did one need to be afraid of death? Death ended the animal existence and brought all suffering to an end. Had we ever seen symbols of the love of life or even a heartily laughing people on our long march in Russia? Under the ice cold of mistrust and the animalistic look of people, the longing for a better life had long died away. The man was robbed of his dignity, without which the outer and inner freedom cannot exist. Now the Russian man also may not have had outer freedom in the Tsarist time, but he could sound and shout out with joy the longing for this freedom in simple and warm-feeling songs of his church. Today even the inner freedom has been taken by the bloodsuckers in Moscow. They pushed down the people to the level of the animal. They take from him every moral feeling for honour and responsibility. The fanatical Red Army man shoots down the opponent from a distance of three meters and possessed the gall to tap his comrade on the shoulder in a friendly way and ask him for a light for his cigarette. I have observed that more than once. If we soldiers also haven't expressed this directly, so we sense, however, that the longed-for paradise in Russia did not meet us. That what we encountered here was the exact opposite!

Anti-Bolshevism and the desire to protect Germany from the imposition of such a regime clearly motivated large chunks of the German eastern army, as did the behaviours and actions of Red Army soldiers and NKVD troops, which only served to legitimize German propaganda.[19]

The German army's string of unbroken victories that conquered continental Europe was finally broken in December 1941 when its last gasp offensive towards Moscow sputtered to a halt. The subsequent Soviet counterattack led to an existential crisis within its ranks, as the exhausted, frost-bitten and severely under-strength army was driven back hundreds of kilometres by the suddenly resurgent Red Army.[20] For the seemingly invincible German army, its first strategic retreat weighed heavily on the troops' morale. The intelligence officer of the hard-pressed 7th Infantry Division distributed the following document to his men some two weeks after the opening of the Soviet counterattack.[21]

The Enemy Situation

The Red Army has now suffered the heaviest defeats in the past six months. It has been decisively weakened in men and material. Russia may have been barely successful in the last hour in constructing a front and holding Moscow, but the losses in territory and industrial areas, in valuable war material and trained troops are too great to decisively change the situation in the coming year. Thus the desperate break-out attempts from the Petersburg fortress matter as little as the continual attacks on single sections of the front, in that while leading to the winning of unimportant terrain, are not capable of influencing the entire situation. The Red Army has suffered defeat after defeat. If it has been successful in recent weeks in forcing back our troops, worn out from months of fighting and in need of rest from a few positions, this has no importance for the larger situation. Large sections of the front have remained spared from attacks and have been able to prepare for the defensive in quiet. The imminent snow period will also shortly lead to a slackening of the Russian attacks on the present relatively unsettled positions.

The German front in the East cannot be shattered.

It is absurd to judge the entire situation of the Eastern Front only from the combat strength of one unit. Not all divisions have been employed in so many focal points, as, for example, our 7th Division. Mogilev, the Roslavl highway, Yel'nya, Vereya, the Moscow highway were points of emphasis. Not all divisions have stood at such decisive spots, many still possess great fighting power. After the long period of quiet that the winter will bring, all will be ready for the decisive battle.

The Russians' calls for help for the support from the side of England and America are no signs of strength. They obviously show that without help from abroad, the Red Army can no longer be brought to full combat strength by its own available military industry. However, now English help is very questionable, [and] American [assistance] has been completely eliminated by the war with Japan. Besides, developments in the Far East may force the Russians to keep the mass of their Siberian troops there.

The situation of the German East front [19]14/17 was occasionally more difficult than now and yet all crises were overcome, crises of completely different dimensions than those that have temporarily occurred on only a few sections of the front. The winter on the Carpathian Front[22] was much more onerous than that of the plains of central Russia. The opponent was never so smashed as today. Even in 1916, two years after the beginning of the war, he could overrun entire fronts and appear before the gates of Hungary in the Brusilov offensive. At the same time, strong German forces were committed in France, and more soldiers bled to death in the battles of Verdun and the Somme than in the entire campaign to date altogether.

One often hears the claim that the Russian of today is different than that of 1914. This is true and false. The majority of the Russians from then was perhaps more uniformly oriented than today when the entire peasantry stands in opposition to the Red Terror. But, then and now, the methods were the same. Then, it was the machine gun that drove the brown columns to attack, today are added the commissars, whose power will finally be broken in the year 1942 with the coming final account with communism.

This war is about the 'to be or not to be' of the Red rulers in the Kremlin. This explains the severity of the fighting. Any other government would have looked for an armistice after the great battles of annihilation during the fall of 1941. In this struggle, there is no armistice, there is only victory or defeat.

The task of the German Eastern Army is to force a German victory with all means and under all circumstances.

In this struggle, Japan has now also entered with completely fantastic initial successes. Japan is also fighting a war of life and death. The soldierly attitude of the Japanese *Volk* guarantees that this war will be carried out unerringly and ruthlessly. The Japanese Army in the Far East ties up strong Russian forces and stops any type of American supply through the Vladivostok harbour. So, the Japanese-American war constitutes a direct relief to our Eastern Front.

In the coming final battle, the remainder of Bolshevik Russia alone stands facing the German Army. And this army will triumph, because it wants to and must win!

This document proves instructive on several levels. First, the present crisis facing the German army was put into the larger context of Operation Barbarossa.

Correctly arguing that the Red Army had suffered much heavier casualties during the course of 1941 than the Germans, the author tried to convince the men that the Soviet army was in worse shape than the German army, a view that was shared by much of the German High Command. Second, by comparing the present struggle to that of the First World War and by specifically mentioning touchstone battles from that conflict such as the Carpathian campaign, the Brusilov offensive, and twin battles of material, Verdun and the Somme, he was specifically playing upon their patriotism and devotion to their family members. By placing the winter crisis of 1941/42 into the larger continuum of defending Germany from its enemies during the twentieth century, he portrayed members of the 7th Infantry Division as heirs to the men who fought in the hellacious battles of the First World War, ones which were well-known to German soldiers fighting in its successor. The fact that many of the men now deep in the Russian heartland were sons and nephews of those who suffered and died at Verdun or in the Carpathians only increased the stakes; in order to reach the near-mythical status of their predecessors in field grey, these men had to do their duty, no matter the cost. Third, the missive argued that the Germany was not alone in the struggle to remake the world. The addition of Imperial Japan and its *Volk* firmly tipped the balance in favour of the Reich, because Japanese intervention in Asia and the Pacific would tie up British and American resources, leaving the Soviet Union alone in its struggle with Germany. The final point that emerges from the document concerns the importance of will. Both the Soviets and the Japanese were fighting a war of 'to be or not to be,' or in other words, 'a war of life and death.' The stakes were clearly as high for the German Reich and they could only be achieved by the army and its men possessing the necessary iron will to achieve its goals. The importance of this requisite will increasingly preoccupied the German High Command, as well as the Nazi political leadership. Even though the army and the National Socialist movement approached the notion of will from different perspectives, as the war continued to progress, both institutions looked to overcome Germany's numerical inferiority through an utterly committed and even fanatical fighting force that shrank from nothing in its quest for final victory.

A report issued by a regimental commander fighting on the northern section of the front in spring 1942 acknowledged the Red Army's fighting abilities, but understood these in the larger context of a mixing of Asiatic blood and Bolshevik ideology.

> No less than the forces of the area's geography, the peculiarity and character of the Soviet people have determined the form and development of the fighting in Russia. The Soviet theatre of war differs from all other European theatres in this war in that the enemy fights with almost animal-like doggedness and cruelty and therefore forces every single German soldier to fight to the last and with absolute severity. The legacy of middle-Asian blood [*Bluterbe*] and the Bolshevik teaching of crass materialism, which strips even life as such of its higher worth and sees it as an objective matter, something functional, so that the failure to reach a goal set from the outside ... means it has no legitimate reason to exist and merits being wiped out, is reinforced by the political and military leadership of all ranks and is also absorbed in numerous simple soldiers of the Red Army to perfection.

We must not forget the spiritual dullness and weak character development of primitive, Russians, made soulless [by the Bolsheviks].[23]

The Nazi ideological belief system based on both 'biological' beliefs and anti-Bolshevism that had framed the invasion with the criminal orders thus continued to provide soldiers with a context to understand their opponent into the second year of war.

The extension of the war into 1942, however, meant that the army now had to take more proactive steps to ensure that its soldiers remained functional in the field. Complementing tangible attempts to keep the men well supplied with appropriate clothing, modern weapons, and sufficient food, it also tried to maintain the men's spirits. While the army's use of Nazi ideological beliefs to steel the minds of its men became increasingly prevalent during the second half of the war, this proved to be only one means of providing spiritual and physical care for the ranks. One concrete manifestation of this policy was the establishment of the *Erholungsheim*, or recuperation centre, for troops who required some rest from the strains of battle. The 205th Infantry Division's guidelines for its recuperation centre were as follows:[24]

Purpose: Front soldiers (officers, NCOs and rank and file) shall *recuperate* in that home in the first place physically through sufficient sleep, good nourishment, [and] personal hygiene (including delousing). The get-together with other comrades shall serve the fostering of comradeship and the understanding of other branches, a proper spiritual care (reading, music playing, visits to the cinema, etc.) for mental strengthening and refreshment. [...]

Recuperation time: Four days; in addition to the day of arrival (arrival from 15.00) and the day of returning (departure before 08.00). Recuperation time will *not* be charged to the home leave due."

[The home has places for 10 officers and 48 NCOs and soldiers.]

Care: One female head and two female assistants of the German Red Cross.

The 7th Infantry Division also established such a recuperative area for its troops in February 1942.[25]

The division clearly understands that only the smallest gaps can be filled with the replacements that have arrived. Nevertheless, the combat strength reached in this way allows for small recuperation centres to be established at the regimental and independent battalion levels.

Purpose of the recuperation centre:
   a) De-lousing of the soldiers with the simplest means
   b) Rest for the soldiers for a few days (2–3 days) with better food
   c) New uniforms. The present clothing situation is not unfavourable to this end.

The soldiers in the trenches are primarily to be considered for these measures, and within a specific period of time, they will be given opportunity to clean themselves up and to relax, even if only for a few days.

Guidelines for the installation of de-lousing devices have been given.

To save time, the recuperation homes are to be established by the regiments and independent battalions within the accommodations area eastwards of the north-south road. An appropriate spiritual care is to be aimed for in the recuperation centres. (Radio, newspapers, card games, skis, etc.)...

The 8th Panzer Division sent five of its men to the *Erholungsheim* in Skugry in late October 1942 with high hopes for their recuperation:[26]

Thanks to its ideal location, the excellent food and the provided spiritual care, the stay in Skurgy invariably has a lasting effect in a physical and spiritual respect on the troops who are sent there.

The events of late 1942 and early 1943, however, clearly signified a shift in the initiative. The combination of battlefield defeats – notably the destruction of the Sixth Army in Stalingrad – with the increasing number of casualties, especially of officers and NCOs, meant the army as a whole experienced a 'leadership and confidence crisis.'[27] With victory no longer assured and Hitler's direction of the war no longer seeming infallible, morale plummeted throughout the Eastern Army.[28] The 126th Infantry Division's commander attempted to provide spiritual succour for his hard-pressed men defending along the Volkhov River in northwest Russia.[29]

Soldiers and comrades of the 126th Infantry Division!

On 30 January 1943, it is 10 years since our Führer was called to the summit of the government by the immortal Reich President, Field Marshal von Hindenburg. At that time, the formerly powerful German Reich found itself in abject humiliation, because the world powers England, France and North America tolerated no new ascent of our Fatherland and had bartered away old German land on our borders to small robber-states, such as Poland, Belgium, Denmark, Lithuania, and Czechoslovakia. Our agriculture, industry, shipping, aviation and trade could therefore not develop. Unemployment and hunger were the result. What has since changed in these 10 years? The Führer has created one, unified German *Volk*that is governed on a social basis and whose work is defended by powerful and strong armed forces. There is no longer any unemployment and no hunger. No German needs to emigrate to foreign lands in order to find his bread. The Saar, the Rhineland, German-Austria, and the Sudetenland returned to the Reich. Now England and France declared war against us, in order to crush us with force.

So came the Second World War, that now rages in its fourth year of war and which is a war of to be or not to be. Tremendous victories have been achieved; Poland, France and Yugoslavia were crushed and the landing attempts of the English in Norway and Greece were bloodily smashed. As soon as our victory appeared certain, the enemy, international Jewry, threw the war machines of Bolshevism and North America into the fight. The mighty Japan entered on our side. The Russians and Americans were forced to swallow heavy defeats in Europe and East Asia, but the fight is still not ended. The enemy also knows that everything depends on the outcome of this war. And so it is now that the great final battle has flared-up in which we, as well as our enemies, are committing our last reserves to achieve victory. We also know what it is for and therefore grit our teeth. The more the enemy attacks, the more we need to strike back. The lord of battles will only give the laurels of victory to the most courageous *Volk*.

Our Führer has in a previous winter, when it was also either do or die, taken over command of the army himself and we have endured. We will also endure now despite a few setbacks, because we are the better soldiers. We receive the better weapons and are better supplied and clothed than our enemies. Fighting with us are our U-Boats on the seas and our air fleets in the skies. Our allies Italy, Romania, Hungary, Finland and the powerful Japan faithfully stand with Germany. We have the previously conquered countries in Europe firmly in our control and again liberated the old German lands on our borders. When we win, Germany will head towards a radiant future. We want to protect our beautiful *Heimat* from Bolshevism; we want to maintain our beautiful houses and gardens, our green forests and meadows for us.

We know therefore, what we are fighting for and thus we will win. Especially on 30 January, we want to remember therefore what we all owe to our Führer. He has always led us upwards, Germany again stands powerful. And as we thank our Führer, we want to pledge that we will stand firm together, to do our duty and to gather all of our forces for the offensive.[30]

Long live the Führer and the Greater German Reich!

Several important themes emerge from this order of the day. First, while it fails to display the virulent anti-Bolshevik ideological slant that permeated similar directives, it does nonetheless advance other Nazi beliefs. The commander points to the 'radiant future' that all Germans would enjoy following victory; this pointedly contrasts to the 'unemployment and hunger' that reigned in Germany following its defeat in the First World War and the loss of territory, resources and people to the 'robber-states' that emerged following its conclusion.[31] He credits Hitler for Germany's revival and, by emphasizing his leadership during the winter crisis, he explicitly emphasizes his confidence in the Nazi regime. Second, while 'international Jewry' is blamed for aligning the United States and the Soviet Union against the Third Reich; the 126th Infantry Division commander's order thus reinforced Nazi anti-Semitic claims. Finally, he paints the war waged against Germany as one designed to keep the Reich in a subordinate position. With the support of its numerous allies, however, the German army could indeed achieve a just victory. Once again, the phrase 'to be or not to be' emerged in a German order: for the army as an institution, the war – especially that in the east – had become a war of existential struggle. At its most basic level, the order was an attempt to convince his men of the bond between army, society and Hitler, in hopes that this would keep them in the field fighting for final victory.

Such directives were meant to assuage the doubts that had begun to creep into the minds of German soldiers across the front. One man wrote to his wife in late January 1943 that:

Now the highly anticipated speech of Göring is over and we know quite well what we can expect from the future that means: nothing more. From the outset, every soldier must be prepared for self-sacrifice [*Opfertod*] and to expect it. Should one really be 'lucky', one can count on being regarded as a fool after the war. In any case, we weren't 100% enthusiastic about the speech. Naturally, everyone possesses a full appreciation of this struggle of destiny and is continually ready to die for it – but why must this be said to the *Heimat* in such a crass way? Well, that the war will still last for a long time, will not shake us further. This is what we have long expected!. [...] This crisis must first be survived!³²

Despite the evident war weariness expressed in this letter, the writer also maintained a steadfast approach to the war: he would stay in the field and do his duty until death. The morale crisis engendered by the defeat at Stalingrad was only exacerbated by the increasingly heavy bombing of German cities during the course of 1943. Soldiers at the front were frustrated and angered by both the suffering of their families and the state's inability to protect them. The previously cited NCO from the Caucasus wrote:

The fearfulness of war time events is now perhaps even clearer than in 1914/18, because now the civilian population is very severely suffering. Hamburg, Nuremberg, [and] Munich were affected in recent days. If a settlement with England isn't reached this year, then all the great cities of the north and west will lay in rubble. In addition to the loss of cultural values, it also means a misery for the civilian population, that we haven't experienced all the way back to the Thirty Years War. This is Judas' revenge, without a doubt!³³

Another soldier wrote a letter to his sister in which he expressed his worries about the bombing of Germany, but also clearly articulated his belief that Germany needed to continue the fight to the end.³⁴

My comrade from Hamburg received mail. Everything is OK. He apparently lives in one of the 180 houses that are allegedly still standing. Having said this, his wife wrote that she couldn't leave her cellar for days 1. because of the heat and 2. because of the continual attacks. All rail stations are destroyed. It is said that no street was spared but the first impression is always worse than the impression one gets once the clearing work has ended. A man returning from leave in Mainz said that while the attacks were continual to be sure, the resulting damage wasn't so considerable. A person returning from his leave in Cologne said the same thing. So there is certainly much exaggeration. The mood is nevertheless catastrophic. I understand this quite well, but I am nevertheless against the slogan: peace at any price!

The people should say what they want and where they want to go and not simply push for senseless mutiny. If this war does not bring a rational decision about the future of Europe, then there will soon again be a new war, because I do not believe that America or England can bring about a better economic or social order for us that will have value for a long time. In any case, I see a truly black future. I can't imagine at all what a peace should look like. Our enemies are in that respect certainly not united, for neither will the Russian give up their aims, nor the American or English concede anything to him if it threatens their interests. We can make use of this if we tip the scales. Perhaps you now understand what I want and why it is that I don't see the situation as so hopeless, if we were to just once display a united political will and choose any direction for us and didn't always want to force through our own ideas, even if by doing so we make the entire world our enemies. Germany is forced by its position to play a role in politics, but we can only have success when the *Volk* politically thinks and acts. In politics, one cannot go through the wall with his head, but rather must twist and turn, lie and cheat, even when it goes against character. If the *Volk* does not see this and act today, then there will be no happy future. Then it will always be the whipping boy and have fairly earned it. This petty bickering and agitation which are now being pushed I can only curse. We must evaluate everything that happens today and tomorrow, not only for the moment, but above all for the future.

Even when faced with a deteriorating situation at the front and at home, however, the ranks of the German army continued to tenaciously fight against the Red Army. Various factors played into the maintenance of German morale and combat motivation, including primary group bonds, unit cohesion based on regional recruitment, a professional commitment to the army and its values, and the increasing importance placed on Nazi ideological beliefs. The latter was due in large part to the introduction of 'military-ideological care' in mid-1942.[35] This new programme amounted to 'the indoctrination and manipulation of the soldiers'[36] with Nazi values, beliefs and fears being used to motivate German soldiers at the front. An order issued by the 8th Panzer Division's welfare officer in late October 1943 highlights this approach.[37]

The German Struggle and Victory against Soviet Slavery

Comrades! Once more, we know what is in store for us after the war if it doesn't end with a German victory.

The British union big shot Sir Herbert Ingram published a letter in the London newspaper 'Daily Telegraph' in which he declared with satisfaction that the Soviets

'after the war will transport all German men up to 25 years old to forced labour in the Soviet Union and during this time period, the entirety of Germany will be occupied by the Bolshevik army.'

At the same time, this British union big shot suggested that the Germans could be used in similar slave labour in other countries and in closing, he let the cat out of the bag in that he wrote:

'Under these conditions, it will take many years before Germany will once again have the opportunity to compete with England and the USA in the world market.'

Such plans are nothing new to us. What the Bolsheviks intend with the German *Volk* is known. It has likewise been long proven that the Kremlin-Jews with their fanatical hatred [*Hassfanatismus*] have been found to be in complete agreement with the Jews in London and Washington. Months ago, one of Roosevelt's favourite journalists declared that no German soldier in the east will see his *Heimat* again, and should instead be shipped away from the battlefield to the Siberian steppe.

That is the 'happiness' after the war promised to us by our enemies. But: they have reckoned without their host, without us!

Comrades! We think about what the Führer said in his headquarters to the
assembled party leadership on 6 October 1943:
*'We will fight everywhere and never tire until our goal is achieved. Take firmly
and unshakeably the belief in your heart that if our will does not waver, then this
war will end with a great German victory.'*
There will be a German victory at the end of this war! As long as this victory
is not achieved, it is futile to speak at all about peace. The expression 'after the
war', which we utter daily, is therefore senseless and aids enemy propaganda. It
can only be said: after the victory! There will be no peace until we have won.
[...]
Three Foreign Ministers around the Conference Table
Eden, Hull and Molotov meet in Moscow
An official announcement in elevated diplomatic language about the 'complete
agreement' of opinion will be produced at the conclusion of the discussions
between the three foreign ministers of the enemy powers Great Britain, the USA,
and the USSR. This announcement is opium for the Soviet Union's peoples.
In reality, the differences between the participants fiercely collided. Stalin
repeatedly asked: where are your divisions?
Hull, Roosevelt's representative, pointed out the heavy casualties of the
so-called Second Front and demanded [of the Soviets]: advance faster, attack
more determinedly. To be sure, this meant even more destroyed cities and villages
and even more dead, but you [the Soviets] must understand that the loss of one
American soldier weighed just as much as 1,000 dead Soviet soldiers.
Eden attempted in vain to facilitate what his secret directives said: to do
everything to promote the mutual bleeding-white of the Soviet Union and
Germany, in order to avoid a domination of the victor.

In this document, two different tracks were taken. On the one hand, the division
welfare officer attempted to inspire his men to fight to the end based on Soviet
plans for Germany, which allegedly had the support of the British and Americans.
Working within the context of the omnipresent Jewish conspiracy propounded by
the Nazi leadership, he argued that the Soviet Union planned to destroy German
society and decimate its male population through slave labour in Siberia. On the
other hand, the document also portrayed a fractured enemy alliance, playing up
the widely believed split between the western Allies and their Soviet counterparts.
In concert, these two ideas worked to both instil fear of Allied victory in the
German army's ranks, as well as provide the men with a sliver of hope that the
Allied coalition was destined to fray.
Such ideas were also expressed by the men themselves in letters written home.
While obviously not every German soldier identified with the Nazi programme,
some did find much of value in National Socialism. One soldier wrote to his wife:

How can a man who had leading role in party and no doubt wants to continue to
be so disgraceful in his attitude, especially now as a soldier?!! And then in the end
still ask me for an assignment!!! I now recognize the correct and unshakable basic
ideas of National Socialism and avow that I see them not as a party program but
rather as an expression of my and the German nature![38]

Though the transmission of ideological material was an important part of the welfare officer's duties, it constituted only a portion of his daily routine. A report submitted by the 126th Infantry Division's welfare officer in autumn 1943 highlighted the various, often mundane, ways that the army attempted to maintain morale.[39]

I) Work and measures for spiritual care and for military-ideological leadership

In the reporting period, the division remained in its positions on the north-wing of Eighteenth Army in front of Leningrad. The favourable conditions found there facilitated the spiritual care. During this time period there was no large engagements; however, news about the preparations for a large Russian attack led to increased work, in which periodic difficulties with the performing of spiritual care arose as a result. Carried out in particular were:

1) On 12.10, a meeting of the battalion welfare officers took place in which all pending questions were discussed.
   a) In the staffing of the battalion welfare officers, [personnel] stability is needed for a well-ordered work.
   b) As a result of the presence of new battalion welfare officers, a fundamental clarification of the tasks [is once again explained]. Instructions on the necessity of this area of work. Sole responsibility to regimental and battalion commanders as well as company commanders, battalion welfare officers only for support!
   c) The prerequisites for all work are reasonable material living conditions. Then spiritual care can be employed for enlightenment. Not until then is military-ideological leadership really possible.
   d) From this point of view, all areas, as they specifically lay with the division, were discussed:
       Material conditions (shelter, food, etc.): satisfactory,
       Spiritual care: especially favourable conditions, 15 well-equipped care stations.
       Military ideological leadership: much is left to be done in this area.
   e) Subsequently, an orientation of the entire political and military situation as given to him [the D.B.O] at the division welfare officer conference in Kingisepp [Yamburg] by the Army was described in a detailed report.
2) Spiritual Care:
   a) Film. The number of screenings could be increased. 8,691 spectators were recorded in 53 showings. The colour film 'Münchhausen'[40] received particular interest.
   b) Variety shows: The theatre troop's 'Something is happening today!', Soldier's theatre 'Kubu' from the 58th Infantry Division.
   c) Care material: Care material distributed:
       1,250 books out of the OKW library
       1,500 anthologies of 'Soldiers' letters for the Promotion of Occupational Training'
       23,000 field post letters
       200 card games
       Personal effects (mirror, pipes, shoe inserts, etc.) in small amounts.

From the front book store were purchased:

for RM 5,500 – books and 3,680 – recreational games (1,255 units), that can be sent home as Christmas presents

From Lth Army Corps was further allocated:

500 books 'South of Lake Ladoga' with 500 picture books '10 Weeks'

The Reich Ministry for Popular Enlightenment and Propaganda's Troop Entertainment Department donated for the excellent contribution of the division to the WHW [*Winterhilfswerke* or Winter Relief Help]:

    10,000 cigarettes

    500 cigars

    200 parcels of tobacco

    3,000 field post letters

    40 writing pads

    120 various games

    100 skat games

    200 books

    100 'We are with You'

    2000 short novels

    2 piano-accordions

d) On 15.10, Nr. 9 of the 'Lake Ilmen Voice' and Series 2 of the 'Tradition Sheets' came out.

3) Military-Ideological Leadership

a) The 'Instructions for Military-Ideological Leadership' were still issued for the instruction of unit commanders. 'Communication for the Troops' and the 'Communication for the Officer Corps' were regularly distributed. 'Education and Guidance in the Army' and 'What Moves Us' were issued in an increased amount.

b) Within the units, numerous educational and presentation hours took place. Headmaster Niggel was available for the division with lectures about the demographic-political situation of Germany. The themes chosen by the troops ranged over all areas, for example:

    'The Wisdom of the Soldier'

    'The German Soldiers and the Woman from a Foreign People'[41]

    'Marriage in War'

    'The Position of the Non-Commissioned Officer'

    'The Fight of the 126th Infantry Division'

c) Special attention was bestowed to the withdrawal in the south of the Eastern Front and, in conjunction with it, the rumours about such measures on the north front. The consistently surfacing claims about a voluntary pulling-out of the positions in front of Leningrad were successfully combated. The development of the situation in Italy also received further vigorous attention.

II) *Hilfswillige*

The development of the situation naturally brings with it a strain for the volunteers. In contrast, informative lectures by the leader of the Russian care staff and other Russian propagandists were held. The delivery of newspapers occasionally left something to be desired. In general, the attitude of the volunteers remains proper and loyal.

III) Occurrences that have special meaning for the troops' attitudes!
   a) Material:

Positive	Negative
Good accommodation	Absence of everyday items
Good food	(razor blades, shoe polish,
Good personal hygiene	lighting devices)
Good leave situation	

   b) Spiritual:

Sufficient supply with film and variety shows
Sufficient allocation of literature
The establishment of university courses in Tartu [Dorpat] and Tallinn [Reval]

   c) Combat events

Positive	Negative
Positive development in Italy and in the Aegean, Repeated defence of strong storm troops in our own sector.	Continual terror attacks against the homeland, continual withdrawals in the south of the Eastern Front. Little success in the U-boat war.

IV) Rooms are generally available in sufficient amount.

V) Wishes of the troops:
   More radio receivers, more light reading material, table tennis, musical instruments of all types. Improvement of the field postal service.

VI) Special:
   The commemoration day for the founding of the division on 15.10 played a special role. After careful preparation, the day was festively celebrated by the entire division. In addition to musters and commemorations that took place in every unit even in the most forward line, a celebration that took place at the divisional headquarters stood at the centre. In the presence of the commanding general of IInd Army Corps, *General der Infanterie* [Wilhelm]Wegener, and in front of delegations from all troop sections, a large military concert and a celebration in a closed hall with a collective meal, music, and variety shows took place. This celebration substantially contributed to the further coherence of the unit.

This report proves instructive on several levels. First, it highlights the army's increasing reliance on ideological instruction for the troops, as one of the document's primary emphases was the creation of a framework to ensure the men were receiving the proper information. It was also clear that the war in the east stood at the centre of the propaganda effort. The army was trying to convince the men not only of the great importance of the conflict for Germany's future, but also of the special role played by the 126th Infantry Division in this struggle.

Such ideological material, however, was not delivered in a crude fashion. This leads to the second point: working within the larger context of Nazi propaganda practices that believed that the most effective means of transmission was through subtle means, the army utilized seemingly neutral methods to spread Nazi ideas and values. Books, films and theatre groups all combined entertainment with education. And this flows into the third important point: alongside the ideological material were more banal, yet perhaps more important items that maintained the troops' morale: cards, cigarettes, pipes and mirrors, among others. The availability of everyday articles was recognized by the welfare officer as having the utmost importance in keeping the men's spirits high; as noted in the report, the soldiers' greatest desires were for more basic items, such as razors and shoe polish.

The report also examined how the men understood the larger context of the war. This was reflected in its observations on how the troops reacted to news of the war in Italy and the North Atlantic. Its discussion of the use of *Hilfswillige* also explored this topic, though in a way that hit much closer to home for the division. While the suspicion of these Russian volunteers clearly emerged from the document, the attempt to ideologically mould them into conscientious soldiers for the German cause was seen as an absolute necessity; *geistige Betreuung* was thus utilized at all stages of the division's develop, from its initial training, as discussed in chapter 6, all the way through to its deployment at the front.

In June 1943, the 8th Panzer Division's welfare officer submitted a report on his activities over the preceding months. While the report is focused on the primary messages he shared with members of the division, detailing the various meetings he participated in, and the complaints of the troops (including SS-army tensions), perhaps the most interesting aspect of the document concerns his lectures in Minsk.[42]

> During the reporting period, I held lectures before 72 units with altogether 146 officers, 894 NCOs, and 4,407 men about the following themes:
> 1) Political and military development during the war.
> 2) Enemy propaganda and rumours.
> 3) The spiritual orientation of soldiers before and after leave.
> 4) The military situation.
> 5) The political task of the German soldier towards the Russian population.
> 6) Causes and goals of the Second World War
> 7) Political Soldierly

> On 14. and 15.5.43, participation in a meeting of Third Panzer Army's division care officers in Vitebsk.
> The same thing on 28. and 29.6.43.
> On 16.5.43, lecture in Vitebsk theatre for the units stationed there about the theme 'Causes and Goals of the Second World War and Enemy Propaganda.'
> The same thing on 25.5.43.
> From 8–11 June 1943, lectures in the division's rehabilitation home and at the maintenance company in Minsk.

The audience's interest was great, the subsequent debate was lively. The following questions were repeatedly asked:

'Did we need to shatter ourselves and occupy all of Europe?'

'Was it correct to march so deeply into Russia?'

'Why haven't the Japanese begun the war against the Soviet Union?'

'How will Turkey act?'

'Is it even possible to defeat the Bolsheviks militarily?'

The existence of SS-units per se and their frequent appearances in illustrated magazines and the weekly news reels were criticized.

Complaints were directed on the part of the men from the entire division, that despite the orders of the Führer and the *Reichsmarschall* to the contrary, men are ordered to attend mass and those who did not attend voluntarily were ordered carry out especially dirty work and the indirect form of address for superiors is still customary.

In individual cases, the unfair distribution of personal goods and leave cards and a better life for officers has been complained about.

As the report indicates, by summer 1943 doubts about Germany's victory in the war permeated the ranks, and it was precisely this phenomenon that so alarmed the German political and military leadership. As detailed above, part of the army's approach to this morale crisis was to ratchet up the ideological indoctrination. Complementing this was an increasingly politicized judicial system, which served two purposes. In the literature, German military justice has been described as traditionally severe. While this was certainly the case in the days of Frederick the Great, the Imperial German army took a much less violent approach to discipline than many of its contemporaries. During the First World War, the Italian, French, and British armies executed far more men than the *Kaiserheer*. By the time of the Second World War, this was no longer the case and only the Soviet Union shot more of its own soldiers than the German army's 19,600 victims from its own ranks.[43]

On the one hand, the military justice system utilized terror as a means of coercing German soldiers to man their positions in the face of enemy superiority by recourse to the death penalty as a pedagogic tool. On the other hand, it also attempted to 'use the labour power of a man for as long as possible' and troops whose offenses were not seen to fundamentally threaten the army's cohesion were funnelled back to the front.[44] This dual nature was made clear in a report issued by the 8th Panzer Division's divisional court for the first half of 1942.[45]

In the reporting period, 208 criminal proceedings were carried out. Of these, 36 cases led to convictions. The rest of the proceedings were dismissed or settled in a different way. The number of carried out proceedings was small, especially during the time of the advance. The enforcing of the punishment was predominantly suspended especially during the time of operations in order to avoid convicted soldiers being preserved in prisons while unpunished soldiers found themselves at the front.

The following military offences emerged as the most common during the reporting period: military theft, breach of guard duty, and unauthorized absence.

The total number of criminal cases was higher than in the previous half year, though it must be considered that during the reporting period, the troops found themselves more stationary.

In one case, a death sentence was pronounced.

Elements of military necessity emerge from this document; while the army needed to impose discipline in the ranks to keep its organizational integrity, it also realized that locking men in prison deprived the front of much needed manpower, and since sentenced soldiers would stay in the safety of prisons, this could also influence troops' morale negatively. German military justice increasingly radicalized during the conflict, but it is clear that the war in the east provided the real impetus to this process. This was partially due to how soldiers viewed the struggle: as a seemingly interminable conflict that simply ground them – and their enthusiasm for war – down to a blunt edge. A report issued by the 205th Infantry Division commander drew attention to a company where professionalism and discipline had clearly been eroded under the strain of war in the east.[46]

On 5.12.42 from 11.00 to 13.30 the divisional commander inspected the positions of the 3rd/*Jäger* Battalion 6 at the anti-tank ditch near Kashino. On the previous evening, the troops were informed of the appearance of 300 trucks north of Velizh and had been advised for increased attentiveness.

The divisional commander walked along the length of the whole anti-tank ditch, without meeting a soldier or discovering any footprints in the snow. The ditch and the branching-off saps were covered in snow drifts, the ditch was in places buried by earth works and was no longer an absolute tank obstacle. Weapons lay around, unsecured and filthy.

No sentry reported in the forest corner eastward of the ditch despite repeated loud calls. The *Jäger* (riflemen) Bolzer just left his sentry position before the *Jäger* Urbanke relieved him. The light machine gun 42 positioned there was unguarded in this time span.

Neither the aforementioned *Jäger* nor the group leader, *Oberjäger* Gruber, who was brought to the area, were knowledgeable about the enemy situation. Contact to the left had been established by a patrol until eight days ago. The divisional commander caused an alarm to go off at an available wire line. When he left after 5 minutes, no man had yet arrived.

The company chief, *Oberleutnant* Hieselt, who had been brought to the area (older officer, First World War participant), reported after a quarter of an hour and stated that he had been in another part of his sector. He declared that he had informed his platoon leaders about the enemy situation.

Shortly afterwards the battalion commander, *Hauptmann* Rheinheimer, reported without shoulderboards. The divisional commander made him aware of the contradictory order and walked with him along the position again. In the shelters and on the sentry positions, great disorder predominated. Wooden cover panels were broken out, shells laid around in large quantities. When the divisional commander wanted a heavy machine gun sentry to open fire (the machine gun was unloaded), it turned out that this one was not trained on the heavy machine gun and could not open fire. Two German hand grenades lay in the snow. Russian hand grenades that were never tried were placed in a case. The soldiers had no confidence in them.

In response to the division commander's question, *Oberleutnant* Hieselt reported that the night patrols had a strength of 2 men and patrolled at the top of the ditch in contradiction to the divisional order, according to which the patrols must have sufficient combat strength and must use the ditch to avoid unnecessary losses.

The *Jäger* were partly unshaven. No formal report was given at all.

As this report indicated, even front-line units failed to always take their duties seriously due to the burnout suffered by men continually manning their positions. In the particular case of this battalion, the situation was exacerbated by it being independently formed during the winter crisis and immediately thrown into battle in early 1942. The high command feared that the erosion of discipline would eventually result in an army that was both unwilling and unable to defend the Reich against the Red Army. Thus, its need to keep its men in the field, combined with the growing influence of Nazi beliefs and values, led to a transformation of the army's judicial system into one that routinely employed terror against its own men. Relatively minor offenses, such as falling asleep on sentry duty, were viewed through the prism of ideology, while an entire series of offenses – including desertion and self-inflicted wounds – was grouped under the heading of *Wehrkraftzersetzung*, or subversion of the war effort. The act of desertion struck both the army and the Nazi state at their core; for the former, deserters abandoned their comrades and increased the likelihood of defeat on the battlefield, while the latter viewed them as race traitors who betrayed the living organism of the Third Reich. The army's view of deserters – one that clearly connects the military and social problems together – is perhaps best encapsulated in a document issued by 8th Panzer Division in October 1942.

1) Measures against Deserters

In a time of the highest mental and physical exertions on the front and in the *Heimat*, the criminal elements and psychopaths who want to evade their duties to this *Frontgemeinschaft* must be prevented with the use of all means.

The nastiest military crime is desertion. At the same time, its combating serves the general fight against crime, because as experience shows, deserters commit numerous of the gravest crimes. A sustained combating of desertion is only possible when Wehrmacht agencies and the general Security Service desertion authorities know the tricks that deserters have often successfully used previously in order to make possible and continue with desertion. Then deserters will quickly be seized and convicted more successfully than before. That is the most important measure to combat desertion.

The report also included examples of deserters and their techniques in hopes of the army recognizing and stopping such infractions in the future.

In the following, 2 typical cases are named. They show that great mistrust is appropriate everywhere and the active collaboration of every superior is necessary to combat this crime.

Before *Gefreiter* W. deserted, he stole numerous already stamped but not signed forms for marching orders and Wehrmacht train tickets, as well as two leave passes from his unit's orderly room. Before his numerous trips, he drew up the corresponding march orders each time. He was able to travel by train unchallenged:

Lemberg-Berlin-Breslau-Lemberg
Lemberg-Breslau-Hamburg
Hamburg-Paris
Paris-Berlin-Breslau-Hamburg
Hamburg-Posen-Breslau-Hamburg

Due to his passes, he continually received food.

Over time, he donned the badge of rank of an *Unteroffizier* and later that of a *Feldwebel*. He entered the promotion he gave himself into his pay book. Despite numerous controls, the falsifications were never discovered. One day, he appeared at a dockyard. He passed himself off as an *Oberfeldwebel* from the Reich Air Ministry and declared he had the task of reviewing suspicious holders of military passes.

During the examination of his pay book when he showed it, the false entries were immediately detected and this prompted his arrest.

As deserters, *Gefreiter* P. and *Kanonier* Z. stayed for many months among the Russian inhabitants of Kharkov. They identified themselves to patrols through stolen pay books.

In the vicinity of the city, they one day discovered a defective Russian truck. At a divisional motor transport squadron, they acquired a motor for the vehicle. There, they passed themselves off as members of a corps map production unit and asked for a suitable motor for the vehicle. The motor was handed over without verification. They subsequently fitted the motor into the vehicle to make it drivable. In the following period, they frequently used the vehicle to get paid by a Russian town administration for delivering goods.

The deserters were sentenced to death.

Announcement of Sentences (Military Theft)

A soldier has the assignment as a messenger to bring the field post to his deployed company. He used the opportunity to misappropriate numerous field post packages addressed by and for his comrades. He continues his thievery when later the mail is brought forward from the company-troop vehicle. Amongst other things, he steals 20 packages from a postal sack earmarked for wounded soldiers. Within 4 months, he steals no less than 120 packages with items from loved ones at home and also valuables of all types. He is sentenced to death as a *Volksschädling* and shot.[47]

The concluding section of the document publicized the execution of a *Volksschädling* – someone whose behaviour damaged the *Volk* as a whole – for theft. This was actually one of the more common crimes punished by the army on the Eastern front, alongside the more explosive crimes of desertion or self-mutilation.

The following report, issued by the 83rd Infantry Division in autumn 1942, gives a flavour of the discipline issues the army chose to punish.

Activity Report of the 83rd Infantry Division's Court for the Months of August and September 1942

Punishments have been handed out in accordance with the following breakdown:

NCOs in 7 cases

Enlisted Men in 42 cases [...]

Enquiries of death were completed in 8 cases (including 5 suicides). [...]

Punishments:

1) Lange, Friedrich, *Schütze* 1./Security Battalion 343. Breach of guard regulations. 1 year and 3 months prison. [He] did not take to sentry post in partisan-threatened area, but instead went to sleep in a house out of his sentry area. [...]

3) Schulz, Wilhelm, *Unteroffizier*, 1./Security Battalion 336. Breach of guard regulations. 1 year and 6 months confinement in a fortress. Due to heavy rain, a fork in the road that his group was to secure by night was not permanently manned, and instead the fork in the road was 'secured' by a patrol while his troops withdrew some 700m. The fork was occupied by the Russians and had to be retaken by a relief force with the loss of one man.

4) Johannsen, Alfred, *Gefreiter*, 8./Infantry Regiment 251. Absence without leave. 6 months prison. Exceeded his home leave by 8 days to initiate his divorce.

5) Ninkerken, Karl-Heinz, *Schütze*, 14./Anti Tank/Infantry Regiment 251. Breach of guard regulations and insubordination. 5 years penitentiary and *Wehrunwürdikeit*.[48] [He] had stable guard and was to observe a forest edge 300m away. He left his position, went to his quarters, and went to bed. Furthermore shortly afterwards during a Russian attack, after delivering a message he did not go as ordered to his gun position, but rather lay in a trench and slept. [...]

8) Küllsen, Karl, *Gefreiter*, 7.Infantry Regiment 251. Cowardice in concomitance with breach of guard regulations. 5 years penitentiary and *Wehrunwürdikeit*. Due to fear of danger to himself, [he] did not move to his security post.

9) Koschnitzki, Wilhelm, *Kanonier*, 4./Artillery Regiment 183. Theft from a fellow soldier. 3 months prison. Stole a pullover jacket and a lighter from a comrade. [...]

11) Ingelmann, Edmund, *Gefreiter*, 8./Infantry Regiment 251. Careless handling of weapons. 5 months confinement in a fortress. [He] caused the death of a comrade through the careless handling of a submachine gun.

12) Schulz, Helmut, *Kanonier*, 1./Artillery Regiment 183. Careless handling of weapons. 3 months confinement in a fortress. [He] caused the death of a comrade by loading his rifle contrary to regulations.

13) Herzogenrath, Hubert, *Gefreiter*, 9./Infantry Regiment 251. Continued breach of guard regulations, insulting and threating a superior. Total punishment 1 year and 6 months prison. [He] left his guard position three times at night and went to the rear position, to find the relief inadvertently forgotten to be sent forward, and while there insulted and threatened the responsible commander.

14) Rof, Willi, *Gefreiter*, 4./Artillery Regiment 183. Theft from a comrade. 6 months prison. [He] stole breeches, a fur coat and a map case from a room in which two military police men lived.

15) Wischniewski, Roman, *Reiter*, Veterinary Company 183. Recidivism of theft, military embezzlement, plundering. 3 years and 6 month prison and loss of *bürgerliche Ehrenrechte*[49] for 3 years. [He] has continually stolen from his comrades and superiors and appropriated a comrade's wallet that he found, as well as stole 10m of linen and a scarf from a Russian house.

16) Schoknecht, Reinhold, *Obergefreiter*, 7./Infantry Regiment 251. Recidivism of military theft. 6 months of prison. As cook [he] sent some 800 grams of coffee from the allotted inventory to his family members, furthermore from army inventory he sent to his wife 2 towels, 2 handkerchiefs, 3 pairs of stockings and bootlaces. [...]

18) Weidner, Kurt, *Gefreiter*, 7./Infantry Regiment 251. Careless handling of weapons. 3 months confinement in a fortress. After finishing weapon cleaning and the insertion of the magazine, [he] touched the trigger of the submachine gun and thereby fired several shots which killed one comrade and severely wounded another comrade. During the sentencing, his good conduct, his youthful age, and his lack of training with the submachine gun were taken into consideration in favour of the punished.

[...]

21) Tiede, Berthold, *Gefreiter*, 5./Infantry Regiment 251. Fraud. 2 years prison. While filing an application for family support, he concealed that he received 12 RM monthly for sublease from his father and claimed a surplus amount of 352 RM. His punishment was increased due to consideration of his criminal record and the fact that he attempted during the investigation to send letters to his family in order to prompt false testimonies by his family members.

22) Jakobs, Fritz, *Gefreiter*, Headquarters Battery II./Artillery Regiment 183. Breach of guard regulations. 9 months prison. [He] left his guard position, allegedly to get his coat, and went to his quarters, where he was found sleeping.

23) Meyer, Walter, *Unteroffizier*, 5./Infantry Regiment 251. Careless handling of weapons. 2 months confinement in a fortress. [He] loaded a machine gun with live ammunition during training and carelessly fired, which severely wounded a comrade.

24) Flemming, Hans, *Kanonier*, 2./Artillery Regiment 183. Military theft. 5 months prison. [He] stole 2 kilo tins and four iron ration tins of meat from the provisions area.

[...]

26) Beckmann, Walter, 14./Infantry Regiment 257. Careless handling of weapons. 3 months confinement in a fortress. [He] activated a Russian hand-grenade in a closed room, which detonated due to careless handling and wounded the punished, as well as 5 comrades.

[...]

28) Buhmann, Otto, *Gefreiter*, 2./ Infantry Regiment 277. Military embezzlement. 6 months prison. [He] took two army postal packets for a comrade during mail distribution and stole their contents.

29) Heideman, Helmut, *Unteroffizier*, Headquarters Company./Infantry Regiment 251. Disobedience. 6 months prison. [He] did not carry out an order for a sentry position.

[...]

31) Dohmann, Max, *Gefreiter*, Butchery Company 183. Breach of guard regulations. 6 weeks confinement. [He] left his guard position in a drunken condition and lay down in a carriage 20 meters away to sober up. Mitigation was considered, in that the neighbouring sentry looked after the punished's area.

33) Krebs, Walter, *Gefreiter*, 3./Security Battalion343. Falsification of documents. 3 months prison. [He] modified leave entries in his pay book to obtain preferred leave.

34) Vasterling, Heinrich, *Wachtmeister*, Headquarters Battery IV./ Artillery Regiment 183. Recurrence of military theft with fraud. 3 years prison and loss of rank. [He] sold his service pistol in Vilnius to a member of the Lithuanian police for 140 RM and traded another borrowed pistol with an *Obergefreiter* for 4 bottles of schnapps and cigarettes.

[...] Several proceedings on self-inflicted injuries have, despite strong suspicions, led to no conclusions, because a later clarification from the Replacement Army was no longer possible. Soldiers, who are suspected of self-inflicted injuries due to the nature of their wounds, are therefore held back in the divisional area until the facts of the case are clarified. Furthermore, one has to report immediately to the military tribunal when the suspicion arises of self-inflicted injuries.[50]

The infractions listed in this report highlight the various discipline issues that plagued the Wehrmacht, from mundane issues of simple thievery and improper handling of weapons, to more important offenses such as insubordination, absence without formal authorization and self-mutilation. It was the latter that most offended Nazi ideological tenets and one which the army punished fiercely, either through execution or long stints in military prisons.[51] As the war dragged on into 1944 and 1945, and a new generation of German commanders rose to positions of real power, the symbiosis of motivation, ideology, and military justice was perhaps best represented by *Generalfeldmarschall* Ferdinand Schörner.

Described as 'a fanatical loyalist from ingrained Nazi conviction, a believer in "triumph of the will" and the need for a revolution of the spirit in the army,' Schörner had deserters hanged, leaving their corpses dangling in the wind as a deterrent to others.[52] His quick recourse to terror was complemented by his belief that only through a thorough indoctrination of the men with Nazi ideological tenets could Germany win the war. The following order was issued in early 1943 when Schörner commanded a corps; by the end of the war, he had been named commander-in-chief of the German army in large part due to the fanaticism he demanded of his men as captured by this document. The fact that the order was issued while his corps was deployed on a relatively quiet section of the front betrays the severity and ideological rigour that permeated Schörner's command.[53]

This order should not be read through the first time during the usual office hours, but rather studied in quiet concentration outside of work. In the process, consider in what form and which time increments the content should be taught to our soldiers.

I

Our comrades have stood for months on the Eastern Front in tough combat with varied fortunes. The more serious tone of our *Wehrmachtberichte*[54] characterizes the highpoint of the 1942/43 winter war.

In this hour, I turn to every officer of my area of command and oblige him to intervene as a leader with true spirit and persuasiveness and to more intensively exert influence in education and enlightenment on the German men entrusted to him.

II

Every soldier must know that in this type of colossal struggle, there are not only shining victories, but that setbacks can also occur. No soldier should let himself be mistaken in his spiritual attitude by the whims of battlefield luck, but rather should await with quiet confidence the war's further development and the tasks that will also confront us one day.

An officer's word can only be borne from a rock solid belief in the justice of our task and from a faith in victory that cannot be shaken by anything, as it corresponds to our soldiers' healthy optimism and the unparalleled efforts and successes of our army.

The officer must make his soldiers immune to an unsoldierly emotional stress. He must convince them to squelch rumours and gossip because no one runs as fast as a rumour, especially when it is bad. Enemy propaganda will more or less skilfully begin. It is therefore necessary that even the soldier, who is still indifferent and apathetic to things, is spiritually led by the officer and somehow knows what the war is about.

Every one of our soldiers must have a notion of our *Volk*'s war of destiny and for the magnitude of his tasks. Men on leave and letters go to the *Heimat*; the success of this education by the officers must therefore make an impact on the People's Arm to the anchoring of the ideas and the teachings of our Führer. The soldier must clearly discern the national socialist idea and fight for it with passionate conviction in word and deed.

Belief is the strongest vital force. Success in life is always with those who happily and constantly believe in it and fate loves these believers, the cheerful and the brave.

Decisive is the loyalty that we maintain for our Führer and our *Volk*. Victory grows out of it.

III

To awaken this idea for our country and our decisive struggle is easy in our situation because:

1. At this time, things are good, very good for us.[55]
2. Our front's closed community of fate of gives us the strongest possibilities for the education of our soldiers. All undesirable distraction or influence is missing. Therefore, a strong need for affection exists for every real leader to solve the smaller and larger problems of the day, to grasp the great inner upheaval of our time.
3. It can be made quite clear to our people that we are fighting in the struggle with the Soviet Union for our most elemental existence, not only in a national, but also in an individual sense. Naturally, these concepts must be translated for the simple man and be made familiar to them that we are fighting for the existence of our house, home, and family.

   In this great struggle, two extremes clash against one another that are irreconcilable. Here, is a struggle about *Weltanschauungen*, about two types of seeing and living life.

IV

The officer must orient himself and his soldiers towards the final decision.

We must constantly keep in sight of our soldiers that the campaign against the Soviet Union is not like that against Poland, against Norway, against France, or in the Balkans, but rather, that this war is, in reality, completely different. At the same time, we must say to them again and again what it means to have achieved success, such as the German Wehrmacht can offer, against such an armed, fanatically led and bestial-fighting opponent. We must explain to them what the occupied territories mean for the future of Germany and for the life of our people, so that even the sceptical or half-hearted recognize that the rigorous concentration of all strength for final victory has never been more necessary, but has also never been more rewarding, as it is now in the hour of the final decision.

Modern wars do not last for decades, the weaker must be smashed under the force of the stronger's better weapons. It all depends, however, on these weapons being used by men whose bravery, enthusiasm for combat and will to persevere cannot be exceeded by any enemy.

As for the rest, history teaches that in a war victory invariably goes to the one who, next to the greater military efficiency, carries the firmer belief in the righteousness of his cause and is willing to ruthlessly commit to this conviction.

In this enormous struggle to be or not to be, there is no compromise solution. There is only an increase in the sense of duty and the cold will to win or to die. Everyone must understand: fate is hard and merciless; it inclines toward those whose inner strength and confidence is stronger. We can and we will win, but in this enormous struggle it needs an enormous exertion of force. No one can be excluded; everyone is involved. No one can exist 'outside of it'.

V

The personal example of the officer stands out front.

The best instruction content-wise and methodologically or the best-led discussion remains groundless when the deed doesn't follow these persuasively spoken words and this deed is called: *example*. According to a word of the previous world war, dying as an example is therefore a piece of it. An officer, who teaches a national socialist solution and then deviates from it in practice has forfeited his belonging in my corps just as anyone who today sees in National Socialism an imposed form of intellectual-spiritual attitude.

For his soldiers, the officer is there daily, hourly. I expect that during my troop visits I will receive from every company, platoon, and group leader complete answers to the last question regarding the mental attitude, conduct, family background, district of origin and other such things about every single soldier in his unit. The long nights and the dreary solitude in bunkers offer the best opportunity to dutifully concern oneself with that.

In the evening, the officer also always belongs in the circle of his soldiers where he can speak informally with them. I expect considerably more success from such discussions than from such social evenings where true camaraderie loses out. True camaraderie has absolutely nothing in common with the shallow social gathering of the masses; it proves itself in the inner unity of life and death.

The soldier has a pronounced sensitivity to these things and if his superior possesses leadership values or not. He wants to be led, clearly and fairly; he also bears severity, whose necessity he especially recognized in this war as already being beneficial many times. But he also has a legitimate right that one accepts his worries and problems. I would like to know the correctly educated and led German soldier who breaks his loyalty.

One thing that is self-evident is that one cannot demand more effort and sacrifice from the soldiers than the leader himself is prepared to give. When a *Leutnant* or NCO indeed gets up later than the soldier, takes liberties that the simple soldier does not have, and doesn't exceed them in conscientiousness and conception of duty, then the matter is rotten.

The greatest concern is for the young replacements, which for the most part consist of ethnic Germans. These people are capable of being educated and must be turned into good Germans. A special education and training appears necessary that, next to the return to Germandom, aims for the absolute dependability in soldierly respects. [...]

VI

Implementation of National Socialist education

1. As leader of his men in battle, the officer is also the bearer of national socialist education. This constitutes the foundation and prerequisite for his training work, which has proven itself under heavy fire and in long deployment. [...] *There is no splitting of military and spiritual leadership.*

The harder and longer the war is, all the more adamantly arises the question about the war's meaning. All the more clear, however, is that the war could not have been won alone with the indispensable iron discipline of the old army. 'The soldier of today's army wins with the weapon and with the *Weltanschauung*.' (From my special order Nr. 3 from 6.3.42).

Schörner's order contained numerous threads that ran through the German army's experience in the east. He repeatedly emphasized the importance of officers in ensuring that their men knew why the war was essential to Germany's future. The hardness and the strength of the individual's will that had become such vital components of the army's self-understanding permeated the order. And finally, the conviction that Nazi beliefs were the only means to ensure a soldier's confidence in the war effort meant that the melding of military and National Socialist values and ideas that Blomberg had first pushed for in the 1930s now became standard practice for at least some German field commanders and their units. This was supplemented by the introduction of the National Socialist Leadership Officer in December 1943. Hitler, believing that the army's officer corps still refused to submit fully to the Nazification of the army, ordered the creation of this position; similar to Soviet commissars, they were to provide the ideological framework of the war to the rank and file. So, despite the efforts of commanders such as Schörner, the army's loss of sovereignty and independence was clearly noticeable in this area.

Conclusion

During its war with the Soviet Union, the German army approached the peak of its powers as a military force and underwent a steady grinding away of both its combat strength and its principles until the army that surrendered to the Allied powers in May 1945 was scarcely comparable to the one that invaded in June 1941. This documentary collection has attempted to show how the German army appraised its own situation and what attempts it made to salvage it after it became apparent that the Soviet invasion had developed completely differently from previous campaigns. During the opening months of the war, the German army displayed all of the hallmarks that made it such an effective fighting force. Led by an officer corps that valued decisiveness, boldness and aggression, the army utilized speed and mobility in a blitz campaign designed to defeat the Soviet Union quickly. Initially, the German army appeared destined to achieve its goals; encirclement battles at Bialystok, Minsk and Kiev led to some one million Soviet prisoners of war and numerous smashed and mangled Soviet armies. Even during the summer months of great victories, however, it was clear that the army faced numerous serious obstacles and that the German way of war was threatened from multiple directions. And once the German onslaught was stopped and the war degenerated into one of attrition, the chances of a German military victory decreased rapidly.

The German system of command – which was primarily responsible for the army's victories from tactical to operational level – was significantly damaged by the campaign on two fronts. First, the tremendous number of casualties suffered not just by officers, but also by NCOs (who were given much more authority in the German army than in other contemporary forces) caused shortages of well-trained and able leaders that persisted throughout the remainder of the war. This necessarily made it more difficult for a system of war based on commanders making a decisive, yet thoughtful and more importantly sound decision on the spot, to function effectively. Second, the theatre of war's immense size – the fabled *Ostraum*, which translates as eastern space, but which suggests a hostile land without end – combined with the wide-ranging actions of panzer formations led not just Hitler, but also the Army High Command to tighten up the lines of command on several different occasions; in other words, the *Auftragstaktik* that had traditionally given the army its flexibility in the field was continuously shorn away by the political and military leadership. This most notably occurred in December 1941 when Hitler issued his famous 'Halt Order', effectively denying his field commanders the ability to act as they saw fit, but it was a trend that continued throughout the remainder of the conflict and spread to lower command levels. In both cases, however, enough traditional German leadership practices survived to ensure that the army remained proficient on the battlefield at least through late 1944. One essential point here was the will to adapt to the changing circumstances. German military leadership demonstrated a high level of flexibility in developing new approaches, especially in the tactical, but also in the operational spheres. Less effective were learning processes in intelligence and logistics.

This last area was perhaps the largest problem that the army had to contend with. Neglect played an important role, but the German army simply lacked the means for supplying a far-reaching advance. Confident that the war would indeed be quick, the Germans believed that their logistic weakness would not be too damaging; this assumption proved entirely incorrect, and the Germans struggled throughout the entirety of the campaign – though especially in 1941 – to bring sufficient supplies of ammunition, clothing and food to the front. As the war changed into one of attrition, the transportation problem was exacerbated by a growing need for supply goods of all types, which the German war economy proved increasingly unable to produce. Shortages of most items lowered German combat efficiency – dramatically at times – and the German army consistently found itself operating at a material disadvantage compared to its Red Army opponent. One solution to this problem was to exploit Soviet resources; while captured weaponry became an increasingly important component of German forces in the field – particularly artillery – it was the plundering of Soviet agriculture that proved most detrimental to the German war effort. While living off the land gave the Germans some short-term advantages during the advance in 1941, plundering Soviet peasants only drove them into the arms of a burgeoning resistance movement, thus adding yet another task to an already overburdened and undermanned force.

The German response to any manifestations of popular resistance in the Soviet Union was centred on violence, and while such policy sat squarely in the army's institutional history, it received an injection of venom from Nazi ideological beliefs. For Hitler and the Nazi leadership, the Soviet Union's destiny was to serve as the foundation for a German racial empire. As noted in the text, the Germans planned a literal war of annihilation against Soviet state and society, a war which targeted millions of Soviet citizens – from Jews to prisoners of war, from Roma to urbanites – with death. The army's complicity in this ideological war is well-established, particularly at the higher levels. At the lower levels of the field army, it is clear that various formations, as well as individual men, participated in the war of annihilation; the motivations behind their actions, however, ranged from ideological congruence with the regime, to policies that fit, one way or another, into the concept of military necessity. No matter the reasoning, the army's anti-partisan, food requisitioning, and scorched earth retreat policies all substantially contributed to the Nazi attempt to decimate the Soviet population and destroy the state.

In an attempt to rectify these issues, the army resorted to ad hoc policies throughout the course of the war. It instituted wide-ranging training courses at the front so that men being trained as officers and NCOs could understand the intensity of the war in the east before being thrown into the front lines. Such attempts to mould *Ostkämpfer*, or 'Eastern Fighters' who were veterans that possessed the necessary hardness, tenacity, and decisiveness to survive in the *Ostraum* behind the front underscored the seriousness with which the German army took training, and this was ultimately one of the reasons why the army was able to stay in the field despite persistent shortages of men, weapons, and equipment. Another solution to the manpower problem was to enlist Soviet auxiliaries – the *Hilfswillige* – into the army, generally in rear-area positions to free up German soldiers for combat roles, but occasionally for frontline service. Of course, integrating Soviet citizens into the army's ranks called for a readjustment of German attitudes towards Soviet civilians as a whole, and lower level army formations attempted to do just that, knowing that only through the mobilization of the occupied territories' manpower and resources could the Germans achieve victory. Though some units truly strove to reverse course in occupation policy, the radicalization of the army's behaviour – including that of the individual soldier – during the course of the war and the certainty among Soviet civilians by mid-1943 at the latest that the Red Army would be returning, meant that such programmes had little chance of success.

The experience of the German army during its war with the Soviet Union was one that consistently evolved over time. At the front, the army transitioned from fighting a mobile, offensive war to one based on grinding positional defensive battles. In the rear, the army oscillated between arbitrary violence, conciliatory policies and destruction – during scorched earth retreats and large anti-partisan operations – on a wide scale. While the majority of these policies were designed to maintain the army's combat efficiency, the size of the Soviet opponent – in terms of manpower, geography, and, more abstractly but no less importantly, will-power – proved too great for the German army to overcome. Despite achieving operational victories unprecedented in modern military history during the second half of 1941, the strategic goal of defeating the Soviet Union proved too great for the army to accomplish and, in the end, its military failure complemented its moral failure.

Appendix A
Glossary

Bundeswehr: Armed forces of the Federal Republic of Germany, formed in 1956

Frontgemeinschaft: front society. Has its roots in the romanticisation of front soldiers' war experience in the First World War. In Nazi rhetoric, the term referred to a classless, egalitarian society of soldiers at the front which was to serve as the basis for German society after the war.

Härte: a key value in the German army. Dual meaning that suggested 'toughness' in the face of the enemy and a 'hardness' in dealing with the privations and problems of war.

Heimat: roughly translates as 'home'. Dual meaning that referred both to one's country, as well as one's home region or town. German soldiers could therefore argue that they fought for multiple 'homes' during the war.

Hilfswillige: volunteer, literally 'willing to help'. Denotes Soviet citizens and primarily prisoners of war who served in the ranks of the German army during the war.

Jagdkommando: special ad hoc units assembled by various German formations to carry out anti-partisan sweeps

Kaiserheer: Unofficial name for the German army between 1871 and 1918. Official names were the '*Deutsche Heer*' (German Army) and the *Reichsheer* (Imperial Army).

Manneszucht: Older German term for discipline, mainly used in the military arena, connecting discipline to masculinity.

Reichsführer-SS: Created in August 1934 as highest rank of the SS.

Reichswehr: German armed forces of the Interwar Period, officially renamed Wehrmacht on 1 June 1935.

Weltanschauung: A belief system (literally: world view) usually used to denote an ideological programme.

Winterhilfswerk: Winter Relief of the German People. This was an annual charitable collection carried out by the Nazi state to help finance the state-run charity, the National Socialist People's Welfare Organization.

Volk: roughly translates as 'people', though it has multiple meanings. During the Third Reich, the term was used to denote an 'ethnic people' who constituted a distinct nation with equality of all members (*Volksgemeinschaft*). Linked to notions of rootedness in the soil and thus permanence.

Appendix B
Organization of a German Infantry Division Staff

Divisional commander: Responsible for the command and condition of the division.

Command section (*Führungsabteilung*)

Ia: First General Staff Officer and deputy of the divisional commander (staff above the divisional level had a separate deputy commander, the Chief of Staff). Supported the divisional commander in the deployment and command of the division and led the staff work of the divisional staff. Supported by the *O1* (First Ordonnance Officer), who wrote the divisional war diary and kept the command papers (i.e. maps) updated.

Ic: Third General Staff Officer. Responsible for Intelligence and Counter-intelligence, but also for troop care until the creation of a special troop welfare staff officer (*Divisions-Betreuungs-Offizier*). Supported by the *O3* (Third Ordonnance Officer) and one or more interpreters.

The command section also included the divisional map section, a motorcycle platoon and officers advising the divisional commander about their arms, such as the commander of the artillery regiment for artillery questions.

Personal group of divisional staff section (*Adjutantur*)

IIa: Divisional adjutant, responsible for personnel affairs of the division's officers .

IIb: Responsible for personnel affairs of the rank and file as well as for the divisional staff office.

III: Divisional martial court. Also worked on requests for judicial assistance from civil courts, i.e. divorces.

Filing department (*Registratur*): Responsible for receiving and distributing orders and other documents and administering classified files.

Commander of the divisional headquarter (*Kommandant des Stabsquartiers*): Responsible for exploring, establishing and securing the divisional headquarter and command post.

Quartermaster Section (*Quartiermeisterabteilung*)

Ib: Second General Staff Officer, responsible for the complete logistical affairs of the division, including supply, POW transfer to rear installations, management of traffic and air protection in the rear area. Supported by the O2 (Second Ordonnance Officer).

Ib/WuG: Officer for weapons and equipment, responsible for supply and maintenance of weapons, ammunition and equipment except for special equipment such as that of engineers or medical services.

Ib/Kfz (or *V*): Divisional engineer, responsible for motor vehicle park, including spare parts and fuel supply.

IVa: Divisional intendant, responsible for supply of rations, fodder, clothes and individual equipment. Also responsible for gaining resources from occupied territory.

IVb: Divisional physician. Responsible for the deployment of the medical units, transport and care of wounded, hygiene and preventive measures for the troops and possibly civilians in the divisional area, supply of medical equipment.

IVc: Divisional veterinary, responsible for divisional horses, the butcher company and for food safety.

IVd: Chaplain (*K* = Catholic, *P*= Protestant, depending on the division's origins). Spiritual care for the troops.

IVz: Divisional paymaster, responsible for the field pay office.

    With the quartermaster section were also the *Divisions-Nachschubführer* (*Dinafü*) (divisional supply leader) with his staff, the leaders of the baggage trains, and the divisional Army Postal Master.

Table of units and their size

Note: the numbers given of men and material are authorised strengths. After the start of the war in the East, most units never approached these strengths again. From 1942 on, most units reached only 50-75% of the authorised manpower strength. The same was true with material, but here numbers of tanks were often lower due to maintenance problems.

Unit name	Men	Tanks	Guns (Artillery)
Heeresgruppe (army group)	1-4 armies		
Armee (army)	2-4 corps		
Korps (corps)	2-5 divisions		
Division (division)	15,000-18,000	100-350	
Regiment (regiment)	2,000-3,000	72-180	48
Abteilung (battalion)	500-750	36-60	12-18
Kompanie/Schwadron (company)/Batterie (battery)	150-200	12-20	4-6
Zug (platoon)	30-50	4-5	
Gruppe (squad)	8-12		
Trupp (team)	3-5		

Appendix D

Table of ranks

Note: The *Luftwaffe* (Air Force) and the *Kriegsmarine* (Navy) had a similar structure to the Army, but while the *Luftwaffe* used more or less the same names, the *Kriegsmarine* had very different rank names for traditional reasons.

	German Army	Waffen-SS	US Army
Generals	Generalfeldmarschall	SS-Volksmarschall (planned)	General of the Army
	Generaloberst	SS-Oberst-Gruppenführer (from 1942 on)	General
	General[1]	SS-Obergruppenführer	Lieutenant General
	Generalleutnant	SS-Gruppenführer	Major General
	Generalmajor	SS-Brigadeführer	Brigadier General
Staff officers		SS-Oberführer	
	Oberst	SS-Standartenführer	Colonel
	Oberstleutnant	SS-Obersturmbannführer	Lieutenant Colonel
	Major	SS-Sturmbannführer	Major
Subaltern	Hauptmann Cavalry: Rittmeister	SS-Hauptsturmführer	Captain
	Oberleutnant	SS-Obersturmführer	First Lieutenant
	Leutnant	SS-Untersturmführer	Second Lieutenant
NCOs	Stabsfeldwebel	SS-Sturmscharführer	Master Sergeant
	Oberfeldwebel Oberfähnrich[2] (OA)	SS-Hauptscharführer SS-Standartenoberjunker (FA)	Staff Sergeant
	Feldwebel[3] Fahnenjunker-Feldwebel	SS-Oberscharführer SS-Standartenjunker (FA)	Staff Sergeant
	Unterfeldwebel Fähnrich (OA)	SS-Scharführer SS-Oberjunker (FA)	Sergeant

	German Army	Waffen-SS	US Army
	Unteroffizier Fahnenjunker-Unteroffizier (OA)	SS-Unterscharführer SS-Junker (FA)	Sergeant
Enlisted Men	Stabsgefreiter		Specialist
	Obergefreiter	SS-Rottenführer	Lance Corporal
	Gefreiter	SS-Sturmmann	Private First Class
	Obersoldat	SS-Oberschütze	Private
	Soldat[4]	SS-Schütze	Private

OA/FA: Offizieranwärter (Army)/Führeranwärter (SS) = Ranks for Officer candidates.

Notes

Chapter 1

1. Stephen Fritz, *Ostkrieg: Hitler's War of Extermination in the East*, p. 470.
2. Ibid., p. 471.
3. Elements of Army Group North that retreated into East Prussia and Latvia following the Red Army's offensive that liberated Leningrad were eventually pushed into what became known as the Courland Pocket, where some 500,000 men – though only half could be counted as true front line troops – held out until the end of the war in May 1945; see Karl-Heinz Frieser, 'Die Rückzugskämpfe der Heeresgruppe Nord bis Kurland,' in Karl-Heinz Frieser et. al, *Die Ostfront 1943/44: Der Krieg im Osten und an den Nebenfronten*, volume 8, *Das Deutsche Reich und der Zweite Weltkrieg*, pp. 623-678.
4. The best examination of the decisive panzer thrust – that of Army Group Centre's Panzer Groups 2 and 3 – during Operation Barbarossa is David Stahel's *Operation Barbarossa and Germany's Defeat in the East.*
5. A balanced analysis of these issues is found in Gerhard P. Groß, *Mythos und Wirklichkeit: Geschichte des operative Denkens im deutschen Heer von Moltke d.Ä. bis Heusinger*, pp. 225-232.
6. See Ernst Klink, The Conduct of Operations,' in *Germany and the Second World War*, vol. 4, *The Attack on the Soviet Union*, pp. 525-569, Ben Shepherd, *Hitler's Soldiers: The German Army in the Third Reich*, pp. 134-141.
7. Panzergruppe 3/Ia, Gefechtsbericht vom 22. – 29.6.41, 29.6.41, Bundesarchiv-Militärarchiv, hereafter (BA-MA) RH 21-3/46. The authors graciously thank Dr. David Stahel for providing a copy of this document.
8. Oberkommando des Heeres or Army High Command.
9. See the chart 'Casualties for all Divisions per Month,' in Christian Hartmann, *Wehrmacht im Ostkrieg: Front und militärisches Hinterland 1941/42*, pp. 212. For more on how German divisions experienced the opening days of the campaign, see Jeff Rutherford, *Combat and Genocide on the Eastern Front: The German Infantry's War, 1941-1944*, pp. 84-5.
10. Fritz, *Ostkrieg*, p. 88.
11. 8. Panzer Division/Ia, KTB, 6.7.41, National Archives and Record Administration hereafter (NARA) T-315, Roll 483; KTB, 19.10.41, 31.10.41, NARA T-315, Roll 484.
12. For more on this issue as it relates to logistics, see chapter 4.
13. XXXXVII. Panzer Korps/Ia, Kriegstagebuch Nr.2., 19.7.41, BA-MA RH 24-47/2. The authors graciously thank Dr. David Stahel for providing a copy of this document.
14. 7. Infanterie-Division/Ia, Kommandeur-Besprechung, 15.8.41, NARA T-315, Roll 374.

15. The commander was stating that a linear defence necessarily concentrated the men at the front, leaving very few in reserve. Without a reserve that could eliminate any enemy penetration of the defensive front, any breakthrough threatened the position as a whole.

16. David Stahel, *Kiev, 1941: Hitler's Battle for Supremacy in the East*, p. 302.

17. [7. Infanterie-Division/Ia], Betr.: Kurzbericht über die Kämpfe im Jelnja-Abschnitt, 29.9.1941, NARA T-315, Roll 397.

18. The document referred to the ongoing encirclement battle centered on Kiev.

19. David Stahel, *The Battle for Moscow, 1941*.

20. 14. Panzer Division/Ia, KTB, 21.11.41; 29.11.41, NARA T-315, Roll 656.

21. Panzer-Regiment 10/Kommandeur, An 8. Panzer-Division/Ia, 14.12.1941, NARA T-315, Roll.

22. Fritz, *Ostkrieg*, p. 205.

23. VII. Armeekorps/Ia., Betrifft: Lage und Kampfführung im Osten, 3.1.42 NARA T-316, Roll 376.

24. VII. Armeekorps/Ia, Korpsbefehl für die Kampfführung in der Winterstellung, 3.1.42, NARA T-315, Roll 376.

25. 7. Infanterie-Division/Ia, KTB, 4.1.42, NARA T-315, Roll 372.

26. 126. Infanterie-Division/Ia, KTB, 22.1.42, BA-MA RH 26-126/34.

27. The most authoritative examination of the Stalingrad campaign from the German perspective remains Bernd Wegner, 'The War against the Soviet Union, 1942-1943,' in Horst Boog, et. al, *Germany and the Second World War*, volume VI, *The Global War*, pp. 843-1172.

28. XXXXVIII. Panzer Korps/Ia, KTB, 6.9.42, NARA T-314, Roll 1153.

29. On 5 December 1757, Frederick the Great's small, yet more mobile and better-drilled army maneuvered around the flank of the much larger Austrian force near the town of Leuthen and decisively smashed the Hapsburg forces. The battle passed into Prussian and later German lore as the triumph of skill, determination, and will in the face of superior forces.

30. 71. Infanterie-Division/Ia, Kampfstärken der 71. Div. am 19.9.1942 (Anlage), o.D., BA-MA RH 20-6/212.

31. For a detailed calculation, see Adrian Wettstein, *Die Wehrmacht im Stadtkampf 1939-1942*, pp. 306-315.

32. XI. Armeekorps/Kommandierender Generanl, Dem Oberbefehlshaber der 6. Armee, 27.9.1942, BA-MA RH 20-6/213.

33. *Führererlass* (literally: leaders decree) is an order given directly by Adolf Hitler.

34. Pionier-Bataillon 179, Angriff auf den Nordwestteil der Martinofenhallen des Roten Oktober (Halle 4) am 11. November 1942. Gefechtsbericht, 12.11.42, BA-MA RH 26-79/61.

35. For further discussion of the former, see Rutherford, *Combat and Genocide on the Eastern Front*, pp. 307-315; for an examination of the latter, see Christopher Rass, '*Menschenmaterial*': *Deutsche Soldaten an der Ostfront*, pp. 381-82.

36. IX. Armeekorps/Ia, Betr.: Zerstörung im Falle 'Büffel,', 20.2.1943, NARA T-315, Roll 388.

37. 126. Infanterie-Division/Ia, KTB, 21.3.43, BA-MA RH 26-126/153.

38. 8. Panzer-Division, Kommandeurbesprechung am 5.6.43, NARA T-315, Roll 499.

39. For more on German efforts to destroy the partisan movement, see chapter 5.

40. For more on large-operations, see Ben Shepherd, *War in the Wild East: The German Army and Soviet Partisans*, pp. 1 2 1-24 and Christian Gerlach, *Kalulierte Morde, Die Deutsche Wirtschafts und Vernichtungspolitik in Weißrußland 1941 bis 1944*. pp. 884-958.

41. Auffrischungsstab 3/Ia, Tagesmeldung 6.6.1943, NARA T-3 1 5, Roll 390.

42. The term 'gangs' (German: *Banden*) refers to partisans in the National Socialist and military terminology of that time and was officialy used from 1942 on, as for example in the *Führerweisung* No 46. See Walter Hubatsch, *Hitler's Weisungen für die Kriegsführung. Dokumente des Oberkommandos der Wehrmacht*. See also chapter 5 for some discussion of this issue.

43. In his study *Hitler's Army: Soldiers, Nazis and War in the Third Reich*, Omer Bartov states that the 18th Panzer Division's participation in the operation led it to suffer "only a few casualties"; p. 92.

44. For recent examinations of the Kursk battle, see Karl-Heinz Frieser, 'Die Schlacht im Kursker Bogen,' in *Die Ostfront 1943/44*, Roman Töppel, *Kursk 1943: Die größte Schlacht des Zweiten Weltkriegs*, Dennis Showalter, *Armor and Blood: The Battle of Kursk, the Turning Point of World War Two*.

45. 7. Infanterie-Division/Ia, Zustandsmeldung vom 1.8.1943, NARA T-3 1 5, Roll 392.

46. *Hiwi* is the short form of *Hilfswillige*, or volunteer, used to describe Soviet citizens who worked within the ranks of the German army.

47. 306. Infanterie-Division/Kdr, An Gruppe Schwerin mit der Bitte um Weitergabe an Gen.Kdo. LVII. Pz.Korps und 1. Panzer-Armee, 4.12.43, BA-MA RH 2 1-1/1 20a.

48. German infantry units up to the level of regiments were renamed as "Grenadier" units in October 1942. The term is French, but it had a long tradition in the German army going back to Frederick the Great.

49. Schreiben von [Oldwig von] Natzmer, Oberst i.G [Ia PzGrenDiv GD] an [Oberst Hellmuth] Laegeler, 1.12.1943, BA-MA RH 2 1-1/1 20.

50. Alarm units (*Alarmeinheiten*) were units organized in rear units to be used in case of emergency, normally for defensive deployment to free real combat forces for counter-attacks. Usually, these were of platoon or company strength. Because most of the men in the rear units had limited tactical and weapon training, there was a need for additional training. From 1943 on, most rear units had to form such alarm units, in particular to act against airborne operations or partisans.

Chapter 2

1. Auszüge aus den vom Oberkommando der Heeresgruppe Süd an O.K.H. eingereichten Berichten über die Hebung der Kampfkraft der Infanterie, 1943, BA-MA RH 1 1-I/44

2. Cited in Marco Sigg, *Der Unterführer als Feldherr im Taschenformat: Theorie und Praxis der Auftragstaktik im deutschen Heer 1869 bis 1945*, p. 1 1 6.

3. 7./I.R. 2 1 1, Schilderung der Kämpfe um Kiew in den Tagen vom 6.-9.8.41, 28.9.41, BA-MA RH 24-29/29.

4. Fernschreiben Chef des Generalstabes an die Herren Chefs der Generalstäbe der Heeresgruppen und Armeen, 6.1.42, BA-MA RH 20-16/80.

5. OKH/GenStdH/Ausb.Abt. (II), Betr.: Kampferfahrungen, 10.6.42, BA-MA RH 2/2853.

6. Armeeoberkommando 4/Ia, Nr. 166/42 geh. (Abschrift), 23.1.42, BA-MA RH 2/2854.
7. Stellvertretendes General-Kommando VII. Armeekorps/Ia/Id, Betr.: Ausbildungsanregungen nach Fronterfahrungen, 27.7.42, BA-MA RH 53-7/v 234b.
8. Auszüge aus den vom Oberkommando der Heeresgruppe Süd an O.K.H. eingereichten Berichten über die Hebung der Kampfkraft der Infanterie, 1943, BA-MA RH 11-I/44.
9. Panzer-Grenadier Division Grossdeutschland/Ia, Gliederung, Führung und Ausbildung unterster Einheiten der Panzergrenadiere, 24.5.1943, BA-MA RH 26-1005/41.
10. 58. Infanterie-Division/Ia, Divisionsbefehl für die Führerausbildung Winter 1941/42, 14.11.41, BA-MA RH 26-8/37.
11. Anlage zum Divisionsbefehl für die Führerausbildung der 58. Infanterie-Division im Winter 1941/1942, BA-MA RH 26-58/37.
12. Combat motivation will be discussed in chapter 7.
13. 58. Infanterie-Division, Anleitung als Ausbilder etc., Winter 41/42 , BA-MA RH 26-58/37
14. Generalstab des Heeres/General der Infanterie, Richtlinien für die Ausbildung der Unteroffiziere bei der Feld-Unteroffiziers-Schule, 24.3.42, BA-MA RH 53-7/v.234b.
15. GenStdH/GendInf, Richtlinien für die Ausbildung der Unteroffiziere bei der Feld-Unteroffiziers-Schule, 24.3.42., BA-MA RH 53-7/v.234b.
16. Numbers according to OKW/AWA/WVW(V), Gesamtausfälle der Wehrmacht, Stand 31.12.1944, in: BA-MA, H. 6/737. The research of Rüdiger Overmans indicates even higher numbers as the German reporting system on losses had some defects.
17. Omer Bartov, *The Eastern Front 1941-45: German Troops and the Barbarization of Warfare*, pp. 12-18.
18. 8. Panzer-Division/Divisions-Nachrichten-Führer, Betr.: Nachrichten-Lage der 8. Panzer-Division, 27.11.43, NARA T-315, Roll 504.
19. Radio net traffic in which several stations communicated one at a time with the net control station, while the other stations listened in.
20. The German army used portable radio sets, typically carried on the back of soldiers like backpacks, from which the German name *Tornisterfunkgerät* came. They could transmit messages up to 25 kilometres and weighed more than 20 kilograms.
21. Armee-Oberkommando 6, Fahrten des Oberbefehlshabers vor Stalingrad am 15.10.42, BA-MA RH 20-6/225.
22. Armee-Oberkommando 6, Frontfahrt des Oberbefehlshabers am 29.10.1942, BA-MA RH 20-6-227.
23. Armee-Oberkommando 6, Frontfahrt des Oberbefehlshabers am 1.11.42, BA-MA RH 20-6-227.
24. Merkpunkte (anlässlich des Besuchs des Div.Kdr. in Welish) am 5.10.42, BA-MA RH 26-205/32.
25. The following is from Herr's personal file, BA-MA Pers 6/191. While much of his service information can be found in the literature or on the internet, the date

generally given for his wounding (25th September 1942) is wrong (31st October 1942), stemming from the passing over of divisional command to his successor on that date. His personal file contains a medical report, briefly describing the action.

26. Sönke Neitzel, *Abgehört. Deutsche Generale in britischer Kriegsgefangenschaft 1942-1945*, p. 11.
27. Personal File in BA-MA RH 6/300324.
28. Information about Werner Ziegler's career from BA-MA Pers 1/99823.
29. 73. Infanterie-Division/Ia, KTB, 6.9.1942, BA-MA RH 26-73/18.

Chapter 3

1. Panzer-Aufklärungsabteilung 13/Ia, Gefechtsbericht für den Angriff des Zuges Sassenberg am 19. Aug. 1941, 24.8.1941, BA-MA RH 27-13/46.
2. While focusing on Panzer tactics, Rudolf Steiger, *Panzertaktik im Spiegel deutscher Kriegstagebücher 1939-1941*, provides a good introduction into German tactical thinking. See also Gross, *Mythos und Wirklichkeit*.
3. See Williamson Murray, *Adaptation in War*, pp. 74-118. Alexander Hill's *The Red Army and the Second World War*, also argues along these lines.
4. A profund study on German military learning culture before 1914 can be found in: Markus Pöhlmann, 'Das unentdeckte Land. Kriegsbild und Zukunftskrieg in deutschen Militärzeitschriften,' in Stig Förster (ed.), *Vor dem Sprung ins Dunkle. Die militärische Debatte über den Krieg der Zukunft 1880-1914*, pp. 21-131.
5. Armee-Oberkommando 6/Ia, Nr. 4387/42 geh., 5.11.42, BA-MA RH 20-6/228.
6. For a more detailed approach on German experience reporting, see Wettstein, Die *Wehrmacht im Stadtkampf*, pp. 245f and 317-325.
7. Oberstleutnant Freiherr von Uslar-Gleichen (Wa Prüf 1), Verbindungstrupp zur Heeresgruppe Nord, Abschlussbericht über das Kommando zur Heeresgruppe Nord vom 9.6.-18.7.42, 25.7.1942, BA-MA RH 19-III/780.
8. This was a questionnaire given by the Second Department of the Army Ordonannce Office, responsible for infantry weapons and equipment.
9. This refers to the Fourth Deparment of the Army Ordonance Office, Group for Development and Testing, responsible for artillery, often abbreviated to *Wa Prüf 4* in German.
10. This refers to the Fifth Department of the Army Ordonannce Office responsible for fortresses and engineer weapons and equipment.
11. The *Stielgranate 41* (literally 'stick shell') was an fin-stabilized shell with a hollow charge bigger than that of the barrel of the weapon, with which the German army wanted to upgrade its outdated 3.7cm ATG. Its low velocity, as well as the need to load it from the front of the barrel, rendered it relatively ineffective.
12. For an overview on the development of the *Sturmartillerie* and its changing tasks, see: Adrian Wettstein, 'Sturmartillerie – Geschichte einer Waffengattung,' http://portal-militaergeschichte.de/wettstein_sturmartillerie.
13. Markus Pöhlmann, *Der Panzer und die Mechanisierung des Krieges. Eine deutsche Geschichte 1890 bis 1945*, pp 404-407.
14. Armee-Oberkommando 6/Ia, Betr.: Sturmgeschütze Sfl. mit s.I.G., 3.11.1942, BA-MA RH 20-6/227.

15. The development and the use of the Assault Rifle 44 has produced a considerable amount of literature, though much of it consists of technical books. Few have examined the testing process. The most comprehensive work is Dieter Handrich, *Sturmgewehr 44*.

16. 1.Infanterie-Division/Ia, Erfahrungsbericht über Grossversuch mit M.Pi. 44, 14.9.44, BA-MA RH 12-2/139a.

17. Less is known about German small unit tactics. A brief but comprehensive approach is Gerhard Elser, 'Von der "Einheitsgruppe" zum "Sturmzug" : Zur Entwicklung der deutschen Infanterie 1922 bis 1945', in *Truppendienst* 36/1997, pp 118-124. 'Small unit action during the German Campaign in Russia' , anonymously published as part of the studies produced by German officers and generals under the US Army's Historical Division after World War II, also provides numerous insights into German tactical thinking at the lowest levels.

18. *Das Deutsche Reich und der Zweite Weltkrieg*, Volume 5/2, p. 688. The effects of that flood of modifications on production is discussed in the same book, pp. 684-688 and p. 918f.

19. More detailed in Pöhlmann, *Die Mechanisierung*, pp. 420-423

20. For a comprehensive approach to German urban warfare practices in the early war, see Wettstein, *Die Wehrmacht im Stadtkampf 1939-1942*.

21. 305. Infanterie-Division/Ia, Merkblatt für den Ortskampf, o.D. (Herbst 1942), BA-MA RH 26-305/14.

22. VI. Armeekorps/Kommandierender General, Nr. 2939/42, 29.11.42, BA-MA RH 26-205/32.

23. Anlage zu XIII. Armee-Korps/Ia, Nr. 725/42 g.K., 30.11.42, BA-MA RH 24-13/100.

24. XXXXVIII. Panzer Korps/Kommandierender General, Erfahrungen aus den Angriffs- und Abwehrkämpfen im Raume Shitormir-Berditschew vom 15.11.43-21.1.44, 26.1.1944, BA-MA RH 10-125.

25. This meant a ratio of 1 NCO to 7 soldiers. On higher levels, the notion was normally officers/men (including NCOs).

26. *Kampfstärkennachweis* is comparable to the US Table of organization and equipment (TOE).

27. This references the German Kursk summer offensive in 1943, codenamed Operation 'Citadel', in which the XXXXVIIIth Panzer Corps also participated.

Chapter 4

1. The classic study on the German army's logistics in the East is still Martin van Creveld, *Supplying War. Logistics from Wallenstein to Patton*. The issue is also discussed for the Eastern Front in 1942 in *Germany and the Second World War*, Volume 6, pp. 878-882. We still lack both detailed studies and a general overview of the German supply situation on the Eastern front.

2. 7. Infanterie-Division/Ib, Leistungen der Versorgungstruppen während der Kämpfe um Mogliew (20.-26.7.41), 16.8.41, NARA T-315, Roll 376. For

a more detailed approach to the battle, see Wettstein, *Die Wehrmacht im Stadtkampf*, pp. 121-134.

3. Army troops were units subordinated to the Army High Command and temporarily attached to other formations to create a main point of emphasis for various operations. Important army troops included the heavy and heaviest artillery units, engineer units and anti-tank units. Later in the war, tank hunter and heavy tank units were also formed as army units.

4. OKH/Generalquartiermeister/Gruppe Munition/IIa, Munitionsverbrauch in to. Osten, 10.12.1944, BA-MA RH 3/135. For an analysis see also Heinz Rullkötter, 'Munitionseinsatz des deutschen Heeres im Zweiten Weltkrieg,' in *Wehrkunde*, Dezember 1973 (22), pp. 648-651.

5. For the most comprehensive approach to German war production, see the sections by Rolf-Dieter Müller in *Germany and the second world war*, Volumes 5/1 and 5/2 with many helpful tables and charts. A very readable, though sometimes too pointed, account is Adam Tooze, *Wages of Destruction. The Making and Breaking of the Nazi Economy*.

6. In his *Waffen und Geheimwaffen des deutschen Heeres 1933-1945*, Volume 1, pp. 147ff., Fritz Hahn lists 49 types and versions of 10.5cm light field howitzer shells. While many of those were special training shells or prototypes, around 20 were in production for longer periods of time and sent to the front.

7. Anlage 4 zu 24. Panzer-Division/Ia, Nr. 365/42 geh. v. 10.11.42, BA-MA RH 27-24/3.

8. FES was the abbrevation for *Führungsbänder Eisen Sinter* (Driving band Iron Sinter). Sinter iron, which replaced copper that was always short in supply, was not liked by the troops.

9. o.M. means *ohne Mundlochbuchse* (without adapter).

10. Vorgeschobener Offizier/OKH bei Armee-Oberkommando 6, An OKH/Op.Abt., 20.9.1942, BA-MA RH 20-6/212.

11. Due to its great range, the 10cm canon 18 was especially needed for counter-battery fire. This lack of ammunition meant that Soviet medium and heavy artillery could not be silenced.

12. The Sixth Army had some 60 10cm canon. As a result of this shortage, each gun had only six to seven rounds available, which in a period of normal use could be fired in two to three minutes.

13. For a detailed discussion on German urban warfare tactics, a numerical comparison and the supply situation in Stalingrad, see Wettstein, *Wehrmacht im Stadtkampf*, pp. 268-349.

14. 87. Infanterie-Division/Kdr., Betr.: Munitionseinsparungen, 11.7.1943, BA-MA RH 26-87/163.

15. *Jäger* (literaly: hunter) was a traditional German military term for light infantry.

16. See the detailed account in Wettstein, *Wehrmacht im Stadtkampf*, pp. 121-134 (Mogliev) and pp. 142-168 (Dnipropetrovsk).

17. Eugen Kreidler, *Die Eisenbahnen im Machtbereich der Achsenmächte während des Zweiten Weltkrieges. Einsatz und Leistungen für die Wehrmacht und Kriegswirtschaft*; Alfred Gottwaldt, *Deutsche Eisenbahnen im Zweiten Weltkrieg. Rüstung, Krieg und Eisenbahn*; Klaus Friedrich Schüler, *Logistik*

im Russlandfeldzug. Die Rolle der Eisenbahn bei Planung, Vorbereitung und Durchführung des deutschen Angriffs auf die Sowjetunion bis zur Krise vor Moskau im Winter 1941/42.

18. See Creveld, *Supplying War.*

19. 198. Infanterie-Division/Ib/V, Betr.: Kfz.-Lage, 9.11.1941, BA-MA RH 26-198/91.

20. A German battalion-level supply train consisted of three subunits: The combat train (*Gefechtstross*) with additional ammunition and combat equipment, the provisions train (*Verpflegungstross*) with field kitchen and an additional supply truck and finally the luggage train (*Gepäcktross*) with a truck for additional equipment as well the troops' luggage, such as additional clothes and personal items. Typically, trucks from the latter one were the first drawn away for other, more important purposes.

21. The division was the highest level of a fixed unit in the German army. Corps consisted of several divisions, which changed according to tasks and situations, with divisions sometimes remaining under a certain corps' command for only several days. Each change meant a new chain of commands and was a source of friction.

22. 8. Panzer-Division/Ib, Entwurf, 26.10.1943 (sent with minor revisions included here on 28th October 1943 to Panzer Army 4), NARA T-315 R 503.

23. See Williamson Murray, *Strategy for Defeat. The Luftwaffe 1933-1945*, p. 156.

24. Luftwaffenkommando Ost/Ia, Gefechtsbericht über die Schlacht von Welikije Luki vom 24.11.1942-19.1.1943, 26.3.1943, BA-MA RL 7/549.

25. This was the command agency responsible for all *Luftwaffe* units in Army Group Centre's sector between 1 April 1942 and 6 May 1943, when it was re-designated as *Luftflotte 6.*

26. The Go 242 was a transport glider built between 1941 and 1944, which could transport up to 23 men or an equivalent of cargo.

27. The Junkers Ju 87 was the famous Stuka. The Bf (Bayrische Flugzeugwerke) 109 (better known as Messerschmitt Me 109) and Focke-Wulf FW 190 were the standard German fighter planes, while the Heinkel He 111 and the Junkers Ju 88 the were the standard German bombers and the Junkers Ju 52 was the standard transporter. The Focke-Wulf FW 189 and the Henschel Hs 126 were reconnaissance planes and the DFS (*Deutsche Forschungsanstalt für Segelflug*, German Research Institute for Sailplane Flight) 230 a glider.

28. Murray, *Strategy for Defeat*, pp. 94-96.

29. LIX. Armeekorps/Qu., KTB, 15.1.1943, BA-MA RH 24-59/180.

30. Anlage 4 zu Der Kampf um Welikije Luki, zusammengestellt vom Oberkommando der Heeresgruppe Mitte, o.D., BA-MA RH 24-59/70.

31. For a general introduction, see: Ekkehart Guth (ed.), *Sanitätswesen im Zweiten Weltkrieg.*

32. 14. Panzer-Division/IVb, Übersicht über die Tätigkeit der Sanitätsdienst der 14. Panzer-Division vom 22.6.1941 bis 31.8.1941, 1.9.1941, NARA T-315, Roll 656.

33. 123. Infanterie-Division/IVb, Bericht über den Gesundheitszustand der 123. Inf.-Division, 14.11.41, BA-MA RH 24-2/100.

34. 87. Infanterie-Division/IVb., o.T., 3.7.1943, BA-MA RH 26-83/163.

35. 306. Infanterie-Division/Kommandeur, An Gruppe Schwerin, 4.12.1943, BA-MA RH 21-1/120a.

Chapter 5

1. Jürgen Förster, 'Securing "Living Space"' in Horst Boog et. al, *The Attack on the Soviet Union*, volume 4, *Germany and the Second World War*; Dieter Pohl, *Die Herrschaft der Wehrmacht: Deutsche Militärbesatzung und einheimische Bevölkerung in der Sowjetunion 1941-1944*; Shepherd, *War in the Wild East*.

2. Rolf-Dieter Müller, 'From Economic Alliance to a War of Colonial Exploitation,' pp. 118-224, esp. pp. 150-186 and 'The Failure of the Economic "Blitzkrieg Strategy"', pp. 1081-1188, esp. pp. 1141-1179, in Boog, et. al, *The Attack on the Soviet Union*; Alex J. Kay, *Exploitation, Resettlement, Mass Murder: Political and Economic Planning for German Occupation Policy in the Soviet Union, 1940-1941*; Christian Gerlach, *Kalkulierte Morde*. See chapter 6 on issues of food and supply.

3. Felix Römer, *Der Kommissarbefehl: Wehrmacht und NS-Verbrechen an der Ostfront 1941/42* and Felix Römer, 'The Wehrmacht in the War of Ideologies: The Army and Hitler's Criminal Orders on the Eastern Front,' in Alex J. Kay, Jeff Rutherford, and David Stahel (eds.), *Nazi Policy on the Eastern Front, 1941: Total War, Genocide and Radicalization*, pp. 73-100.

4. Richtlinien für das Verhalten der Truppe in Rußland, BA-MA RH 26-126/25.

5. 7. Infanterie-Division/Kommandeur, An alle Kommandeure und Chefs, 5.7.1941, NARA T-315, Roll 376.

6. The word 'organize' referred to the requisitioning measures carried out by the individual German soldiers without authorization from their superiors.

7. Der Ortskommandant Cholm, den 19.8.41, BA-MA RH 26-123/187.

8. Karel Berkhoff, *Harvest of Despair: Life and Death in Ukraine under Nazi Rule*; Pohl, *Die Herrschaft der Wehrmacht*.

9. The term 'black butcher' originated within the black market and referred to someone who slaughtered animals without permission.

10. Fr[anz] Schaback, Der Todesmarsch nach Leningrad: Ein Kampfbericht 7./II Battaillon IR 407 im Rahmen der 121. Infanterie-Division aufgezeichnet an Hand des Kriegstagebuches vom 22. Juni bis zum 15. September 1941. Geschrieben im Ortslazarett Modlin im März-April 1942, 28.7.41, BA-MA Msg 2/2580.

11. Armeeoberkommando 16/Ic A.O./O.Qu./Qu. 2, Betr.: Flüchtlinsgbewegung, 20.10.1941, BA-MA RH 26-123/189.

12. Shepherd, *War in the Wild East*; Jeff Rutherford, *Combat and Genocide on the Eastern Front*.

13. David Stahel, *Operation Barbarossa and Germany's Defeat in the East*.

14. Artillerie-Regiment 126, 24. Juli 1941, BA-MA RH 26-126/116.

15. See chapter 2 on issues of command.

16. Peter Longerich, *Holocaust: The Nazi Persecution and Murder of the Jews*.

17. Christopher Browning, *The Origins of the Final Solution: The Evolution of Nazi Jewish Policy, September 1939 March 1942*.

18. Waitman Beorn, *Marching into Darkness: The Wehrmacht and the Holocaust in Belarus*; Shepherd, *War in the Wild East*.

19. 123. Infanterie-Division/Ib, Nr.1146/41 geh., 2.10.41, BA-MA RH 26-123/189.

20. Sicherungs-Division 221/Ia, An Feld-Kdtr. 549, 18.7.41., NARA T-315, Roll 1672. The authors graciously thank Dr. Ben Shepherd for providing a copy of this document.

21. Sicherungs-Division 221/Ia, KTB, 12.9.41, NARA T-315, Roll 1666. The authors graciously thank Dr Ben Shepherd for providing a copy of this document.

22. Johannes Hürter, 'Die Wehrmacht vor Leningrad: Krieg und Besatzungspolitik der 18. Armee in Herbst und Winter 1941/42,' *Vierteljahrshefte für Zeitgeschichte*, 49 (2001), 377-440; Jörg Ganzenmüller, *Das belagerte Leningrad 1941-1944. Die Stadt in den Strategien von Angreifern und Verteidigern*; Anna Reid, *Leningrad: The Epic Siege of World War II, 1941-1944*.

23. XXXIX Armee-Korps (mot.)/Ia, Korpsbefehl Nr. 44, 7.12.1941, NARA T-315, Roll 482.

24. 8. Panzer-Division, KTB, 7.12.41, NARA T-315, Roll 484.

25. 126. Infanterie-Division/Ic, Betr: Wach- u. Sicherungsdienst gegenüber Partisanen, 6.1.1942, BA-MA RH 26-126/118.

26. See Christian Streit, *Keine Kameraden. Die Wehrmacht und die sowjetischen Kriegsgefangen 1941-1945*, p. 136; Hartmann, *Wehrmacht im Ostkrieg*; Christian Gerlach, *Krieg, Ernährung, Völkermord: Forschungen zur deutschen Vernichtungspolitik im Zweiten Weltkrieg*.

27. 207. Sicherungs-Division/Ib, Anlage zu Besondere Anordnungen Nr. 103, 29.12.41, NARA T-315, Roll 1085.

28. Timothy Mulligan, *The Politics of Illusion and Empire: German Occupation Policy in the Soviet Union, 1942-1943*; Manfred Oldenburg, *Ideologie und militärisches Kalkül: Die Besatzungspolitik der Wehrmacht in der Sowjetunion 1942*.

29. Panzer-Armee-Oberkommando 3/Ic/A.O., Richtlinien für die Behandlung der einheimischen Bevölkerung im Osten, 31.5.42, NARA T-315, Roll 382.

30. Rutherford, *Combat and Genocide*; Shepherd, *War in the Wild East*.

31. 7. Infanterie-Division/Ic, Betr.: Deutsche Propaganda in der russ.Bevölkerung, 1.3.42, NARA T-315, Roll 382.

32. 8. Panzer-Division/Ib/, Besondere Anordnungen für die Versorgung Nr. 95, 2.5.1942, NARA T-315, Roll 491.

33. Rolf-Dieter Müller, "Menschenjagd: Die Rekrutierung von Zwangsarbeitern in der besetzten Sowjetunion," in Hannes Heer and Klaus Naumann (eds.), *Vernichtungskrieg: Verbrechen der Wehrmacht, 1941-1944*, pp.92-103; Rutherford, *Combat and Genocide on the Eastern Front*; Rass, "*Menschenmaterial*".

34. Armee-Oberkommando 4/Ic/IVa/IVb/A.Wi.Fü./Qu.2, Einsatz von Zivilarbeitskräften, 22.11.42, NARA T-315, Roll 388.

35. 123. Infanterie-Division/Ic, Betr.: Überwachung der Zivilbevölkerung, 6.10.1942, BA-MA RH 26-123/98.

36. 126. Infanterie-Division/Ic, Kurzer Inhalt des Vortrages an die Starosten am 19.4.43, BA-MA RH 26-126/128.

37. On Vlasov and his army, see Rolf-Dieter Müller, *The Unknown Eastern Front: The Wehrmacht and Hitler's Foreign Soldiers*, pp. 226-236.

38. 126. Infanterie-Division/Ic, Abschrift von Gedanken zum totalen Arbeitseinsatz der russischen Zivilbevölkerung, 2.4.1943, BA-MA RH 26-126/128.

39. 7. Infanterie-Division/Ia, Betr.: Hilfswillige, 17.4.43, NARA T-315, Roll 389.

40. 24. Panzer-Division/Ia, 5. Tätigkeitsbericht der 24. Panzer-Division für die Zeit vom 20.9.-31.10.1942, 10.11.1942, BA-MA RH 27-24/3.

41. Gruppe Weiss/Qu., Besonder Anordnungen für die Erfassung der Kriegsgefangenen, Arbeitskräfte und der Beute, sowie für die Militärverwaltung, 7. Mai 1943, NARA T-315, Roll 393.
42. 407. Infanterie- Division [7. Infanterie-Division]/Ic, Betr.: Arbeitskräfte und Rohstoffe, 19.6.43, NARA T-315, Roll 390.
43. The weapons referred to here are the Soviet 122mm Howitzer M1938 M-30 and 152mm Cannon-Howitzer M1937 ML-20.
44. Der Chef des Oberkommandos der Wehrmacht/WFSt/Op (H), Betr.: Bandenbekämpfung, 16.12.1942, NARA T-315, Roll 387.
45. 207. Sicherungs Division/Ic, Betr.: Bandenmeldung für die Zeit vom 27.12.42 bis 6.1.43, 26.1.1943, NARA T-315, Roll 1607.
46. Anlage zu 126. Infanterie-Division/Ia, Hinweise für die Bandenjagd, 4.12.1943, BA-MA RH 26-126/107.
47. 7. Infanterie-Division/Ib, Besondere Anordnungen für die Versorgung für 'Büffel', 21.2.1943, NARA T-315, Roll 388.
48. 8. Panzer-Division/Ia, Betr.: Behandlung von Zivilbevölkerung, 3.10.1943, NARA T-315, Roll 505.

Chapter 6

1. Der Oberbefehlshaber des Heeres/Generalstab des Heeres/Ausb.Abt. (Ia), Betr.: Ausbildung im Ersatzheer, 26.10.1941, BA-MA RH 53-7/234b.
2. A combat firing exercise (*Gefechtschiessen*) was a type of exercise in which the infantry trained together with all of its weapons (rifle, hand grenade, machine gun, mortars, infantry gun) and with live ammunition.
3. A more thorough analysis of that system can be found in Rutherford, *Combat and Genocide on the Eastern Front*, pp. 197-208.
4. See *Germany and the Second World War*, Volume 5/1, pp. 1100-1 for the numbers and a critical discussion on the reliability of the numbers.
5. Pionier-Bataillon 173, Betr.: Zustandsbericht, 2.11.42, BA-MA RH 26-73/22.
6. 8. Panzer-Division/Ia, Betr.: Bericht über den Ausbildungsstand des Ersatzes, 12.6.42, NARA T -315, Roll 488.
7. Grenadier-Regiment 186, Betr.: Zustandsbericht, 2.11.42, BA-MA RH 26-73/22.
8. Comparisons between the US and German army from 1939 to 1945 have led to many publications. The classic work is Martin van Creveld, *Combat Power*; for a comparison suffering from the problems mentioned above, see Keith Bonn, *Where the Odds were Even*.
9. 8. Panzer Division/Ia, Betr.: Ausbildung, 7.1.42, NARA T-315, Roll 484.
10. 125. Infanterie-Division/Ia, Anlage einer Muster-Kampfschule, [1943] BA-MA RH 26-125/26.
11. OKH/Generalstab des Heeres/Ausb.-Abt./Org.-Abt., Betr.: Ausbildungsmöglichkeiten im Feld-Ersatz-Bataillon der Divisionen im Osten, 1943, BA-MA RH 24-59/80.
12. The German army's table of organization used a letter to signify all positions, marking which rank the man in the position should normally possess. B stands for *Bataillonskommandeur* which corresponds to the rank of *Oberstleutnant* or *Major*.

13. When possible, German units had a small reserve of officers and NCO not posted to positions, but ready to take over any command when officers or NCOs were killed, wounded or otherwise lost, to avoid long vacancies in ongoing operations. Often, the forming of such a leader reserve was not possible due to the general shortage of officers and NCOs, and even if such a reserve existed, it was frequently depleted after a few days of operations.

14. Armee-Oberkommando 6/Ia, Betr.: Erfahrungen 300er Divisionen, 26.10.1942, BA-MA RH 20-6-227.

15. For a detailed study on the 385th Infantry Division and its leadership, see Marco Sigg, *Der Unterführer als Feldherr im Taschenformat*, pp. 262-323

16. 5. Panzer-Division/Ia, Betr.: Erfahrungen mit neu aufgestellten Einheiten im Einsatz, 2.1.44, BA-MA RH 20-2/557.

17. Armee-Oberkommando 6/Ia, Betr.: Erhöhung der Kampfkraft, 6.10.42, BA-MA RH 20-6/220.

18. Armee-Oberkommando 6/Ia, Vom AOK 6 befohlene Massnahmen zur Hebung der Gefechtsstärken, 28.10.42, BA-MA RH 20-6/22.

19. OKH/GenStdH/General der Osttruppen/Org.Abt, Landeseigene Hilfskräfte im Osten, 29.4.43, BA-MA RHD 7/8a/3.

20. Armee-Oberkommando 6/Ia, Betr.: Erhöhung der Kampfkraft, 6.10.42, BA-MA RH 20-6/220.

21. Antony Beevor, *Stalingrad: The Fateful Siege, 1942-43*, pp. 161.

22. *Germany and the Second World War*, volume 5/2, p.943

23. Armee-Oberkommando 6/Ia, Betr.: Erhöhung der Kampfkraft, 6.10.42, BA-MA RH 20-6/220.

24. Numbers in *Germany and the Second World War*, Volume 6, pp. 865-7.

25. Numbers in *Germany and the Second World War*, Volume 5/2, p. 1013.

Chapter 7

1. H.R., 29.01.1943, Feldpost Sammlung, Museum für Kommunikation (hereafter MfK), 3.2002.0985.

2. E.A Shils, and Morris Janowitz, 'Cohesion and Disintegration in the Wehrmacht in World War II,' *POQ*, 12 (1948), 280-315; Creveld, *Fighting Power*.

3. Ronald Smelser and Edward J. Davies II, *The Myth of the Eastern Front: The Nazi-Soviet War in American Popular Culture*; Wolfram Wette, *The Wehrmacht: History, Myth, Reality*.

4. Hans-Adolf Jacobson, 'The Commissar Order and the Mass Execution of Soviet Prisoners of War,' in Hans Bucheim et al., *Anatomy of the SS State*, pp. 163-283; Christian Streit, *Keine Kameraden. Die Wehrmacht und die sowjetischen Kriegsgefangen 1941-1945*; Jürgen Förster, 'Operation Barbarossa as a War of Conquest and Annihilation,' in Boog et. al, *The Attack on the Soviet Union*.

5. Bartov, *Hitler's Army*.

6. Sönke Neitzel and Harald Welzer, *Soldaten: Protokolle von Kämpfen, Töten und Sterben*.

7. Sven Oliver Müller, 'Nationalism in German War Society 1939-1945,' in Jörg Echternkamp (ed.) *German Wartime Society 1939-1945: Exploitation,*

Interpretations, Exclusion, volume 9/2, *Germany and the Second World War*, pp. 11-93; Nicholas Stargardt, *The German War: A Nation under Arms, 1939-1945*.

8. Hürter, 'Die Wehrmacht vor Leningrad,' *Vierteljahrshefte für Zeitgeschichte*, 49 (2001), 377-440; Rutherford, *Combat and Genocide*, Oldenburg, *Ideologie und militärisches Kalkül*.

9. Jürgen Förster, 'Ideological Warfare in Germany, 1919 to 1945' in Jörg Echternkamp (ed.) *German Wartime Society 1939-1945: Politicization, Disintegration, and the Struggle for Survival*, volume 9/1, *Germany and the Second World War*, pp. 485-669.

10. Hew Strachan, 'Ausbildung, Kampfgeist und die zwei Weltkriege,' in Bruno Thoß and Hans-Erich Volkmann (eds.), *Erster Weltkrieg. Zweiter Weltkrieg*, pp. 265-286; Frank Vossler, *Propaganda in die eigene Truppe. Die Truppenbetreuung in der Wehrmacht 1939-1945*, pp.19-37.

11. 8. Panzer Division/Kommandeur, 25.3.1943, NARA T-315, Roll 498.

12. Wilhelm Deist, *The Wehrmacht and German Rearmament*, p. 34.

13. Anlage 4 zu Ob.d.H./GenStdH/O.Qu.I, Nr. 500/40 g., 7.10.40, BA-MA RH 26-123/173.

14. 7. Infanterie-Division/Ia, Besondere Anordnungen zum Divisionsbefehl für 2.7.41, 1.7.1941, NARA T-315, Roll 373.

15. Chronik der 2. Kompanie Nachrichten-Abteilung 121, BA-MA RH 44/381.

16. 121. Infanterie-Division/Ic, 21.6-19.11.1941, Abschrift: Zusammenstellung von Beobachtungen über die Rote Armee (von A.E. Frauenfeld), o.D., BA-MA RH 26-121/70.

17. Alfred Frauenfeld was an Austrian Nazi who served with the Luftwaffe's propaganda troops in France, in the Balkans and the Soviet Union and later became *Generalkommissar* for Crimea. See Werner Bräuninger, 'Meisterstück falscher Behandlung. Alfred E. Frauenfeld und die Probleme der Verwaltung der besetzten Ostgebiete,' in Werner Bräuninger, *Hitlers Kontrahenten in der NSDAP. 1921–1945*, pp. 247–257.

18. Der Todesmarsch nach Leningrad, BA-MA MsG 2/2580, pp. 151-2.

19. For more on the spiraling of violence on the Eastern front as a result of both German and Soviet atrocities, see Römer, *Der Kommissarbefehl*, pp. 226-275.

20. Mark Edele and Michael Geyer, 'States of Exception: The Nazi-Soviet War as a System of Violence, 1939-1945,' in Michael Geyer and Sheila Fitzpatrick (eds), *Beyond Totalitarianism: Stalinism and Nazism Compared*, pp. 345-395.

21. 7. Infanterie-Division/Ic, Die Feindlage, 19.12.1941, NARA T-315, Roll 376.

22. During the First World War, Austro-Hungarian, Russian, and German forces clashed in the Carpathian Mountains, in the northwestern section of the Habsburg Empire. The fighting in 1915 was particularly hellish for the belligerent armies and their soldiers. See Graydon Tunstall, *Blood on the Snow: The Carpathian Winter War of 1915*.

23. Infanterie-Regiment 407/Ia, Erfahrungen über die russ. Führung und Kampfesweise während des Ostfeldzuges, 1.3.1942, BA-MA RH 26-121/18.

24. 205. Infanterie-Division/Ic, Betr.: Fronturlauberheim, o.D. (Entwurf), BA-MA RH 205-26/31.

25. 7. Infanterie-Division/Ia, Betr.: Errichtung von Erholungsheim, 19.2.1942, NARA T-315, Roll 382.

26. 8.Panzer-Division Tätigkeitsbericht Abt Ic, 1.10.42-30.4.43, NARA T-315, Roll 497.

27. Förster, 'Geistige Kriegsführung in Deutschland 1919 bis 1945,' p. 560.

28. Rutherford, *Combat and Genocide on the Eastern Front*, pp. 346-354.

29. 126. Infanterie Division/Kommandeur, 30.1.1943, BA-MA RH 26-126/94.

30. The last section of this sentence is drawn from Johann Wolfgang von Goethe's, poem *Feiger Gedanken* (Cowardly Thoughts).

31. For more on how German soldiers responded to the 'positive' aspects of Nazi propaganda, see Stephen Fritz, *Frontsoldaten: The German Soldier in World War II*.

32. H. S. to his wife, 31.01.1943, MfK, 3.2002.1214.

33. H. R. to his wife, 11.03.1943, MfK, 3.2002.0985.

34. H. S. to his sister, 18.8.1943, MfK 3.2002.0827.

35. Volker Berghahn, 'NSDAP und "Geistige Führung der Wehrmacht,"' in *Vierteljahresheft für Zeitgeschichte*, Jahrgang 17 (1969), vol. 1, pp. 17-71; here p. 37. See also Förster, 'Motivation and Indoctrination in the Wehrmacht,' in Paul Addison and Angus Calder (eds.), *Time to Kill*, pp 263-73; here, p. 271.

36. Rass, "*Menschenmaterial*", 316.

37. 8. Panzer-Division/DBO, 31.10.1943, NARA T-315, Roll 505.

38. W. P. to his wife, 01.02.1943, MfK, 3.2013.355. It should be noted that this officer was never deployed to the Eastern front. His enthusiastic acceptance of the Nazi programme, however, was typical for large numbers of German soldiers.

39. 126. Infanterie-Division/Ic/DBO, Arbeitsbericht des Divisions-Betreuungs-Offiziers, Berichtzeit: 15.9.-14.10.43, 14.10.1943, BA-MA RH 26-126/130.

40. This German film combined Nazi ideological ideas about pastoral life with fantasy elements, offering German soldiers some escape from the rigours of the front.

41. This issue became an increasingly worrisome one for the Nazi leadership, which feared that relationships between German soldiers and Soviet women would inevitably result in 'inferior' children. For more on this topic, see Regina Mühlhäuser, *Eroberungen: Sexuelle Gewalttaten und intime Beziehungen deutscher Soldaten in der Sowjetunion 1941-1945*.

42. 8. Panzer-Division/DBO, Tätigkeitsbericht des Divisionsbetreuungsoffiziers für die Zeit vom 1.4. bis 30.6.1943, 30.6.1943, NARA T-315, Roll 505.

43. Shepherd, *Hitler's Soldiers*, p. 384.

44. Rass, "*Menschenmaterial*", p. 191.

45. 8. Panzer-Division/III.,Tätigkeitsbericht der Abt. III für die Zeit vom 1.1. bis 30.6.1942, 30.6.1942, NARA T-315, Roll 491.

46. 205. Infanterie-Division/Kommandeur, ohne Titel, o.D. [1942], BA-MA RH 26-205/32.

47. 8. Panzer Division/Ic, Betr.: Ic-Angelegenheiten, 29.10.1942, NARA T-315, Roll 497.

48. *Wehrunwürdikeit* translates as 'ineligibility for military service'. Since military service was regarded as an honourable service to the Fatherland, groups that were prosecuted by the Nazi regime, such as homosexuals, Jews and Jehovah's witnesses were excluded from military service, which was a form of discrimination. Criminals sent to prison also lost their right to serve, but they could regain it by serving in so-called *Bewährungeinheiten*, or probation units.

49. *Bürgerliche Ehrenrechte* translates as 'civil honours right'. This included, for example, the qualification to hold office.
50. 83. Infanterie-Division/III., Tätigkeitsbericht des Gerichtes der 83. Inf.-Division für die Monate August und September 1942, 4.10.1942, BA-MA RH 26-83/69.
51. See Rass, "*Menschenmaterial*", pp. 180-1 for a discussion of this issue as it relates to the 253rd Infantry Division.
52. Ian Kershaw, *The End: The Defiance and Destruction of Hitler's Germany, 1944-1945* (New York), p. 50.
53. XIX. (Geb.) Armeekorps/Kommandierender General, Sonderbefehl Kommandierender General Nr. 10, 1.2.1943, NARA T-315, Roll 505.
54. The *Wehrmachtberichte*, or Armed Forces Reports, were daily summaries of military events that were framed in such a positive way, that they were viewed as having a great propaganda value by the regime.
55. The XIXth Mountain Corps was stationed in Lapland, a relatively quiet front in February 1943.

Appendix D

1. General was combined with the branch, i.e. *General der Infanterie, der Artillerie*, and so on.
2. *Oberfähnrich* were already wearing officers' insignia, such as officers' uniforms and caps.
3. Note that the artillery and the cavalry used the rank name *Wachtmeister* instead of *Feldwebel* for all NCO ranks.
4. Note that this rank was different according to the arm: in the infantry it was *Schütze* and from 1942 on *Grenadier* (riflemen), in the artillery *Kanonier* (gunner), in the cavalry *Reiter* (horsemen) and so on.

Index